The United States and the Americas

Lester D. Langley, General Editor

This series is dedicated to a broader understanding of the political, economic, and especially cultural forces and issues that have shaped the Western hemispheric experience— its governments and its peoples. Individual volumes assess relations between the United States and its neighbors to the south and north: Mexico, Central America, Cuba, the Dominican Republic, Haiti, Panama, Colombia, Venezuela, the Andean Republics (Peru, Ecuador, and Bolivia), Brazil, Uruguay and Paraguay, Argentina, Chile, and Canada.

The United States and the Americas

Haiti and the United States

Brenda Gayle Plummer

Haiti and the United States: The Psychological Moment

The University of Georgia Press

Athens and London

© 1992 by the University of Georgia Press
Athens, Georgia 30602
All rights reserved
Set in 10 on 14 Palatino

The paper in this book meets the guidelines
for permanence and durability of the Committee on
Production Guidelines for Book Longevity of the
Council on Library Resources.

Printed in the United States of America

96 95 94 93 92   C   5 4 3 2 1

96 95 94 93 92   P   5 4 3 2 1

Library of Congress Cataloging in Publication Data

Plummer, Brenda Gayle.
    Haiti and the United States : the psychological
moment / Brenda Gayle Plummer.
        p.   cm. — (The United States and the Americas)
    Includes bibliographical references (p.   ) and index.
    ISBN 0-8203-1422-6 (alk. paper). — ISBN 0-8203-1423-4
(pbk. : alk. paper)
        1. United States—Relations—Haiti. 2. Haiti—Relations—
United States. 3. Haiti—History.
    I. Title. II. Series. E183.8.H2P55 1992
303.48′27307294—dc20   91-34105
                                                  CIP

British Library Cataloging in Publication Data available

This book is for Robert Baldwin Plummer

Contents

Acknowledgments

This work is in many ways a collaborative project. Many people have been involved in its diverse incarnations. Franklin Knight's careful reading of the manuscript and useful commentary greatly assisted the task of organization. I am also grateful to the staffs of various libraries and archives in the United States and abroad. Special thanks are owed to Walter LaFeber, Jennifer Radke, Donald Culverson, and Lester D. Langley for their attention and helpful suggestions on particular chapters and areas of concern. Thanks are also due to the editors of *Cimarrón*, where parts of Chapter 7, *Le Vogue Nègre*, were first published as "The Golden Age of Haitian Tourism," vol. 2 (Spring 1990).

This volume owes a special debt to the pioneering work of the late Rayford W. Logan. Logan's 1941 diplomatic history of Haitian-U.S. relations made the most comprehensive use to date of the rich Haitian sources. Logan's gracefully understated arguments challenged prevailing biases in an era when Jim Crow still held sway.

The United States and the Americas

Haiti and the United States

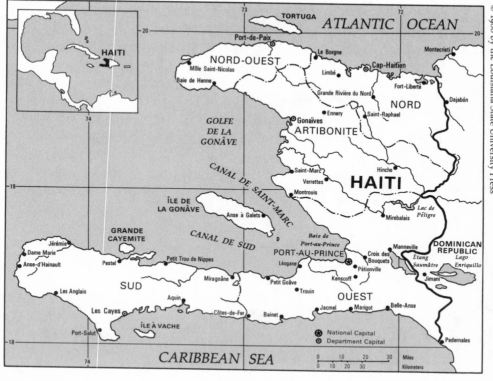

TORTUGA

ATLANTIC OCEAN

Port-de-Paix

Le Borgne

NORD-OUEST

Môle Saint-Nicolas

Limbé

Cap-Haïtien

Montecristi

Baie de Henne

Grande Rivière du Nord

Fort-Liberté

Dajabón

GOLFE DE LA GONÂVE

Gonaïves

Ennery

Saint-Raphael

NORD

ARTIBONITE

Saint-Marc

Hinche

HAITI

Verrettes

Montrouis

CANAL DE SAINT-MARC

ÎLE DE LA GONÂVE

Anse à Galets

Mirebalais

Lac de Péligre

GRANDE CAYEMITE

CANAL DE SUD

Baie de Port-au-Prince

Manneville

DOMINICAN REPUBLIC

Jérémie

Dame Marie

Anse-d'Hainault

Pestel

Petit Trou de Nippes

PORT-AU-PRINCE

Croix des Bouquets

Étang Saumâtre

Lago Enriquillo

Léogane

Pétionville

Jimani

Miragoâne

Petit Goâve

Kenscoff

OUEST

SUD

Aquin

Trouin

Les Anglais

Côtes-de-Fer

Bainet

Jacmel

Marigot

Belle-Anse

Les Cayes

National Capital

Department Capital

Port-Salut

ÎLE À VACHE

Pedernales

CARIBBEAN SEA

Miles

Kilometers

HAITI

Introduction

"From the palm-fringed shores a great mass of mountains rose, fantastic and mysterious," W. B. Seabrook wrote of his first impressions of Haiti. As sunset melted into night, "only the jungle mountains remained, dark, mysterious; and from their slopes came presently far out across the water the steady boom of Voodoo drums."[1] The aura of drama and menace Seabrook created reflected enduring perceptions of Haiti among North Americans. These persist into our times, even though the imagery of tropical luxuriance has yielded to the stark reality of environmental devastation. Today, dry gullies and arid plains rather than palms fire the visual imagination, coupled with age-old fears and fantasies about savage blacks inhabiting a nightmare world of their own making. These fears stem in part from the cataclysmic slave insurrection that so changed the Western Hemisphere, and from psychic tensions deeply embedded in U.S. culture and society. When coupled with a history of political turbulence, repulsion led the U.S. public to see Haiti as a doomed land, beyond comprehension, beyond help, and outside history.

Haitians' perceptions of the United States were not flattering either. Slavery dominated impressions of the northern republic before the U.S. Civil War. The view from Port-au-Prince took in an expansionist power bent on spreading slavery and racism into the tropics. After emancipation, the persistence of racism in its most egregious forms—lynching, disfranchisement, peonage—confirmed earlier mistrust. The few Haitians who traveled to the United States in the early twentieth century sometimes experienced discrimination firsthand. The commercialism of a booming industrial economy, moreover, did not always please those who regarded the United States as grossly materialist and lacking in spiritual values. Educated Haitians in a position to compare cultures had adopted the traditions of the French

1

bourgeoisie. They preferred French civilization to the raw and often cruel society of Anglophone North America.

The racial chasm that historically divided Haiti and the United States was not merely a matter of black and white. Race and color also played a role in Haitian society that confused many North Americans. In the U.S. context, race traditionally served as a simple dividing line in a country that did not admit fine distinctions. Only very marginal groups, like American Indians, were neither black nor white. Latin America constructed racial identity differently. It recognized a spectrum of colors, physiognomies, and hair types, which it associated with a somewhat parallel system of class stratification. Diversity in classification and ascription among different countries depended on such variables as the number of Africans or Indians in any one locale. Haiti was indeed a black republic, but it configured blackness differently.

Haitians tried to supplant the Latin American model of multiraciality with another social construction derived from their revolutionary history. They proclaimed themselves *noirs*—"blacks," and admitted to this category any Indians or mulattoes who considered themselves Haitians. Even renegade Polish mercenaries, stranded in Haiti after the expulsion of the French army, shared this attribute. Revolutionary leaders intended *noir* as a unifying concept that would undermine the social conflict begotten and nurtured by colonialism and racial slavery. They did not fully succeed, however, and color consciousness survived.

Like racism in the United States, its persistence owed much to its ability to transcend the original conditions that engendered it and to attach itself to other social dynamics. The revolution successfully destroyed slavery ideology but did not completely eradicate the belief in the superiority of European somatic norms and culture. The early concentration of mulattoes in urban areas, their relative Western acculturation, and the economic advantages they enjoyed from inheriting the wealth of French forebears highlighted other divisions in society. It was easy enough to polarize: French versus Haitian Creole, citizen versus peasant, Christian versus pagan. Civil wars, campaigns of repression and extermination, and coups d'état took place under such ideological banners. There was nevertheless enough ambiguity in the Haitian experience to warrant closer examination.

Some Haitians were neither mulatto nor black. Others had physical characteristics that would identify them as mulattoes, for example, but lacked the corresponding class standing and cultural attributes. All understood Creole and had absorbed some part of the indigenous cultural and religious milieu. Many North Americans, accustomed to the flattest and most sterile generalizations about people of color— among whom they failed to differentiate clearly—preferred easy dualities to careful observation. The overlay of fear and fantasy further discouraged detached analysis.

These problems were not apparent when contact began between the United States and the people of what would eventually become Haiti. When British colonials traded with the wealthy French of Saint-Domingue, they did business with merchants and planters not unlike themselves, white people who chafed at the mercantile restrictions of empire. Direct transactions between the thirteen colonies and Saint-Domingue cut across traditional national barriers but were tolerated for reasons of expediency. Saint-Domingue offered its molasses and coffee at lower rates than did the British islands; and the mainland colonies provided staple provisions to the French island dependency.[2] The Franco-American alliance of 1778 against Britain, and the subsequent U.S. reliance on French-supplied munitions during the Revolutionary War further bolstered this trade. The French also sent a naval expedition to assist the colonists at Savannah in 1779. The Fontages Legion, a volunteer unit of 545 mulattoes and blacks from Saint-Domingue, participated in the battle of Savannah.[3]

The American Revolution was the first of three successful insurgencies leading ultimately to the disintegration of Caribbean slavery. The French Revolution isolated the island planters from their mainland peers, and the Haitian Revolution destroyed Haitian slavery and the sugar economy. Powerful West India lobbyists in Parliament no longer enjoyed North American support after 1776. In French America, class divisions among the whites of Saint-Domingue reduced their political clout. Later, the defeat of Napoleon's army by black insurgents led France to sell Louisiana to the United States. Island whites thus lost a supportive mainland colony of white planters. The French Revolution also ensured that democratic thought circulated in the region and would be accessible to slaves. Despite the usual precautions, the Rights of Man provided a coherent political ideology that had wide currency in the late eighteenth century and helped discredit chattel slavery. The economic liberalism accompanying faith in natural law had already begun to undermine mercantilist organizing principles of overseas empires.[4]

The vigor and proximity of the United States and the size of the U.S. market further subverted imperial preference systems. Once independence had placed it beyond the conventional restraints to free trade, weaker Caribbean economies increasingly looked to the U.S. market for cheaper and more readily attainable provisions. Canadian supplies provided an alternative, but Canada could not surpass the United States, whose gradual ascendancy as a metropole in its own right hastened Europe's exodus from the Western Hemisphere.[5]

The three revolutions provided the impetus for conflict among the great powers in Europe as well as in the New World. A Franco-American alliance of 1778 precipitated fighting between Britain and France in the West Indies, and monarchy entered the lists against the French revolution both in the Caribbean and on the European continent. The Haitian Revolution incubated in the period of prolonged hostilities that pitted the principal powers against one another. They established rival armies on Española and assisted the creation there of a combat-toughened generation of black military leadership. These revolutions inspired ongoing debates about the meaning of the revolutionary phenomenon, which continued to shape political culture and expectations in the three countries. They also deeply influenced the historical development of Latin American countries, with Haiti materially supporting the rebellions against Spain.

The American Revolution offered inspiration to the Haitian, but the revolutionary generation in the United States feared Caribbean upheaval. Eighteenth-century conservatives perceived Haiti as a source

of subversion and a threat to slaveholding societies. Royalists everywhere hoped to suppress republicanism but realized that a white
landed and commercial gentry would retain the values of patriarchy,
proprietorship, and white supremacy even while insisting on its political independence. The Haitian Revolution, however, threatened not
only the political but the social structure of an imperial domain. Blacks
were now not only masters but strategists and executioners.

To the slaveholding world, the cultural differences between the
black (Creole or African) and the white "common man" exacerbated
the unbearable political implications of black ascendancy. Though few
countries were as dissimilar as the United States and Haiti, a fur-
tive ideological bond linked eighteenth-century republicanism in U.S.
political culture with that articulated by the Saint-Domingue rebels.
For the white yeomanry of the United States, the stability of the polity
rested in freeholders operating in their own interest, detached from
the corruption engendered by dependence. Despite the efforts of indigenous rulers to perpetuate some form of unfree labor, Haitians also
preferred the division of property in freehold. Land ownership and
the right to bear arms remained crucial to the definition of liberty and
personal honor in both societies.[6]

Membership in a republic also necessitated hard work and virtue
from those deemed capable of responsible citizenship. The U.S. political elite thus eliminated free people of color from citizenship, claiming
that inferiors could not execute civil duties. Most proponents of deporting blacks from the United States invoked this argument. Advocates of repatriation to the tropics often contended that a properly
working republic required some measure of cultural and racial homogeneity. In an early Haitian application of this idea, authorities conferred citizenship on persons of African and Amerindian descent and
barred those of exclusively European ancestry.[7]

Such parallels did not mean that peasants and yeomen in these diverse societies responded to the same political impetus. Individual
freedom did not always signify equality. Deference could be a republican characteristic, for virtuous republics supposedly bred a meritoc-
racy that would produce "natural" rulers. To the Founding Fathers

of the United States and moreover to the most zealous French Jacobin, democracy was always in some degree representational, rather than direct. The existence of the Rights of Man did not even guarantee full freedom to dissent, for republican theory equated factionalism and partisanship with rebellion. In Haiti, the general public knew less about republicanism than the leaders did. Here the division of land into small holdings reflected not only the general distaste with which republicans everywhere regarded concentrated power, but also the demands of a newly constituted peasantry.[8]

Revolutionary Saint-Domingue's relationship to the political challenges of the eighteenth century fin de siècle rested as much on the local sociocultural milieu as on ideas that filtered into the society from abroad. The colony remained highly militarized, and officers of the various insurgent, counterinsurgent, and mercenary forces exercised extraordinary powers over both common soldiers and civilian populations. Hierarchical social relations lay embedded in the slavery legacy, which rested on a foundation of traditional deference based on age, gender, skills, and reputation. Spanish interlopers thus retained the loyalty of rebels Toussaint, Jean-François, and Biassou by depicting the French as atheists and regicides to people who firmly believed in God and in the legitimacy of secular authority.[9]

When French forces attempted to reimpose slavery on Saint-Domingue, they executed hundreds who disobeyed General Charles Leclerc's order to disarm. French policies, including that of calculated atrocity, led to widespread popular rebellion that manifested itself long before such leaders as Dessalines, Pétion, and Christophe defected from the consular government. Those chieftains followed rather than organized the revolutionary unrest of the masses.[10] Their most singular accomplishment, recalling the French Revolution, was the politicization of daily life. "By politicizing the everyday," Lynn Avery Hunt wrote of the French experience, "the Revolution enormously increased the points from which power could be exercised, and multiplied the tactics and strategies for wielding that power. Power itself "created previously unsuspected resources."[11]

Like the North Americans, independent Haitians required national myths that validated their own political authority, discourse, and culture. They created rituals similar to those associated with the invention of the French Revolution. They renamed cities and bestowed the identities of classical heroes from the Greek city states and Roman republic on children. Heraldry played a role in the design of the national flag, insignias, and mottoes. The Haitian idea that the *Tricouleur* and cockade represented the three races of Saint-Domingue—the black, white, and mulatto—derived from the use of red, white, and black flags by French terrorists. During the war for independence, Dessalines cut the white out of the flag, thus demonstrating that whites no longer had a place in the emerging society. In 1805 as emperor of Haiti, he changed the traditional blue field to black.[12]

Dessalines realized that the ignorance of the newly emancipated citizens necessitated closely monitoring their contacts with foreign cultures. Efforts to relocate them away from the coasts and confine them to agriculture reflected the need to ensure continued production and a desire to maintain the supremacy of a specifically Haitian discourse. The emperor did not oppose commerce per se. The problem lay with the relationship between the market and the polity.[13] The dependent character of the slaveholding societies of the Americas, including Saint-Domingue, had abetted the hegemonic rise of the liberal worldview. Republicans had originally rejected power aggregations that undercut the independence of individual freeholders. Nonslaveholding white settler groups in the late seventeenth century found themselves either marginalized or forced to emigrate to areas where land cost less and chattel slavery did not predominate. Many independent communities of white yeomen and artisans in the U.S. South deteriorated in the face of the planter onslaught. Conflict between *grands blancs* and *petits blancs* in Saint-Domingue forms one of the well-known motifs of the prerevolutionary configuration.[14]

Western liberalism gradually replaced the republican community with the marketplace as the basic social system. Whereas republicanism had had no room for the capitalist as a citizen, liberalism deflated the importance of citizenship itself, privatized civil society, and raised the market to primacy. Nineteenth-century Latin American debates between liberals and nationalists, and between southern Whigs and Democrats in the United States, reflected the strains that inability to balance agriculture and commerce—and their attendant ideologies— had placed on these underdeveloped countries. In the end, the fierce attachment to a society of shared values, which required constant political activism and vigilance of all, was lost.[15]

The internal struggles of each society and the relative isolation in which it evolved masked these common elements. Differing percep- tions of the world also conditioned the mentality with which each pursued its historical destiny. Early in the twentieth century, U.S. policymakers viewed the political instability then current in Haiti with increasing distaste. As they observed the seemingly endless suc- cession of palace revolutions through lenses clouded by racial and cultural prejudices, they thought of militarily intervening to "clean house." One of them, Theodore Roosevelt's Secretary of State, Elihu Root, realized the difficulties involved in trying to influence Haiti. He nevertheless anticipated the day when U.S. intervention in Haiti would prove timely and effective: "The Haitians are suspicious of us. They are densely ignorant and really believe that we want to gobble up their country, and we have to be very careful about volunteer- ing any interference in their affairs lest we be met with an outcry of protest. Of course, they have some pretty good reasons for doubting the advantages of too close an association between the United States and a black man's government. I have been watching every move in Haiti for several years very closely in the hope that a situation would arise in which we could give that help in such a way as to establish the right sort of relations. We have done something in that direction, but for any positive step I think we must wait for the 'psychological moment.' "[16]

Root's statement was prescient, because much of the Haitian-U.S. relationship has turned on matters of consciousness. The cultural dis- parities between the two republics are all the more ironic as their common experience of anticolonial rebellion and nationhood during the revolutionary epoch in some ways converged. The casual observer of Haitian affairs—impressed by tales of political violence, voodoo, and stark deprivation—may be distracted by those divergent qualities in Haitian and U.S. histories respectively. Students of foreign relations understandably take these differences for granted and concentrate more intensively on matters of state than on the evolution and character of civil society in these countries. Yet, it is in that crucible that the Haitian-American relationship acquired its distinct form. U.S. and Haitian history share certain themes, but the nations' separate identities, and the sociohistorical context in which they figure, required them to approach slavery, self-rule, and economic development differently. Their mutual relations reflect in microcosm many of the grand themes of the Western Hemisphere: wars for empire, struggles for independence, the slavery and freedom duality, conflict between liberal democracy and authoritarianism, and the dilemma of race.

The roots of foreign policy in both countries are intimately linked to the development of domestic policy and conditioned by the character of civil society. Inevitably, conflict between the states has been a natural by-product of their differences, and the search for common ground, while prescribed by critical elements in their histories, has rarely taken place. This book addresses that task.

Latin Americans have quite justly resented the proprietary use by the United States of the adjective "American." Haitian usage of the term reflects a French language tradition and outlook in diplomacy, in which "American" specifically means the United States. French, unlike Spanish, has no equivalent of *estadounidense*. I have refrained from using the term *American* to mean resident of, or pertaining to, the United States wherever possible. I have instead substituted *U.S.* where clarity permitted.

The proper name for the island on which Haiti and the Dominican Republic lie is another bone of contention. The original Amerindian name is Haiti—"mountainous land"—but the adoption of the name by the republic of Haiti is a source of confusion. An alternative is Española—"little Spain"—sometimes corrupted as Hispaniola. Neither of these have suited Haitians, and neither is in fact accurate, but Española at least serves the purpose of distinguishing the geographic land mass from the two countries that occupy it. The term Española is used here.

1   The Foundations

Slaves in what is now northern Haiti, responding to the disorder among local whites engendered by the French Revolution, and
to a tradition of native resistance, revolted in 1791. Under the leadership of the Vodun priest Boukman, they seized arms, burned estates,
assassinated planters, and proclaimed themselves heirs to the promise of Liberty, Equality, and Fraternity. Rebellion soon spread through
the colony. Boukman died in combat early in the rebellion, and a
second generation of secular leaders, including Toussaint Louverture,
succeeded him. Troops from the French republic arrived in Saint-
Domingue in July 1792 as the revolutionary government sought to
salvage the remains of this once vital plantation dependency, wracked
by white dissension and servile revolt. Insurrections inspired by the
French Revolution and the events in Saint-Domingue occurred in
Jamaica, Dominica, St. Vincent, Guadeloupe, and St. Lucia by 1795.[1]

Neither the French government nor the bitterly divided resident
whites could restore order. Mulattoes, the majority of free people of
color, had rapidly identified their own interests as a caste, demanded
full citizenship, and staked claims among the warring parties. Other
European states, seeing an opportunity to expropriate the rich sugar
colony, jumped into the breach, recruiting slave mercenary armies
against France. Britain, opposed to French republicanism, fearing the
spread of insurgency to Jamaica, and covetous of the island's wealth,
intervened in 1793. Acting on the invitation of anti-Jacobin French
settlers, it established a five-year occupation of the southern and western provinces. This period of incessant warfare among blacks, col-
oreds, resident whites of various classes, and the French, British, and
Spanish governments destroyed the old society of Saint-Domingue
and its core institution, chattel slavery.[2]

Spanish and British assaults following Louis XVI's execution in
1793 reversed the effect of earlier victories against slave insurgents

as French troops regrouped to repel seaborne invaders and Toussaint allied himself with Spain. The genuine possibility of losing the colony led French commissioner Léger Felicité Sonthonax to proclaim the abolition of slavery in August 1793. The National Convention in Paris ratified his action on 4 February 1794.[3]

Recognizing the latent slaveocratic and imperialist interests of his British and Spanish allies, Toussaint lost no time in defecting. He swiftly consolidated the rebel forces and established himself as the one politician who could control the turbulent black masses for France. Colonial armies under Toussaint's direction defeated the Spanish and brought them to a separate peace, giving France eastern Española in the short-lived Treaty of Bâle (1795). Three years later Haitian military expertise combined with the effects of yellow fever annihilated at least twenty-five thousand British soldiers. Toussaint then reached an agreement with General Thomas Maitland to spare Jamaica and other slaveholding colonies and to guarantee the safety of British and U.S. trade. Maitland thereafter withdrew the remaining troops from the island.[4]

The French and Haitian revolutions took place at nearly the same moment in history, but antislavery and anti-imperialist revolt in Haiti began long before the calling of the Estates General. Its history starts with the maroons, runaway slaves whose communities possessed varying degrees of social stability, autonomy, and political articulation. Some remained transient groups devoted to sporadic brigandage while others elaborated complex societies. Legally, the maroons were outlaws. In many instances, however, the colonialists honored their de facto autonomy in exchange for territorial concessions, assistance in recapturing other fugitives, or commercial privileges. Commercial and diplomatic relations between maroons and colonial authorities thus developed a pragmatic character.[5]

Scholars frequently perceive maroon communities as artificial reconstructions of a dimly remembered Africa. "It has long been a canon of Western thought," Richard Price and Sally Price observe, "that small-scale, nonliterate societies exist somehow suspended in time and are extremely slow to change (unless impinged upon from the outside)." Price and Price suggest "that such views profoundly under-estimate the creativity of Afro-Americans, their ability to adapt and reshape their collective pasts."[6]

Black resistance retained a specifically indigenous character in spite of the innovations that the *philosophes* and the French Revolution made possible. This is not to suggest a racial mystique, but rather to indicate the eclectic sources of Haitian politics and thought. State formation in Haiti originated in circumstances both cosmopolitan and local. The colonial struggle between Africans and Creoles for cultural dominance exemplifies this diversity. War with France could not end successfully until the resolution of conflict between these elements, which terminated in Creole victory. African guerrillas' strength lay in their tactical flexibility; their capacity to use Vodun as a psychological weapon; and the solidarity created by close ethnic ties in isolated communities. They had been the first to rise against the French. The more westernized Creoles nevertheless brought to the anticolonial movement a battle-tested knowledge of modern military science and the rudiments of political organization.[7]

Despite Africans' bravery, their leaders' indifference to Western meanings of national independence foreclosed the possibility that they would govern the colony. The cults created in their followers the necessary morale to win battles, but a preference for local autonomy rather than central administration compromised African ability to defeat the enemy. Only the displacement onto France of African and Creole mutual hostility and the substitution of abolition for African or Creole primacy as a goal of the freedom struggle would win national liberation.[8] Triumphant Creoles did not want a state predicated on an African cultural base, but they had to face the social reality of those whose fathers, as Dessalines put it, were born in Africa. To the revolutionary generation, national construction required that Creole and African somehow be melded, a task far beyond the capabilities of European political science.[9] They therefore looked to their own milieu for the answers.

The suggestion here is that the relationship between the Haitian and French revolutions and subsequent state-building is full of contrasts as well as comparisons. Haiti and France, for example, both maintained wary postures imposed by the need to defend their respective regimes. "The obsession with conspiracy became the central organizing principle of French revolutionary rhetoric," Lynn Avery Hunt observes. This had two sources: one rooted in the reality of the counterrevolution being mounted against France, and another in the popular culture. "Conspiracy in France was an age-old popular fixation that was fostered by the rigidities of a subsistence economy and easily sustained by a community dependent on oral transmission of news." [10] Both these extensively illiterate, agrarian societies depended heavily on peasant production. A harsh slave regime bore severely on the oppressed colonial majority. Yet the French and Haitian prerevolutionary experiences differed fundamentally. France's provincials did not correspond to the ethnic Africans in Saint-Domingue's Creole-dominated society. Ethnic difference created unique challenges for Haitian leadership.

The policy of an early ruler, King Henri Christophe (1811–20), demonstrates this. Christophe in the 1810s employed an elite police force of imported Africans whom he purchased from European naval vessels interdicting the slave trade. Scholars assume that these reputedly fierce Royal Dahomeys left a profound, if scantily documented, cultural and religious mark on Haiti.[11] It is possible, however, that Christophe did not contemplate a re-Africanization project so much as he sought a counterpart to Britain's African-born West India Regiments. Perhaps he planned to use his troops in the same way the British did: as leverage against potential rivals and to intimidate the Creole population.[12] In any event, the Dahomeyan regiments draw attention to the innate differences between the French and Haitian situations and the ways that specific local conditions mediated them.

The radicalism, social experimentation, and class leveling of the French Revolution disturbed the landed and commercial governing elites in the United States. In the 1790s Franco-U.S. relations cooled in marked contrast to the mutual sympathy of the American Revolution era. Many informed U.S. citizens furthermore resented the crude efforts made by French officials to exert influence in ruling circles during the Adams presidency. Barely disguised behind these gestures, they believed, lay historic French designs on the Mississippi Valley. Grand strategies for empire hatched in Paris challenged the expansionist ambitions of the North American republic. The U.S. view of the Saint-Domingue insurrection as a giant slave revolt took second place to the hope that the conflict would detach an important sugar island from an aggressive interloper.[13]

British activity on the frontier also hemmed the United States in. Emboldened by signs of federal weakness, Britain concluded treaties with hostile Indian nations and established forts in the upper Midwest, hoping to keep Americans out of the Great Lakes region. Alexander Hamilton defused the growing possibility of war by sending Chief Justice John Jay to London in 1794 to negotiate a treaty to settle territorial and commercial questions. Jay's treaty, in which the British ceded little, proved unpopular with the public but succeeded in averting armed conflict. It resulted in an Anglo-U.S. rapprochement and allowed the United States to turn its attention to French and Spanish activity on its southwest border.[14]

The desire to have France out of the way contributed to U.S. nonchalance about Saint-Domingue. When Congress in 1792 prohibited trade with the French empire, the State Department exempted the profitable commerce with the colony. Secretary of State Timothy Pickering insisted that restrictions did not apply to areas not *"under the acknowledged power of France* [his emphasis]." "If the inhabitants of St. Domingo have ceased to acknowledge that power, there will not," Pickering declared, "be any bar to the prompt and extensive renewal of trade between the United States and the ports of that Island."[15]

U.S. commerce with northern Saint-Domingue, where the greatest destruction of estates had occurred, survived the demise of slavery. Yankee merchants clearly profited from supplying the island with the provisions that uncertain agricultural conditions and import dependency made scarce. Authorities furthermore thought it possible to contain revolutionary contagion by proscription. By 1793 the southern states of the Union had closed their ports to Caribbean blacks. South Carolina went so far as to suspend the transatlantic slave trade for two years. A carefully monitored trade and strictly enforced immigration laws would perpetuate the benefits of this commerce and lessen its dangers.[16]

In 1799, the black general Toussaint Louverture became governor-general of Saint-Domingue with the French government's resigned consent. He had earlier effected the recall of the Directoire's representative, Commissioner Sonthonax. Only Toussaint could maintain colonial security. Toussaint's counterpart, Napoleon Bonaparte, had meanwhile become first consul of the republic. In both cases, soldiers filled a political vacuum and, through military means, protected and extended the domain of a French state now firmly controlled by a powerful bourgeoisie. While Napoleon pressed reforms on central Europe, Toussaint recaptured Santo Domingo. Fear of Toussaint's potential led Napoleon to clandestinely support a rival, the mulatto general André Rigaud.[17]

Saint-Domingue continued to produce abundantly during Toussaint's proconsulship, a testimonial to his managerial ability. The epoch also marked the height of commercial relations between the colony and the United States. Flour, fish, and dry goods comprised the bulk of U.S. exports. Merchants could prosper in the provisioning trade even in lean years. Profits depended on the timing of ship arrivals. In August 1801, the large number of U.S. vessels in Cap-Haïtien (formerly Cap Français) reduced the price of North American goods and raised that of local produce. Only a month before, the situation was reversed, as the needs of Port-au-Prince (formerly Port Républicain) siphoned off trade normally enjoyed by Cap Français. During these years, foreign merchants had little control over price fluctuation, no way to coordinate their activities, and small incentive to break with national affiliation. It is apparent, however, that the creation of scarcity in Saint-Domingue could restrain any tendency for local prices to rise.[18]

Commercial policy coordination nevertheless existed, but the motivation was arguably more political than economic. Both Britain and the United States benefited from the windfall the Saint-Domingue revolution showered upon them. Both remained leery of Toussaint's quasi-independence, especially its consequences for Britain's slave colonies and for the U.S. South. Unrestrained trade with the blacks might eventually endanger chattel slavery and the plantations. In early 1799 British and U.S. authorities agreed on a joint plan to limit their shipping to two ports of entry, from which they could engage in a coastwise trade. Cap-Haïtien, easily accessible from the eastern seaboard of the United States, remained the port of choice for North Americans. Port-au-Prince was best for the British, whose trade would reach Saint-Domingue via Jamaica to the south. If a black army from Saint-Domingue should invade Jamaica, Britain would institute a trade embargo to prevent the outfitting of such a force. The U.S. advantage in this cooperative effort, to which Toussaint had assented, lay in the protection afforded by British naval power. Together, they exerted additional leverage on Saint-Domingue through its import dependency.[19]

U.S. commercial agents stationed in Port-au-Prince and Cap-Haïtien, usually merchants themselves, helped direct commerce and kept abreast of market trends. Tobias Lear, for example, based in Cap-Haïtien, realized that a large U.S. merchant fleet in port would reduce import prices and raise those of local produce. A dearth of foreign merchandise would conversely lower the cost of native goods. The structure of trade made the economy vulnerable to manipulation: scarcity could undermine Toussaint's attempts to maintain a consistent and profitable price for indigenous commodities, thus worsening political instability.[20]

The United States evinced a manipulative attitude through its casual neglect of the formalities that characterized commercial relations. Host countries expected consuls and commercial agents to acquire exequaturs, official documents from the host that authorized them to represent their home governments. The U.S. consul in Cap-Haïtien, Tobias Lear, had not bothered to secure this paper. When he first met Toussaint Louverture, Toussaint returned his commission to him unopened. As Lear subsequently recalled, the governor-general "express[ed] his disappointment and disgust in strong terms, saying that his colour was the cause of his being neglected, and not thought

worthy of the usual attentions." Lear quickly denied any such motivation and attributed his lack of an exequatur to his supposed belief
that he did not need one.[21]

In 1800, Napoleon planned to break through the stalemate in the
Americas by launching a French mercantile empire centered on the
sugar producing dependencies of Martinique, Guadeloupe, and Saint-
Domingue. The European powers had conceived of North America
as a vast storehouse from the very beginning of mainland colonization. Lumber, preserved foods, and dry goods from the continent
provisioned the Caribbean islands and permitted the allocation of
greater acreages to cash crop cultivation. Eighteenth-century wars in
the Indies, which originated in European disputes, made northern
supplies critical, for naval blockades and battles at sea periodically
interrupted transatlantic shipping.[22]

Napoleon, in extending this venerable project, had a secret if trans-
parent objective: the restoration of slavery. All Saint-Domingue knew
that he had already reimposed slavery in Guadeloupe. In 1801 he pressured Spain into ceding France the Louisiana Territory, which would
furnish its tropical islands. This arrangement troubled the U.S. president, Thomas Jefferson, who preferred a weak Spain on his borders
to an aggressive, expansionist France. A French Louisiana portended
the loss of frontier markets, the forfeiture of opportunities for western
development, and, for him, the undesirable necessity of forging an
anti-French alliance with Britain. The last possibility repelled Jefferso-
nians nearly as much as the first two. They did not want to participate
in conflicts that had originated in Europe. The United States, moreover, might not be able to stand alone against Napoleon.[23]

Toussaint Louverture, only nominally loyal to France, fully consolidated his power in Saint-Domingue in 1801 and 1802, thus rendering
Napoleon's slavery project impossible. If the United States did not
want a French presence on its borders, it had the option of supporting
Toussaint in order to frustrate Napoleon's plans. Jefferson understood
that Saint-Domingue had implications for the future of all plantation
agriculture and chattel slavery. A wealthy slave owner himself, the
president dared not risk the spread of black insurgency through the

Caribbean and into the U.S. South. His secretary of state, James Madison, however, did not believe that Saint-Domingue posed a grave danger to a country where blacks were so outnumbered. Accordingly, commercial relations with the colony resumed and survived the next round of bloodshed, that of the war for independence.[24]

The Jefferson administration took an officially neutral stance toward the Haitian Revolution and focused instead on the advantages that the fighting offered traders. By secretly providing the rebels with military supplies, and using this as leverage with them, however, it abetted the destruction of French imperial power in the Caribbean. Deprived of the tropical cash crop windfall, Louisiana would mean only so much trackless forest to Napoleon. To ensure this result, Jefferson sent the U.S. Army to garrison New Orleans before the French could get there. He also intended this troop movement to forestall any British sweep down the Mississippi from Canada and readied Great Lakes area forts for war.[25]

Toussaint in 1801 established a constitution and declared Saint-Domingue a self-governing entity under French dominion. Through forced labor laws he attempted to restore the plantations and revive sugar cultivation. Harsh punishment put an end to civil disorder. His agenda promised to return the colony to the kind of prosperity it had previously enjoyed, but without slavery. U.S. merchants approved his conservative policies, which promised a stable business climate, but Napoleon, who by temperament and social background ascribed to the dominant racism of his day, opposed it. The men surrounding Toussaint, he claimed, were "utterly uncivilized men who did not know what a colony was, what France was." Napoleon did not delay in sending his brother-in-law, the slave-owning general Charles Leclerc, with a large army to depose the black governor-general and wrest authority in Saint-Domingue from "these gilded Africans."[26]

When the French landed early in February 1802, they met stiff resistance in Cap-Haïtien, Port-au-Prince, and other towns. Native soldiers blocked their debarkation and killed suspected collaborators.[27] The rebels used armed schooners and barges to traffic with Jamaican and U.S. vessels in the open sea in coastal areas where they did not control the ports. They bartered coffee and other tropical commodities for staple foodstuffs, powder, and bullets, but sometimes simply seized what they needed. The illicit but lucrative maritime commerce joined yellow fever and the dislocations of the Napoleonic wars in weakening legitimate traffic and French pretensions of controlling it. Documented seagoing trade at Cap-Haïtien declined by 50 percent during the revolutionary years, but local and regional markets thrived.[28]

The French hoped to cripple the insurgency by removing Toussaint Louverture from the scene. They did not intend to make him a martyr; they instead engineered his kidnapping in June 1802. Toussaint was transported to a prison in the Alps, where he died.[29] The people of Saint-Domingue nevertheless continued the struggle against re-enslavement, empowering other leaders. In the course of the following year France fought and lost a genocidal war against its adversaries. Napoleon, realizing that he could not subdue the blacks, decided on a campaign of extermination. He could import new Africans to work the estates, he reasoned. Neither French military prowess, the horrendous tortures employed, nor the specially imported entrail-devouring hounds sufficed to break rebel will. Overwhelmed by the revolutionists' superiority in guerrilla warfare and debilitated by fever fatalities—Leclerc himself succumbed in 1802—France withdrew from Saint-Domingue.[30]

Realizing the uselessness of Louisiana without Saint-Domingue and Jefferson's resolve to press the issue, the French sold the mainland colony to the United States for $15 million. The U.S. government raised the mortgage from British bankers. London approved the loan as a small price to pay for France's removal from the North American continent and its reduction in the Western Hemisphere generally. The loan benefited British banking interests and provided a channel for reabsorbing the United States into the British Empire at some future date. Only the War of 1812 eliminated that furtive hope.[31]

The rebels of Saint-Domingue declared their independence from France on 1 January 1804. The chief of state, revolutionary general Jean-Jacques Dessalines, continued Toussaint's pattern of tacitly stressing human equality by emulating the structure of the French government. Dessalines declared himself emperor of Haiti, as Napoleon had made himself emperor of France. Haiti, the product of a thorough social revolution, became the first such modern state to face the awesome tasks of economic development. Constrained by the international politics of slaveholding empires and by the popular insistence on peasant proprietorship, Haitian leaders began the mammoth effort of national construction.

For Haiti, coffee, not sugar, served as the main link to the global economy. Coffee, compatible with subsistence agriculture and family life, joined the country to the West while simultaneously shielding it from the more direct exploitation that plantation agriculture would have entailed. Being simultaneously at the center and the margin of Western experience created a unique and sometimes contradictory consciousness. Commerce could abet a sensitivity to foreign culture that might overshadow pride in one's own. Given the growing inequalities between Western Europe and North America on the one hand and the rest of the world on the other, invidious comparisons were especially difficult to avoid. Persons whose ancestors had fought the French might still revel in Parisian fashions, literature, and commodities. Others consciously and ostentatiously rejected foreign influences. Very often, the same individual expressed these contradictory impulses. The dialogue between the embrace and rejection of the foreign was a recurrent refrain in the political culture of nineteenth-century Haiti, as in many other countries throughout the world.[32]

A legacy of oppression and a hostile environment led to the emergence of a national security state. The 1806 assassination of Dessalines divided the nation as a power struggle erupted between two regional leaders, the black Henri Christophe of the North and the mulatto Alexandre Pétion of the South. Neither could overcome the other, and Henri Christophe established a monarchy in northern Haiti, ostensibly patterned after Britain's, but in reality absolute in character. The republican presidency of Pétion in the South (1807–18) also compromised democratic values as Pétion inaugurated the institution of the lifetime presidency. For both leaders, the arsenal of self-protection comprised armaments, an oversized military force, prodigious works of civil engineering, state terror, and the embellishment of the ruler's already fearsome reputation. It also included a policy of intervention in the Spanish-speaking eastern half of the island.

Both rebels and masters had clearly understood the strategic importance of the East at an early date. Santo Domingo, a sparsely settled land with highly permeable frontiers and a weak administration, was vulnerable to European interlopers, bushwhackers, and local insurgents. From a base in Santo Domingo, another colonial power could threaten the peace of the French redoubt. Control over the entire island, therefore, remained essential to the security of Saint-Domingue. Toussaint Louverture's recognition of this prerequisite led him in 1800 to consolidate his power through the seizure of the capital, Ciudad Santo Domingo. Its significance to Emperor Jean-Jacques Dessalines (1804–6) spurred him to an unsuccessful attempt to reconquer the area in 1805.[33]

Subsequent Haitian rulers pursued the eastern pacification campaigns. During Henri Christophe's reign, Santo Domingo returned to Spanish control, but the French, and especially the planters' lobby, continued agitating for retrocession. In the hopes of effecting such an arrangement, they retained spies and agents to stir up tensions between the northern Haitian kingdom and the southern republic. Conflict maximized the chance that a unilateral agreement with one of the two Haitian governments would ensue. King Henri Christophe's suicide in 1820 raised fears in Haiti that either Britain or France would attempt to regain control of Haiti by establishing a beachhead in the Spanish territory. From such a base they could harass the Haitian population and destabilize the government. The only security rested on a Santo Domingo firmly under Haitian rule.[34]

Until 1844, when the Dominicans finally expelled the Haitian army for the last time, Port-au-Prince mounted a sporadic series of invasions and occupations of the East. While the Haitians failed to ensure Dominican docility, they did achieve island-wide emancipation at the cost of bitter opposition to Haitian cultural domination. Dominicans strongly resented the assaults on such institutions as the church and the university, as well as Haitian army depredations. The price paid for Haiti's success in abolishing slavery and exiling the old master class was an enduring legacy of animosity between neighbors, which continues to the present day.[35]

Arms alone, however, could not solve the problem of national security. Despite its militant posture, Haiti remained a small, weak state for which warfare against a foreign aggressor could only be an ultimate, defensive act. Diplomacy remained the key to achieving and maintaining a tolerable modus vivendi among enemies. The revolutionary generation's experience with European imperialism provided excellent preparation for a statesmanship that emphasized exploiting the differences among superpowers. Haiti generally benefited from circumstances in which there was little agreement among major countries, and soon learned to foster situations that favored its interests and courted those who solicited its views. Christophe, for example, curried favor among the British as a counterpoise to the Franco-Spanish combination. His friendships with noted English abolitionists, and his endorsement of their public pedagogical practices did not derive from antislavery convictions alone. He encouraged British reformers to perceive him as a progressive monarch whose interest in uplift entitled him to the support of those who might otherwise conclude that Haitians were ripe for re-enslavement.[36]

The relationship between national security and international exchange is also mirrored in the contours of Haitian-U.S. commerce. The War of 1812 and subsequent closing of British ports led Yankee purveyors to rely even more heavily on Haitian trade. The ships they used were of small draft and could easily enter creeks and rivers to market contraband as well as buy and sell legitimately at open ports. To avoid the yellow fever and hurricane seasons in the islands, these vessels (mostly brigs) sailed during the winter months. Traders knew what would sell and therefore could risk taking cargoes to Haiti on speculation. Later, some of the larger merchants established permanent relations with resident purveyors in order to assure sales and a return cargo, and regulate voyage itineraries. In the first three decades of the nineteenth century, New England purchased substantial quantities of Haitian coffee.[37]

Completion of the Erie Canal in 1825 opened up the agricultural bounty of the U.S. interior. Grain and lumber shippers found that Haiti, lying outside the restrictions imposed on the West India trade by European mercantile systems, provided a needed outlet. Haitian-U.S. trade in the 1820s surpassed that conducted between the United States and Scandinavia, South America, and the Middle East. This traffic contributed substantially to the development of such seaboard cities as Boston, New York, Philadelphia, and Baltimore.[38]

Haiti did not receive equivalent benefits from this growth, however. The vexing matter of reciprocity surfaced early. "The question has several times been asked me by the 'Native Merchants,'" commercial agent A. Armstrong wrote pointedly to the secretary of state, "how would our vessels be reccev'd [sic] in your ports' to which I have hitherto given evasive answers—Pray let me know how it should be answered." In actuality, black seamen, especially those from the Caribbean, still could not go ashore in many ports of the southern and middle Atlantic states. The ostensible reason was fear that in the wake of the Haitian Revolution, West Indian sailors would contribute to slave unrest in these locales. Free men boasting of the liberty that blacks enjoyed in Haiti, even if they did nothing actively to encourage revolt, constituted a political threat. Haitians perceived the sanctions against their seamen as an insult and retaliated by maintaining a lax policy on defections to Haiti by any black sailors. President Pétion's promise of citizenship to all blacks and mulattoes in the 1810s further encouraged some mariners to jump ship.[39]

As important as trade was to the economy, commercial inequities and racial proscription only reinforced the importance of land and farming in Haitians' calculus. A popular and lasting tradition, that of the nation in arms, illustrates this. "At the first cannon shot," Dessalines had proclaimed, "the cities are destroyed and the nation is on its feet." He referred to the revolutionary willingness to sacrifice everything for freedom and territorial integrity. His statement also suggested the primacy of land over commerce if an embattled population had to resort to peasant subsistence in mountain fastnesses. The foreign invader would meet nothing but hostile fire from bleak ramparts.[40]

Land also provided the fundamental metaphor for the peculiar republicanism practiced in the United States. Here, too, proprietorship conferred the independence and self-interest essential to civil participation. James Madison, one of the most influential North American theorists, called for continental expansion and export trade development as means of guaranteeing the continued security of U.S. institutions. In so doing, Madison broke with the notion of the republic as a spatially contained unit and made it possible for such polities to aspire to imperialist thinking. In Haiti as well, though insular geography constrained citizens' options, politicians realized that land was the foundation on which all political organization had to rest.[41]

The ideal of the yeoman republic did not readily take hold in Haiti. Old ways die hard. During the regimes of Dessalines and Christophe, prized officers received valuable land grants worked by peasants who were little more than serfs on their estates. In this manner, the plantation legacy survived, and a class of powerful proprietors emerged. While this group never became so large or important as to dominate society, its reactionary character placed limits on subsequent rural development. The deference the revolution might have reserved for the man of merit now belonged, as in colonial times, to the man of property.[42]

In the U.S. South, planter values and impact on land prices displaced yeoman communities in newly exploited areas. As freeholder security guaranteed political stability in the federal republic, growing fear of the power over land and labor exerted by slaveholders eventually destroyed the Union.[43] Haiti experienced this conflict differently. Republican ideology, filtered through the French rather than the English tradition, pertained to the small stratum of educated urbanites. The reality of widely distributed property nevertheless entailed similar consequences. Indeed, the old debate between Haitian Liberals and Nationalists resembled that which had engaged Alexander Hamilton and James Madison. Divergent commitments to agriculture and to commerce divided factions in Haiti as in the antebellum South.[44]

An authoritarian tradition and the incomplete development of market forces limited both republicanism and liberalism in Haiti. Each proved compatible, however, with a populism based on identification with personages and events at the core of the revolutionary experience. Haitians preserved a sense of historic grievance, a receptivity to a stylized political rhetoric, and a feeling of inclusion—whether enjoyed or regretted—in a closed society. Those with either republican or liberal predispositions could employ a rich inventory of metaphors and strategies that had accreted over the course of the nineteenth century to demonstrate their particular viewpoint. Certain items in the repertory were identified with particular historical figures, events, or groups, as David Nicholls has demonstrated in the case of color consciousness.[45] Over time, Haitian history itself came to have the immediacy for some Haitians that Southern history still has for unreconstructed great-great-grandsons of the Confederacy.

Born of circumstances unprecedented in the modern world, Haiti had to create itself, as the maroons had done, from the medley of Creole, African, European, and Amerindian elements in their milieu. Haitians also shared with maroons the uncertainty derived from the fundamental insecurity of their position, and the need, for defensive reasons, to develop considerable cultural and political cohesion.[46] Isolation, paradoxically, proved to be both a shield and a handicap. It mirrored the duality that Haiti experienced in the community of nations as simultaneously outcast and cosmopolitan. The duality had a long history. The word Antilles, which describes the islands of the Caribbean, derives from an old word for Atlantis. It indicates the sense of wonder and estrangement with which early European voyagers regarded the transatlantic world. Yet the islands lay at the very center of the imperialist enterprise and played a strategic role in the subsequent devolution of modern history. The Caribbean sustained agricultural capitalism, the factory system, and racial slavery—and undermined them all.

Haiti's mission of survival in a hostile world involved cultural and ideological as well as economic issues. Its precarious position as an independent republic of ex-slaves created a ready-made affiliation with the international antislavery movement. Abolition's vital center in the early nineteenth century lay in England's middle and working classes.

Haitian leaders soon established contacts with British activists. Sympathy for Haiti also resided in British governing circles. Fears that France might reconquer it and reestablish French preeminence in the global sugar economy encouraged this.[47]

Abolitionists frequently expressed the wish that Haiti could in time become a model society, a symbol of what free wage labor could accomplish. The noted British activist Thomas Clarkson maintained an official correspondence with King Henri Christophe over a nine-year period, during which they discussed various ways to simultaneously develop Haiti and crush slavery. Christophe broached the subject of Afro-American emigration to Clarkson early in 1819. He believed that U.S. opinion increasingly favored Haitian over African colonization. Clarkson noted that emigrationism could provide an opportunity for Haiti to acquire sparsely settled eastern Española if Washington purchased it and ceded it to Haiti as a homeland for U.S. blacks. Landed emigrants would thus free the Haitian army from agricultural pursuits, Clarkson argued. Newcomers with skilled trades would provide a nascent middle class, "the connecting medium between the rich and the poor which is the great cause of prosperity in Europe."[48] Clarkson and William Wilberforce, advocates in Britain of a system of acculturating workers to modern proletarian conditions, also supported Christophe's efforts to introduce the so-called Lancastrian system into Haitian public schools.[49]

Most white American support for Afro-American expatriation rested on republican ideology. The black presence spoiled the necessary civic homogeneity, for example, or it debased whites, thereby making it impossible for them to turn their attention to the task of government. Patently racist arguments stressed the permanent unassimilability of an inferior subspecies, which would find its rightful place in Haiti, Liberia, or elsewhere in the tropics.[50] By contrast, the Haitian government supported emigration because it needed more people, especially in the agricultural labor force. It had historically developed various forced labor schemes intended to keep the plantations in operation and export levels high. The first of these was the Rural Code. Similar in intent to the Black Codes, which would later limit the mobility of freedmen in the United States, the Rural Code prescribed hours of work, restricted travel, punished vagrancy, forbade absence from the plantation, enforced deferential behavior toward employers, and even prohibited the formation of associations for the purposes of buying abandoned estates. Designed to keep workers on the land, the code had little effect on distant rural areas that the state did not effectively control.[51]

Afro-American migration to the Caribbean continued at varying rates throughout the nineteenth century. French and Spanish-speaking Creoles in Florida and the Gulf Coast states traveled to and fro, marking a circular path that linked Cuba, Haiti, Mexico, and the gulf states. Aside from the black loyalist war veterans evacuated after the American Revolution, the British moved some black refugees to Trinidad following the War of 1812.[52] Emigration was not an option favored solely by blacks seeking freedom from racial oppression. Many whites also viewed it as a solution to racial conflict. These included proslavery advocates who saw free blacks' removal as a guarantee that slavery, untroubled by their subversive presence, could continue to expand.

Emigration referred to the voluntary expatriation of blacks; colonization to the deportation of "surplus" blacks.[53] Thus, slave masters practiced a qualified abolitionism: they agreed to free certain slaves on condition that they leave the country. In this case, manumission was neither entirely coercive nor voluntary. Many antebellum free people of color resented colonization and the pressure that such organizations as the American Colonization Society (ACS) placed on them. To them, colonization was a scheme to fortify slavery by removing from the United States those who would most militantly oppose it. They looked upon white involvement with suspicion. Others, while eschewing Liberia and the ACS, saw voluntary emigration as a feasible alternative to permanent discrimination and persecution in the United States. For some, Haiti, the first black republic, provided a desirable refuge. Afro-Americans' interest in Haiti did not rest only on admiration of its military accomplishments. As a sovereign republic it was the prototype of the autonomous black state in the modern world. Its fortunes would rise or fall with the waxing or waning of slavery. If prosperous and secure, Haiti represented both a moral and a political check on slavery everywhere. If feeble and anarchic, it encouraged the forces of degradation and destruction.

King Christophe had agreed to pay the transportation costs of an unspecified number of black emigrants, but he died in 1820 before the plan could be put in operation. By that date, his successor, Jean-Pierre Boyer, had already been in contact with emigrationists and in 1824 promised political liberty and economic opportunity to settlers.[54] As the United States was then Haiti's largest trading partner, a black U.S.-born population would further stimulate business by increasing demand for U.S. merchandise. Haiti would be able to pay for these commodities because of the greater agricultural productivity of a larger farm population. The removal of blacks from the United States, the official Port-au-Prince *Télégraph* declared, would afford more opportunities to the poor whites who remained. The *Télégraph*'s article on immigration coincided roughly with the Philadelphia arrival of Jonathan Granville, appointed by the Haitian government to supervise the stateside end of the project.[55]

Port-au-Prince offered to transport an initial six thousand persons unable to pay their own fares. It planned to distribute land in lots of approximately fifteen and a half hectares to each group of twelve persons able to work. Heirs and assigns would have perpetual title. The Haitians agreed to support for four months those seeking titles to land, provided they were farming. Immigrants were afterward expected to be self-sufficient and their plots would be granted in fee simple. Wage earners, tenants, and those who wished to practice a trade would receive an advance of transportation costs but had to reimburse the government within six months. Those intending to become permanent farmers could expect the most generous terms. Granville recruited forty artisans for settlement in the Samaná Peninsula, until 1844 a part of Haiti. This colony of carpenters, blacksmiths, caulkers, rope makers, and sail makers would build small cruisers for coastal duty on government contract. Haiti would give these tradesmen arable land if they had families.[56]

Prospective settlers greeted these initiatives with considerable enthusiasm. In February 1825, seven hundred Afro-Americans arrived at Cap-Haïtien to take up lands assigned them outside the city. By April, however, there were indications that all was not going well. Haitian Secretary-General Inginac announced that his government would no longer pay transportation costs after June 15. He accused ship captains of conspiring to return people to the United States at inflated costs and at Haitian expense. He complained that emigrants often colluded with these schemes and shared in the profits. The outcome marked the virtual end of official Haitian support for such ventures, and subsequent immigrants either had to pay their own expenses or find sponsors before leaving the states.[57]

Black Americans nevertheless continued to emigrate. From two thousand to eight thousand arrived in the 1820s; more than the number who traveled to Liberia during this period.[58] The first flush of interest had abated, however, and the whispers of dissatisfaction in the United States that had begun in 1825 grew louder. Discontent peaked at the end of the decade. Haiti had good soil and a suitable climate, detractors acknowledged, but it remained plagued by despotic government, sloth, and a low birth rate widely attributed to polygyny. Haitians were irreligious people, some maintained, and Afro-Americans should not settle among them.[59]

The emigration experiment did not engender new tensions in Haitian society, but it did exacerbate some preexisting ones. Haiti possessed a small elite of landed proprietors. Some had purchased or inherited their lands; others had received property in payment for military or other service to the state. Estate management proved problematic for this class. Labor costs remained high as Haitians increasingly worked for themselves on small peasant holdings. Labor was available in areas where the Rural Code held sway, but plantation productivity did not reach prerevolutionary levels. Former U.S. slaves—who sometimes arrived en masse from the same plantation—reacted negatively to a perceived lower standard of living. When they demanded as rights what many Haitians viewed as privileges, the elite often reacted with indignation. They saw no reason why newly arrived laborers could not live in a manner befitting their station. Those settlers fared best who could start out as proprietors, professionals, or artisans. They enjoyed a higher degree of social acceptance and consequently, once they had fulfilled their initial obligations, had more options and mobility in Haitian society.[60]

Communications limitations further compromised the emigration experiment in the 1820s. Southern legislatures had passed laws restricting the activities of West Indian seamen, and most commerce between Haiti and the United States took place in middle Atlantic ports. Routing and availability of transport further ensured that the majority of emigrants would hail from the coastal cities of the northeastern states. Haiti wanted agricultural labor, but the emigration movement instead attracted a large proportion of urban blacks.[61]

Many believe that Afro-Americans did not remain in Haiti in sufficient numbers to resist assimilation, but nineteenth-century travelers noted the presence of identifiable groups of Afro-American ancestry. Descendents of Boyer's Samaná Bay colonists still inhabited the area in the late twentieth century.[62] Black migrations outside the continental United States in the 1800s ran counter to the worldwide trend toward metropolitan centers. These movements necessitated both material incentives and strong ideological appeal, which to some degree, Haiti offered. What it could not provide, however, was the promise of enough prosperity and security to offer a wide range of choices to the prospective citizen. Recent scholarship upholds the view that antebellum U.S. blacks were as interested as whites in the accumulation of wealth and property and saw economic security as a partial solution to their plight. The avenues that increasingly restrictive legislation left open were narrow but often seemed more promising than a risky bet on a small, turbulent Caribbean country.[63]

Haiti maintained in the early nineteenth century a foreign policy completely in keeping with its status as an isolated developing state. The refusal of the great powers to extend it diplomatic recognition kept its foreign relations confined to trade. Shifting allegiances and intrigues during the colonial wars and the revolution had taught the value of playing larger powers off against each other to gain time and advantage. Dominican instability remained a source of concern.

As a result of their own problems with national security, Haitians

could fully understand President James Monroe's December 1823 declaration proclaiming opposition to European colonial expansion in the
Americas. They nevertheless found themselves omitted from its supposed protections. The Monroe Doctrine was the fruit of nearly fifty
years of evolving U.S. foreign policy. Revolutions in Spanish America
in the 1810s prompted Great Britain to maintain neutrality so that its
lucrative regional commerce could continue. The United States, also
neutral, waited until after the annexation of Spanish Florida to com-
mence recognition of the mainland republics. Rebuffed when he proposed a joint Anglo-American declaration, Foreign Minister George
Canning approached the French separately. Through the Prince de
Polignac, the French ambassador to the Court of St. James, the British
obtained assurances that France would not intervene in Spain's behalf
in the Americas. The Monroe Doctrine was thus promulgated after
the threat to hemispheric security dissipated.[64]

Incorporated in Monroe's message to Congress, the doctrine asserted that the United States would not interfere in European affairs
but viewed further imperialist ventures in the Western Hemisphere as
a threat to its security. Monroe disavowed any intent to incite colonial revolution but swore to interpret any aggression or intervention
against the nations that had successfully won and maintained their
sovereignty as acts hostile to the United States. This statement, with
the existing opposition to transferring colonies among powers, constituted the basis of a Latin American policy that guided U.S. activity
in the hemisphere for generations to come. At the time of its proc-
lamation, the United States had little independent power to back up
the Monroe Doctrine. The policy's strength rested in reality on Britain
maintaining a similar course of action. British sea power underwrote
Washington's pronouncements in a harmony of interests that dated
back to the years of the Haitian Revolution.[65]

The historian Rayford Logan observed how closely the Monroe Doctrine was conflated with the issue of diplomatic recognition. That
question effectively removed Haiti from consideration as a state that
had gained and conserved its independence. Haiti endorsed the U.S.
stand on South American revolutions. The reduction of French power

in the hemisphere was a boon to Haiti, although neither Britain nor the United States intended the nonintervention principle to apply to it. For Haiti, diplomatic recognition was the only safeguard against French attack. Britain and the United States, meanwhile, having traded for years with Haitians as insurgents and later as citizens, realized that nonrecognition did not impede a long-standing, lucrative commerce.[66]

The Monroe Doctrine thus had less utility for Haiti than for other Latin American states. Excluded from the protected group of independent republics, Haiti remained vulnerable to reconquest. Curiously, the doctrine coincided with the Haitians' own policy prescriptions. They too were jealous of their frontiers and anxious about the disposition of a weak neighbor whose collapse would compromise their sovereignty. Their ambition was to unify the island under Haitian rule and preclude the possibility of foreign infiltration. Not surprisingly, the Dominicans viewed the situation differently. They saw the Haitians as uncivilized aggressors and usurpers, bent on destroying their language, religion, culture, and tenuous claim to membership in the white race.[67]

No metropolitan state after 1825 really wanted the onerous task and dubious reward of defeating and annexing Haiti. Many contemporaneous Haitians, however, would not have accepted such a demurral. External control of Santo Domingo, whether through military invasion or peaceful economic penetration, would narrow Haitian options. This would be so even if the Dominicans and their allies adopted a peaceful coexistence policy with their western neighbor. Consequently, friction between the two states of Española, exacerbated by alien interests, continued to breach the peace of the island. Haitian foreign policy increasingly emphasized multilateral diplomacy, heavy restrictions on expatriate ownership and investment, and a "Monroe Doctrine" for Española. Haiti made clear its opposition to foreign incursions in the East. These nineteenth-century policies comprised the foundation of Haitian relations with the outside world.

2   Race and Nation

Postmedieval Europe was a political construction that rested only partially on the traditional ethnicities that conventionally comprise a nation. The "French," for example, by 1792 had created a central state out of a host of regional and dialect groups, imposing on all of them the language of Ile-de-France. The "British," no less composed of a variety of ethnic groups, also forged a nation-state from often unenthusiastic human material. By 1800, nation and state had ceased to be coterminous, but in almost every Western country a hierarchization of ethnic groups formed the basis of cultural identification and political empowerment. Only in the United States, where a self-conscious doctrine of pluralism prescribed equality for whites, was the conformity imposed by a unitary conception of the state and national culture somewhat relaxed. Even there, however, strong assimilatory pressures made the Anglo-American cultural ideal synonymous with practical citizenship.

The ethnic hierarchy in each Western state led variously to the suppression of separate national subidentities and to the differential valuation of persons according to ethnicity. It was tacitly understood that some groups would permanently remain subject peoples, imperfectly integrated into the cultural and political life of the nation state. Proscription rested on certain social categories. One had to do with such legal conceptions and cultural concomitants of persons as honor, duty, and human and civil rights. In slaveholding societies, these distinguished the free. Modern slavery relied heavily on racial and ethnic identity to define the boundaries of the civil condition, and thus genetics paralleled freedom or bondage.

Proscription also rested on the preemptive rights assumed by states or by dominant ethnic groups within states. The consequences of such arrogation of power fell very heavily on aboriginal populations. The process of delegitimizing the prior claims of earlier settlers to land and

34

other resources necessitated their devaluation as people and ensured their defeat in subsequent transactions with the dominant society. Refusal to conform and submit to these dictates, as encapsulated in the nation-state model, created another avenue for rationalizing hierarchy. Cultural and religious refusal, as evinced by many European Jews, for example, permitted state authorities to treat such nonconformists as offenders and to bar them from full civic participation.

In 1804 when Haiti declared its independence, Europeans and North Americans perceived Haitians as persons who, had they been under the jurisdiction of a colonial power, fit the above proscriptions quite well. These rebel slaves were not civil persons. Most, moreover, remained obstinately attached to African religious beliefs and forms of expression. They refused to acknowledge a universal Christianity. Yet Haitians, by the very act of freeing themselves from bondage, could not be treated as a conquered minority group. To many whites, they had only fortuitously slipped the yoke. Their freedom and pretensions to nationhood were specious, and only force of arms guaranteed their preposterous claims to sovereignty. While Haitians' ability to defend themselves during the early years of independence could not be disputed, their right to do so did not remain unchallenged. Black Haitians and mulattoes, whose dubious descent compromised their claims to humanity, were thought intrinsically unequal to whites and would be so considered in the community of nation-states.[1]

Socioeconomic status at first had little to do with the West's repugnance. A long history of manumissions in Saint-Domingue had created an elite free class of sufficient wealth and refinement to represent Haiti in the most elegant courts and chanceries of Europe. The United States, a slaveholding settler republic, which penalized people of color, did not accept black envoys. Other Western powers that tolerated slavery only in their empires had fewer such qualms. Nonwhites comprised so minuscule a percentage of the population of Europe that the presence of a minister from an independent black state caused no tremor in society. Black diplomats were received at court and regarded not as challenges to the proper order of things but as curious, even exotic, visitors from afar.

For the United States, the demographic facts of life differed some-what. There, the overwhelming preponderance of whites did not alter the perceived need to subordinate blacks or mitigate slave owners' determination to seek out and destroy any signs of servile revolt. By interpreting the slightest sign of black unrest as the beginnings of a rebellion to be suppressed at any cost, slave owners could rally their own forces, instill terror in the slaves, and maintain social security. The result was a peculiar society in the slaveholding districts, one based on fear and the need for mastery. For blacks, it held the possibility of violent death.[2]

Antebellum slavery foreshadowed in some ways the horrors of the modern police state in the Americas. It erected an unassailable authority based on property rights, patriarchy, and labor exploita-tion, all of which a quiescent church sanctioned. "Disappearances," associated in contemporary thought with corrupt and despotic Third World regimes, occurred commonly as slaves were processed through internal markets, moved by their masters to new locales, or privately executed. Society tolerated psychological and physical abuse. Few voices of moral outrage cried out against the system.

With the exception of Cuba, plantation society in North America outlasted its Caribbean counterpart, which took a long time to ex-pire. Nowhere was its demise more dramatic than in Haiti, which uprooted, evicted, and decimated the entire French planter class in little more than a decade. Haiti became anathema in slaveholding so-cieties: the catch phrase "the horrors of San Domingo" connoted the dreaded reversal of the master-slave relationship. It was the revolution in which whites who had abused slaves discovered for themselves the agony of the choke chain, face mask, whip, rack, and pyre. If the Haitian revolution's major feat had merely been the destruction of a small community of planters, its impact, though keenly felt, would not have been as great as it was. The Haitians had not only destroyed the master class but had made it impossible to restore it or the plan-tation. England, Spain, and the United States held no particular brief for French ownership of western Española, as their efforts to wrest control of it attested. Their discomfiture rested instead on the fear that neither they nor France would ever again profit from Haitian soil.

Proslavery advocates furthermore feared the spread of insurgency. Additional harm to the plantations would transform the islands into disaggregated peasant economies from which no whites could benefit. A Caribbean controlled by blacks would continually menace the U.S. South as a source of revolutionary contagion, an asylum for runaways, a base for antislavery filibustering operations, and a center for European intrigues against North American integrity.

Given these considerations, Washington's nonrecognition policy toward Port-au-Prince from 1804, the beginning of Haitian independence, to 1862, when it finally ended, stemmed logically from sectional and national interests and fears. It also reflected the general convictions of the white citizenry. In the United States, even free blacks lacked constitutional protection; they subsisted on the margins of economic and social life, and remained vulnerable to enslavement through caprice, ruse, or the slightest legal inconsistency. To accord members of this race recognition of sovereign status, particularly in light of the way they had achieved it, was unthinkable.

The weight and unanimity of racist opinion dictated the path the United States would take for the first fifty-eight years of Haitian independence. There was, however, a minority voice. Literate members of the free black population knew the Haitian legend. A tiny segment of this group, concentrated chiefly in the Gulf port cities, had fled the revolution and looked on the black republic with disfavor. Others of the same Creole background participated in a pattern of circular migration to and from the Gulf states, Cuba, and Haiti. Many educated Afro-Americans perceived the Haitians as a heroic people who had struggled against slavery and won. Allusions to the Haitian Revolution are pervasive in black antislavery discourse.[3]

Antislavery voices grew louder in the 1830s despite the harsher treatment of blacks that accompanied Jackson administration policies. Militant white settler expansionism and ideology pushed American Indians out of the South and opened new lands to the brutal slavery of the large-scale cotton plantation. The same social forces that made it increasingly difficult for free people of color to practice trades and pursue commerce also proscribed Haitian business operations in U.S. ports. Such transactions within the United States had to be brokered by white intermediaries. Nat Turner's 1831 rebellion in Virginia, which galvanized proslavery advocates, provided the catalyst for renewed efforts to legally control both slaves and free persons of color. In a reciprocal climate of declining receptivity to foreign merchants in general and Yankees in particular, Port-au-Prince imposed a 10 percent surcharge on U.S. goods.[4]

Informed Haitian opinion was generally critical of Jacksonian America. Complaints of U.S. racism from black immigrants, Indian removal policies, the restoration of slavery in Texas (where it had formerly been illegal), the conflicts with Mexico, and the belief that the United States would attempt to annex Canada prompted Haitians to identify their northern neighbor as a ruthless, expansionist power. Washington's refusal to normalize even consular relations with Haiti hampered the conduct of ordinary business, prevented the presentation of reclamations, and created difficulties for those who served as U.S. commercial agents.[5]

The changed atmosphere surrounding Haitian-American commercial relations evoked the attitude toward Haiti expressed by Britain and France. France prohibited Haitian imports in the Antilles, and Britain refused to extend free trade to Haiti, a country capable of exporting to the English colonies, which were not self-sufficient in food production. Such a trade would have strengthened the black republic both economically and politically. Only toward the end of the War of 1812, when the United States could not supply Jamaica, did Britain temporarily drop the ban on Haitian foodstuffs for this hungry—and turbulent—colony.[6]

British emancipation in the 1830s did not bring immediate recognition of Haiti, a policy that the Foreign Office eventually drifted into rather than proclaimed. In any case, Haitian trade with Great Britain remained modest. Under the circumstances, France remained the best outlet for Haitian commodities. It accorded Haiti qualified diplomatic recognition in 1825, pending the settlement of claims presented by the expropriated white planters of the *ancien regime*. While the French discouraged Haitian contacts with Martinique and Guadeloupe, they nevertheless purchased for use in Europe most of the coffee harvest, including the portion that once had gone to New England. French products cost too much for most Haitians to buy, so the United States continued to provide their basic staples, paid for by coffee earnings in Europe. Franc-dollar conversions created opportunities for financial speculators in Port-au-Prince.[7] Port-au-Prince, which previously taxed exporters in kind, began to demand payment in cash, usually in hard currency. Dealers in the United States often bought merchandise ordered for Haiti with drafts on London and Paris, especially when European prices for such tropical commodities as coffee, mahogany, and logwood rose. The results locked Haiti into a growing international financial system, and it felt the effects of the global panic of 1857, when large commercial houses, especially those associated with European trade, collapsed.[8]

Haitians nevertheless proved quick in the 1860s to exploit the market in cotton fiber that the loss of the slaveholding southern states opened up in the Northeast. In the year ending 3 September 1864, the port of Gonaïves alone shipped over 250,000 pounds of cotton to the United States. A gradual trend toward abolition led to improved Haitian-U.S. relations that promised to eventuate in diplomatic recognition. The enduring character of Haitian-U.S. commerce rapidly solidified during these years. No large Haitian mercantile firms capable of operating from U.S. headquarters existed, and maritime business activity continued to move along a track long since delineated by precedent and custom.[9]

Haitian policymakers tried sporadically to protect the local economy from the negative effects of alien domination, utilizing legislation that restrained expatriate commercial activities. Yet such stratagems as progressive taxes for foreigners and the reservation of certain prerogatives to nationals could be defeated by pressure at the consular level, smuggling, and bribery.[10] A burgeoning consumerist ideology also thwarted the desire for economic autonomy. Foreign observers and westernized elites in the Americas took the rising expectations and changing tastes of the postemancipation era as a measure of improved civilization. Haitian peasants, for example, were encouraged to buy and wear shoes. (Indeed, as late as the 1940s and 1950s, appearing in Port-au-Prince without them entailed possible arrest.) Custom obliged freedmen to purchase the accouterments of their altered civil status, for the multiplication of exchange relations were believed to index modernization. Earnest Britons who in the 1830s sought to replace Niger Delta slave traffic with the palm oil trade hoped commerce would serve as an avenue along which rational Christianity and other Western values could advance. Civilization correlated with both commerce and dependency in colonial minds. The world's "backward" peoples, they believed, should pay for their newly acquired consumption patterns by intensifying their agricultural production.[11]

Commerce alone did not suffice, however, to create a community of nations with common goals and values. Aside from its inherently unequal terms, trade did not address Caribbean conditions, where weak republics required freedom from external intervention in order to develop mature political institutions. The limitations of the purely commercial relations that the United States pursued with the Caribbean republics are exemplified by the Spanish occupation of Santo Domingo in the 1860s, the subsequent warfare that resulted, and the involvement of Haiti as a party vitally interested in the outcome of the Dominican-Spanish conflict. Embroiled in its own Civil War, the United States lacked the resources and energy to respond, which clearly demonstrated the need for a less casual regional diplomacy.

The Dominicans had successfully rebelled against Haitian rule in 1844 and established a republic which they defended against successive offensives from Port-au-Prince. Haiti launched large expeditions against the Dominican Republic in March 1849 and June 1850. Warfare continued between the two countries for most of the twelve-year reign of Haitian Emperor Faustin Soulouque I.[12] Washington had remained relatively indifferent to this recurring conflict as well as to great-power meddling in Haitian and Dominican affairs. The disinclination to become involved owed something to the domestic sensitivity of the slavery question, the preoccupation with frontier settlement, and the general acquiescence of European powers in broader U.S. claims of regional hegemony. The United States was also discovering its own interests in the Dominican Republic and would pursue them fully, despite vigorous Haitian protests.

Political instability in the Dominican Republic and chronic tensions with Haiti led Dominican President Pedro Santana, acting without popular consent early in 1861, to arrange the annexation of Santo Domingo as a Spanish province. The arrival of Spanish troops from Cuba aroused general indignation. An organized republican opposition, sheltered by Haiti, took form across the border and made frontier incursions with Haitian assistance. Spain exerted a heavy-handed rule that played directly into the insurrectionists' hands.[13]

Madrid's pique at Haitian involvement in the conflict led to a confrontation on 6 July 1861. The Spanish navy threatened to bombard Port-au-Prince if Haiti failed to offer a twenty-one-gun salute and pay an indemnity of approximately two hundred thousand Spanish dollars for alleged damages resulting from prior frontier invasions. Government officials initially refused these demands and prepared for a siege, but they later capitulated. The local populace was so outraged that authorities had to resort to martial law to restrain antigovernment demonstrations. Spain subsequently forced the Haitians to receive Spanish casualties and refuse asylum to Dominican refugees. It pressured Haiti to agree to its unification with Santo Domingo, a process which, under the circumstances, Port-au-Prince had to reject.[14]

As Spain's pressures continued, U.S. consular representatives in Haiti felt the disadvantage that the absence of a U.S. diplomatic mission caused. They interpreted France as an interested party in the Spanish occupation and believed that both European powers wanted to ensure that the United States would not acquire a foothold in Santo Domingo. Arthur Folsom, commercial agent at Cap-Haïtien, suggested that a U.S. chargé d'affaires be accredited to both Santo Domingo and Port-au-Prince. Such an official, who would travel in circuit to both capitals, would negotiate with all interested parties to restore peace to the island. Now was the time, Folsom believed, for

the United States to assert itself in Española.[15] Unable to quell the insurrection, the Spanish parliament formally renounced its Dominican
claim on 3 March 1865.[16] The United States, itself at war, had not responded to the fighting, but the need to prevent such reoccurrences
clearly depended on greater diplomatic efficacy among the Caribbean
republics. Secession and the establishment of the Confederacy had
created a unique opportunity for Washington to revise its Haitian
policy.

Lincoln had originally perceived the Haitian recognition question
and the concurrent, and recurrent, dilemma of black unassimilability
as linked issues. Only toward the end of the Civil War did he begin
abandoning his commitment to colonization, which he had endorsed
as the solution to U.S. racial problems. He believed that slavery and
the black presence lay at the root of the current U.S. crisis. Removal
of both these sources of discord could restore harmony to what was
intended to be, and what must remain, a white man's country.[17]

Lincoln's desire to appease the loyal slave states and prevent their
secession played a role in coupling the decision to recognize Haiti with
colonization. If the security of the plantation South necessarily rested
on the diplomatic isolation of Haiti, that need was no longer a problem
for the United States. Indeed, as casualties in the Civil War mounted
and exposed the grim savagery of the contest, the Lincoln administration gradually came to enact policies with the express intent of
undermining slavery in the rebel states. The subsequent exodus of the
freedmen would guarantee the South as a homeland for whites. Freed
of the need to conciliate slaveholders, the United States recognized
Haiti on 5 June 1862.[18]

The veteran abolitionist Charles Sumner led the prorecognition debate in the Senate. Sumner did not attempt to engage his colleagues'
rather tenuous sympathies for blacks in his arguments but based his
appeal on pragmatic considerations. He cited the value of Haitian
trade to U.S. commerce, noting that many states regardless of section shared the benefits of doing business with the island republic.
Sumner also argued for consistency in a policy, which traditionally
recognized all de facto governments except Haiti and Liberia. The

arbitrary character of that refusal impugned the "national character" and deprived the U.S. citizens of the usual protections that diplomatic relations normally afford.[19]

Kentucky Whig Garrett Davis opposed Sumner. His principal argument centered on the racial implications of recognizing black states. Polite white society in the capital would have to rub elbows with Haitian or Liberian ministers. "Negro wives and negro daughters" would appear at gala social events. Davis told a story about an incident that had occurred in France. "A few years ago," he narrated, "the refined French court admitted and received the representative of Soulouque. . . . a great big negro fellow, dressed out with his silver or his gold lace clothed in the most fantastic and gaudy style, presented himself in the court of Louis Napoleon and . . . was received. . . . The American minister, Mr. Mason, was present on that occasion, and he was sleeved by some Englishman . . . who pointed him to the embassador [sic] of Soulouque, and said, 'What do you think of him?' Mr. Mason turned around and said 'I think, clothes and all, he is worth $1000.' "[20]

The recognition debate in the House of Representatives divided along partisan rather than sectional lines. Northern opposition to diplomatic relations with Haiti rested not only on racism as such but on the general conception of Haiti as a republic without virtue, that is, a republic without whites. Representative Samuel S. Cox of Ohio was one of recognition's most vehement opponents. His objections echoed the familiar charges of Haitian barbarity and political instability. Noting the modesty of the Haitian trade as a proportion of total U.S. commerce, he opposed establishing missions in a country he regarded as economically marginal. The Ohio congressman based his aversion on his view of proper race relations in the United States. If Washington sent ministers to Port-au-Prince and Monrovia, they would reciprocate with envoys of their own color. The obligation to extend the same courtesies to these foreign representatives as offered to the aristocratic Europeans, who formed the usual diplomatic contingents, would put the State Department in an awkward position. Social equality for black foreigners, moreover, was but the first step toward breaking down racial barriers at home. Cox opposed this and regarded the recognition question as a radical abolitionist ploy to subvert society.[21] "How fine it will look, after emancipating the slaves in this District," he asked, "to welcome here at the White House an African, full-blooded, all gilded and belaced, dressed in court style, with wig and sword and tights and shoe-buckles and ribbons and spangles and many other adornments which African vanity will suggest!" Such an envoy could not be taken seriously. "With what admiring awe will the contrabands [that is, refugee freedmen] approach this ebony demigod! while all decent and sensible white people will laugh the silly and ridiculous ceremony to scorn!"[22] Advocates of recognition sidestepped the question of equality, but conceded that no improvement in relations between the United States and the black republics could take place without it. Representative Charles J. Biddle, Democrat of Pennsylvania, believed that recognition therefore should not be pursued. Racial equality might "be a philosophic idea, an English idea, but it is eminently un-American."[23]

Representative Daniel W. Gooch of Massachusetts argued that good relations with Haiti would grow from the natural U.S. interest in everything that happens in the Americas. In a hemisphere still endangered by European imperialist ambitions, Haiti might prove a valuable ally. The concerns of the commercial state Gooch represented undoubtedly helped shape his viewpoint. New York and Boston merchants had petitioned Congress ten years earlier to recognize Haiti. Gooch suggested that if Congress had followed these recommendations, Spanish intervention in Santo Domingo could have been avoided. Merchants also wished to facilitate a commerce that nonrecognition had hampered. Haiti ranked twenty-first in imports of U.S. goods out of seventy-three nations with which the United States traded. The Haitians bought many stateside products and wanted to buy more. Haiti could also produce cotton, an attractive option, as war had limited revenues from sales of this commodity. Haiti additionally was willing to receive as immigrants the freedmen whose liberty many white Americans found so troubling.[24]

Haitian recognition became a salient issue at a crucial time for the

Republican party and helped to define its notion of republicanism in the Civil War context. The key protagonist was Abraham Lincoln. Lincoln remained committed to colonization at least through the second year of his presidency. He doubted the possibility of social equality between the races, and because he wanted an America for whites and abhorred slavery, he endorsed a country for blacks. The acceptance of Haitian and Liberian sovereignty was a logical corollary to the colonization ideal.[25]

Lincoln advocated the "natural limits" thesis. He saw a productive and populous northern region multiplying its associations with the West while the southern plantation economy developed slowly. The South faced strangulation and the destruction of its institutions because of its structural inability to expand and diversify its economy and its growing weakness in Congress. Lincoln ruled out radical antislavery agitation, inherently distasteful to this conservative, and counterproductive to the "southern strategy" he chose to pursue in the loyal slave states. Time would take care of slavery.[26]

The key to the president's optimism about the future lay in his assessment of the West as a settlement for white yeomen. Abundant land would neutralize their social and political restiveness. Free Soil held out the promise of opportunity for such whites as Lincoln had represented as senator from Illinois. The presence of blacks—slave or free—compromised the dream. At any rate, the greater productivity of northern agriculture and industry seemed to ensure that the developing West would draw population principally from the free states. Slavery, to Lincoln, had no future.[27]

As for Latin America, Lincoln wished to create a favorable climate for U.S. business and influence there, and to retard British progress. He did not favor the creation of a noncontiguous empire; once again, the United States was for whites only. Rule over darker races would only recapitulate the slavery trauma. In Lincoln's version of republicanism, the possession of a vast western hinterland prolonged what western political thought had always seen as the evanescence of republics. The recognition of other, racially alien republics only assured U.S. safety and tranquility. The mutual succor of sister republics, bound by nonroyalist, constitutional principles, would provide a bulwark against aggression from Old World empires.

Lincoln appointed a commission to negotiate the settlement of Afro-Americans in Central America, only to be rebuffed by isthmian governments. The State Department enlisted ministers in European capitals to sound out their hosts on accepting black American settlers in their tropical colonies. Lincoln also considered Haiti as a possible sanctuary. The Haitians had endorsed organized emigration projects before, and sporadic, individual immigration to Haiti had continued throughout the nineteenth century. The desire to remove and resettle the black American population thus forms an integral part of the decision to recognize Haiti.[28]

The Haitian government itself subsidized an emigration project beginning in 1859, when President Fabre Geffrard retained James Redpath as an agent to enroll U.S. and Canadian blacks in a homestead program. Geffrard wanted to rationalize agriculture by increasing labor exploitation. This included reimposing the *corvée*, a system of forced labor for road building and similar projects. Geffrard also sponsored the rural code of 1864, an attempt to suppress "vagabondage" and make agricultural labor more readily available. Geffrard was acting on policies that many tropical regimes instituted during this era. Governments that had eradicated life servitude often resorted to legal stratagems to enhance the survival of plantations. State legislatures in the U.S. South would soon pass Black Codes, designed to limit freedmen's mobility and reap their labor for the benefit of planters. In Jamaica, the British government hoarded public lands so that peasants, having no farms of their own, would have to work for others. Geffrard's interest in black Americans rested chiefly on their utility as plantation laborers. He planned to use them on his personal estates as well as on those of wealthy partisans. As with previous schemes in which emigrants did not receive the homesteads they anticipated, the Geffrard plan came to naught.[29]

During the Civil War, the Lincoln administration fostered another Haitian colonization project. Businessman Bernard Kock had sought and received Lincoln's endorsement of his plan to locate Afro-American cultivators on an offshore island, the Ile-à-Vache. Once Kock's unsavory reputation became known, however, the federal government withdrew its support. Kock thereafter secured front men who successfully obtained federal cooperation for his venture. Kock was keeping the colonists in virtual slavery by summer 1863. The U.S. consul in Aux Cayes described Ile-à-Vache as a charnel house where freedmen perished of disease and starvation while white managers lived in sumptuous luxury. When the emigrants rose in rebellion, Kock defected, the colony was dismantled, and the inhabitants were repatriated to the United States.[30]

Many officials correctly considered the colonization schemes that Lincoln encouraged to be scams organized by unscrupulous hustlers. Those associated with egalitarian attitudes toward blacks, such as John Hay and William Seward, also kept their distance from these projects. Taxpayer resistance to funding large-scale deportations of blacks also played a role in determining the cool reception accorded colonization in government circles. It furthermore became apparent that the black majority lacked interest in emigration.[31] Much of the colonization sentiment indeed rested on white racism and cynical attempts to profit from it, but some Afro-Americans had historically sought alternatives to minority status in the United States. The black nationalist impulse that helped recruit settlers for Liberia and Haiti in earlier decades persisted, abetted by the persecutions of slavery.

Free Afro-Americans began an involuntary exodus from the South in 1850. Demand for slave labor had slowed manumissions, as had renewed enforcement of harsh legislation subsequent to slave rebellion and growing abolitionist agitation. The region's increasing defensiveness about antislavery activism and its growing propensity to violently repress dissent created a political climate that deeply circumscribed the liberties of free black persons. In some cities, white immigration and the growing hostility of native white workers cut into the economic opportunities available to them. Finally, both local and national fugitive slave laws made life difficult for those who could not prove their civil status.[32] Growing repression gave impetus to many to leave the localities where they had long resided. As clientelistic arrangements with white patrons failed during the general crisis, many blacks emigrated, settling at first in the northern states. Later in the decade, the Supreme Court ruled in the Dred Scott case that free blacks' citizenship was unconstitutional and that they had no civil protection under U.S. laws. During these years, thousands fled the United States for Canada, Europe, Africa, and the Caribbean.

The most articulate disciple of a revived Haitian emigration movement in the mid-nineteenth century was the Afro-American Theodore Holly, an Episcopalian missionary who moved to Haiti in 1861. Holly endorsed black emigration as long as he lived, believing that it could have strong reciprocal benefit for émigré and host alike. Haiti was independent and abounded in natural resources, Holly wrote. Its drawbacks included an inadequate labor force, technological backwardness, and a quasi-pagan religion. Black Americans had no government of their own and faced oppression in the United States, where they would never attain social and civil equality. By their energy, capacity for work, knowledge of agriculture, and devout Protestantism, however, Afro-Americans could advance morally and materially in Haiti and make significant contributions to their adopted country. Holly thought ideal a blend of African and European cultural characteristics, contrasting these to the supposed decadence of Haiti's Afro-Latin culture and religion. In Holly's estimation, the black American would "civilize" Haiti—modernize it technically, uplift it spiritually, and place it in the vanguard of the worldwide movement to improve and elevate the black race.[33]

Support for Haiti in abolitionist circles and among black Americans in general did not denote total acceptance of Haitian institutions and society as nineteenth-century reformers found them. None approved of the Afro-Haitian cults and secret societies. All exhorted the government in Port-au-Prince to westernize the populace and raise its intellectual and material level. What chiefly distinguished the pro-Haitian from the anti-Haitian critics was their antislavery commitment and the environmentalism that held that all peoples could advance morally and spiritually once freed of a demoralizing milieu.

Historians have accurately depicted black American sentiment as predominantly antiemigrationist during most of the antebellum period. The brief vogue that emigration to Haiti enjoyed depended on particular situational advantages that Haiti had over other proposed homelands. The Haitian project—unlike the Liberian, which derived financial support from wealthy white philanthropists and federal and state grants—did not depend on government subsidies and was less associated with slaveholders and other eminent whites. Haiti was also close enough to the United States that those who had a change of heart could revise their plans with considerably less difficulty than if they had chosen Africa.[34]

Colonization and emigration continued to have a provisional character during the Civil War years. Aside from the experienced and well-established American Colonization Society, most of the private organizations were ad hoc responses to particular opportunities. The U.S. government during the Lincoln presidency wanted to remove blacks from the United States but could not commit sufficient energy and resources to the project. Ultimately, black labor proved too sorely needed, as the South rebuilt itself, to sacrifice. Haitian interest in black American settlers also seemed sporadic. Haiti required able and energetic agricultural workers but could offer nothing except the possibility of land ownership to draw them. This solitary enticement it appeared reluctant to tender. Interest in Haiti subsequently abated as homesteading within the continental United States became more desirable—and possible—for black Americans after the Civil War. Their admission to citizenship seemed to signal an end to the old system that perceived free blacks as a threat to the integrity of the polity.

The victory of antislavery forces in the U.S. Civil War came as a relief to Haitians. Aside from the transient wartime benefits to local commerce, emancipation temporarily arrested U.S. expansionism and terminated the militancy that the aggressive planters and filibusterers who had greedily eyed Cuba carried southward.[35] Abolition indirectly benefited Haiti by undercutting the rationale on which its universal ostracism had rested.

3   Trade and Empire

For centuries after Spain abandoned total dominion over the West Indies in the late 1570s, the area remained an international waterway. The territories that bordered it were originally prizes in European power contests. Only after the Napoleonic wars ended in 1815 did the islands and littoral of the Caribbean basin cease to be constant staging grounds for European wars. Soon after the Peace of Paris, however, other colonies began following the lead of the United States and Haiti, making concerted efforts to throw off imperial control. Independent republics ringed the Caribbean Sea by 1865. Most of the islands continued to be colonies, however, and great-power military demonstrations in the area aimed more at subordinating subject peoples than at containing the ambitions of rivals. U.S. concerns in the region centered on its long-standing provision trade and its continuing interest in Cuban affairs. Following the Civil War, Washington began to dismantle the U.S. fleet and turned its attention to the tasks of national reconstruction and internal development.

In policymaking circles, some officials remained sensitive to the import of Caribbean issues. One of them, Secretary of State William Henry Seward (1861–69), repeatedly urged Congress to sustain the cause of territorial expansion and the pursuit of privileges in Latin America. Seward's projects included a treaty with Colombia to construct a canal, acquisition of the Danish West Indies, annexation of the Dominican Republic, and establishment of a naval base in Haiti. To Seward, these proposals were strategies, rather than simply ways to acquire real estate. He showed less interest in adding more land to the already formidable U.S. domain than in obtaining what he perceived as commercial leverage. Canal rights and naval stations constituted part of a broader program to build integrated military, commercial, and communication networks.[1] With the exception of Alaska, however, Congress proved unresponsive to his suggestions. Public opinion did not support incorporating peoples of alien races and cultures, nor did it wish the United States to be a colonial power. Many drew the line at annexing noncontiguous territories.[2]

Negotiation of reciprocity treaties formed a key aspect of Seward's foreign policy. Such agreements with noncompetitive countries drew them into the U.S. commercial orbit and integrated them into a growing market. Haiti and the United States concluded a reciprocity treaty in 1864 which resembled those drafted with other Latin American countries during the same period. It placed the citizens of the respective countries on an equal commercial footing. The agreement rested on the false premise that commercial goods were at par with agricultural commodities when in reality the latter had less value. Reciprocity was thus a device to improve U.S. standing in Latin American markets. While Haitians, for example, consumed large quantities of northern foodstuffs and an increasing share of U.S. manufactures, they conducted no stateside business, nor did they market coffee in North America. For years Haiti maintained a favorable trade balance with the United States by illegally exporting hard currency, a device that only masked underlying market inequities.[3]

Expansion of naval and merchant marine operations was another arm of Seward's policy. Maritime commerce required coaling stations in strategic locations. The U.S. Navy favored the deep harbor Môle St. Nicolas, which one officer likened in quality to Newport, Rhode Island. The Môle (which means "breakwater" in French) was additionally attractive in the 1860s because of the general expectation that steamers would soon replace sails in the Latin American trade.[4] The Môle figured in the politics of the rival factions competing for the Haitian presidency in 1865. Warfare had broken out between the supporters of Fabre Geffrard and Sylvain Salnave. Geffrard enlisted British aid and offered territorial concessions if he succeeded in defeating his adversaries. For his part, Salnave approached the United States with a counteroffer, adding that Geffrard's folly would subvert the Monroe Doctrine. The seriousness with which Seward greeted the situation is revealed by his January 1866 trip to Haiti. Seward, ostensibly vacationing, arrived in Port-au-Prince to impress upon U.S. minister Henry

Peck the importance of concessions, though he warned against ac-
quiring the Môle or any similar property secretly. Seward had gauged
the extent of anti-imperialist opinion in Congress and among the public. At the same time, however, he carefully refrained from rejecting
Salnave's proposal outright, preferring to maximize his options.[5]

In mid-1868, after the Salnavist victory, Haiti again secretly offered
the Môle to the United States in exchange for U.S. assumption of its
French debt. The United States would discharge the obligation with
revenues from a customs regime at the Môle. Washington would also
protect Haiti against foreign invasion and internal insurrection. By
essentially offering to accept a protectorate, President Sylvain Salnave
planned to ensure his survival in the midst of an insurgency. Seward
did not like the idea. A Haitian protectorate would be unconstitutional, he told U.S. minister Gideon Hollister, for such a treaty was out
of character for U.S. statecraft and would not gain Senate approval. As
Congress had adjourned when Sylvain made the offer and would not
reconvene until December, the Secretary of State instructed Hollister
to refuse it. He may have sensed that the outcome of the anti-Salnavist
insurgency would be determined by December.[6]

Haitian partisans might cynically dicker with foreign powers over
bits of their own national domain, but as rulers they viewed Dominican cessions differently. Haiti jealously regarded any foreign interest in the eastern part of the island, including President Ulysses S.
Grant's flirtation with Dominican annexation in 1870 and 1871. To that
end, Grant had established a commission of inquiry, including such
Republicans of merit as the Afro-American antislavery activist Frederick Douglass. The commission traveled to the Dominican Republic
in 1871 to report on prospects for incorporating that country as a federal territory. The fact-finding tour also included attempts to evaluate
public opinion. The administration found Haitians worried. Secretary
of State Hamilton Fish regretfully noted a report from Ebeneezer Bassett, the U.S. consul in Port-au-Prince, that anti-American sentiment
had escalated. After "what has been done by the United States for the
African race in the past ten years," Fish asked, how could Haitians
justify their suspicions? Fish understood past Haitian refusal to tol-

erate slaveholder sovereignty, but the United States had made blacks citizens and had even sent a black representative (Bassett himself) to Haiti.[7]

Haitian anti-Americanism also owed something to the popular belief that the United States had abetted Salnave's overthrow in 1870. Haitian insurgents had purchased two ships in the United States and outfitted them in Haitian waters. Fish denied knowledge of these steamers' missions and blamed Haitian diplomatic and consular personnel stationed in the United States for carelessly allowing them to clear port without protest. Washington had observed and would continue to observe, he insisted, a strict neutrality regarding Haitian civil conflicts.[8]

Haitians knew, moreover, that segments of the Dominican ruling class had long advocated colonial status as an alternative to a shaky national independence. In the 1870s, fear of Haitian domination played a role in this preference. The government of Pedro Santana tried to negotiate acquisition of the entire country by the United States. Just as Congress had rejected most of Seward's schemes, it defeated this project, remaining more interested in commercial advantage than colonial rule. Undoubtedly, the growth and maturity of the United States played an important role in the politics of reciprocity, territorial concessions, and annexation. The tensions surrounding these issues cannot be fully comprehended, however, without reference to the Haitian side of the equation. The second half of the 1800s looked very different from Port-au-Prince than it did from Washington.

After mid-century, Haitian trade began to assume the form that characterized it for the next one hundred years and that played a key role in shaping its relations with other countries. The history of the revolution initially influenced the course of commercial development. The fall of the planter class in Saint-Domingue entailed the destruction of its chief economic base, the sugar plantation. Sugar required ample acreage, processing facilities, a large labor force, and animal power for operating machinery and drawing vehicles. All of this necessitated an access to capital possible only for an elite or a government. Sugar production at the end of the eighteenth century demanded a regimen that only slaves would tolerate. It was no longer an alternative after independence.

Following some abortive experiments, the Haitian government found that most free people would not work the sugar estates as formerly. They opted instead for cash crops that complemented rather than competed with foodstuffs and that could be cultivated and harvested without injury to provisions. Tree crops appeared. Haitians cultivated cacao and felled logwood (*campèche*) and mahogany when sporadic demand for these forest products arose. Coffee trees, planted on many colonial estates as a secondary crop, rapidly became the principal source of both popular and governmental revenues.[9]

Peasant smallholders continued to make decisions they believed to be in their own interest. Crop substitution in times of declining prices was a common stratagem. Just as they had earlier substituted coffee for sugar, peasants began chopping down coffee trees or substituting banana palms in response to a poor market. Some, countering the fraudulent weighing practices engaged in by buyers, added small stones to coffee sacks before shipment. Producers sold their coffee to middlemen (*speculateurs*), who forwarded it to urban merchants. It went from the cities on consignment to European markets. Havre or Hamburg brokers warehoused the coffee for later auction.[10]

The web of Haitian commerce connected rural buyers and sellers to wholesale vendors and brokers. In his 1901 novel *Thémistocle Labasterre*, author Frédéric Marcelin gracefully evoked the urban merchant's world in fictional form. He wrote of a subculture that he knew intimately, as he himself descended from a trading family. Labasterre's father, a cloth purveyor, employed his wife as a walking cashier at his market place stalls. She collected the proceeds from the peasant women who peddled his goods. Saturday morning was a big market day in Port-au-Prince and Mme. Labasterre rose early to pray for success in business. On Monday morning, the Labasterres paid off their creditors. The wives of wholesale and consignatory merchants did not work, and this distinction marked off the social distance among these groups within the merchant class.[11]

A small group of twenty Haitian and foreign mercantile and banking houses controlled the rate of exchange, discounted paychecks, and set commodity prices. Members of these firms retained offices in Port-au-Prince's Bord-de-Mer commercial district. The work day ended at 5:00 or 6:00 p.m., when businessmen repaired to villas in leafy districts fifteen minutes by horse and buggy from the waterfront, creating a small rush hour in the late afternoon.[12] Commerce rested on an agricultural base that expanded little in the late nineteenth century. While coffee, cotton, and logwood exports did increase slightly—often in response to short-term demand—larger production simply compensated for the generally declining prices of commodities during the worldwide agricultural depression. Repayment of the French debt and various brokers' commissions also consumed a considerable slice of the economic pie.[13]

The Haitian trade was often a precarious business, but those with ample resources profited from it. Local realities set limits to ambitions. There could be little foreign exploitation, for example, of Haitian land. With a few exceptions, most entrepreneurs found it more lucrative to import provisions for urban areas than to absorb the long-term risks associated with cash crop production.[14] The government responded to commercial problems by creating a tariff structure that made it cheaper to import luxuries than staples, thus shifting the tax burden from the small wealthy groups to the large and impoverished productive classes. A related policy placed urban inhabitants' demands above those of the rural majority. The pattern is familiar today in many developing countries. Where rural dwellers are scattered, badly organized, and impoverished, central governments need not respond as quickly to their needs as to those of a volatile city population much closer to hand. Port-au-Prince knew only too well what mobs could do, especially when aroused by dissatisfied civil servants and other restless urban elements.[15]

The volume of Haitian-American trade decreased after the U.S. Civil War. This deterioration had to do with the general slump in agricultural prices and the devaluation of silver experienced by all developing countries during the epoch. Coffee, Haiti's major export, met stiff competition from such countries as Brazil and from colonial producers. The failure of silver and bimetallist policies in the principal finance capitals of the world worsened its chronic monetary difficulties.

Haiti shared another symptom of the worsening market for tropical producers: a gradual contraction of credit. The advent of the steamship and regularly scheduled sailings lowered import-export costs while multiplying the number of suppliers. Certain Caribbean and West African traders had attained considerable wealth, but tropical merchants generally proved vulnerable to market changes and could not properly insulate themselves from the effects of crop failure and political unrest. Credit restriction resulted from more frequent failures among this group by the 1890s. Lenders came to prefer business transactions with overseas agents of home firms.[16]

Two factors offset the worst of this for Haitian merchants. One was the comparatively better prices paid for Haitian coffee and logwood in Europe, an advantage that allowed U.S. merchants to exchange goods in Haiti for gold or drafts on London and Paris.[17] Haitians also looked forward to the technological breakthrough that would eventually result in the construction of an isthmian canal. The canal, it was widely believed, would inaugurate a new age of commercial prosperity.

Growing independence at the consumer end of the coffee trade led major European buyers to attempt regulation of the commerce as a means of insurance. Coffee can be readily stored and preserved, so Havre brokers, like Haitian peasants themselves, handled it like currency: they bought large quantities, hoarded it, released it to manipulate the price, and extended credit to producers.[18] Havre dominated the Haitian export trade throughout the nineteenth and most of the twentieth century. Around 1900, however, German firms began a small but serious competition in tropical commodity sales. Certain German businessmen had already established themselves as employees of French mercantile houses in Haiti and knew the market. Haiti's modest harvests meant little in absolute terms, but they were steady, and gave the cartels sufficient margin to discipline such large producers as Brazil, whose own price manipulation efforts met with indifferent success.[19]

The coffee exchange financed consumption of Western commodities in the developing countries, which purchased manufactured goods to an unprecedented degree.[20] London, Paris, and New York made short-term loans to Third World buyers. Merchants from Germany and European states without colonies also utilized the French and British money markets to do business in Africa, Asia, and Latin America. Some transactions were farmed out to dependent institutions in these areas. Haiti's national bank, in actuality a French firm staffed by French officers, operated with French capital. The National Bank of Haiti did not normally extend commercial loans, but the advantage of financing trade through such an establishment was that the farther away a country from the seats of power, the higher the interest rates. As Paul P. Gourvitch noted, "A draft drawn on a European center from such a distant country is paid only on arrival, some 20 or 30 days later, during which time the buying house can use the money gratuitously."[21]

Europeans had clearly engrossed important parts of Haitian commerce and finance. The United States dominated only the staple provisions trade. It competed vigorously with Britain in dry goods but did not succeed in ousting its textiles.[22] Haiti, a poor country, provided generous money making opportunities for foreigners and nationals with ready access to capital. The economic systems that developed in mid-century facilitated the exploitation of national resources, and created the illusion—at least in the cities—that prosperity was within reach of many and had indeed been attained by some. Publicists equated progress and civilization with the adoption of western tastes and habits, an idea that has persisted. As in other societies, consumption in Haiti was mandated not only by the desire for material display, but also by a wish to modernize the country.[23]

Economic problems underlay many internal conflicts. President Fabre Geffrard's experiment with black American immigrant labor, for example, derived from a desire to accelerate agricultural production in a manner that would not revive the indigenous peasantry's rebellious instincts. Haitian politicians shared similar concerns with colonial authorities on other islands who, following emancipation, tried many stratagems to create an agricultural proletariat, from vagrancy laws to restricting access to public lands.

Haitians recognized these regional trends, and particularly as they developed in Jamaica. Exploited peasants and workers in both countries experienced disaffection during these years. Haitians strongly objected to the violent suppression of dissent following the Morant Bay protest in Jamaica in 1865. Several Haitians resident in Jamaica were caught up in the police dragnet and arrested for conspiracy. A rising sentiment coupled opposition to President Geffrard's domestic policies with criticism of British imperialism.[24]

Aversion to Geffrard's program went beyond its economic impact. Geffrard, a mulatto, was identified with French language, culture, and religion. An enemy of Vodun, he led a campaign to destroy shrines and discredit priests. In 1864 his government effected a rapprochement with the Vatican to bring more foreign priests to Haiti. Many opposed this because of the close past association between the Roman Catholic Church and French neocolonial aspirations. The many Haitian Freemasons, for example, resented papal condemnation of their organization and practices.[25]

In March 1867 a coalition of Geffrard's enemies forcibly deposed him, and after two months of indecision and provisional authority, installed Sylvain Salnave of Cap-Haïtien as president of Haiti. Salnave, a northern populist, based his widespread support on dissatisfied grassroots elements. Rural immigrants to cities, the urban poor, female market vendors (*marchandes*), and devotees of Vodun numbered among his adherents.[26] Anti-Geffrardists had wanted a puppet governor whose intimacy with the masses would neutralize popular discontent while business proceeded as usual. "Business," of course, meant the continued domination of the Haitian economy by foreigners, and a comfortable niche in the system for the indigenous upper classes. The use of demagoguery to appease the masses without disrupting the system was not new in Haitian politics. It was referred to as *la politique de doublure* (understudy politics). Occasionally, however, the understudy had an agenda of his own.[27]

Salnave intended to use the United States as a cat's-paw to prevent the hostile British and French from gaining excessive influence. By withholding confidence from the gourde, foreign merchants could disrupt local trade. Salnave countered by establishing a network of state stores, issuing an inflationary paper currency, and nationalizing exports. Now, only Haitian merchants with shops in the impoverished "popular quarters" could engage in a retail commerce with prices fixed by the government. In this way, Salnave made inroads into the European import-export sector and rewarded his indigenous constituents at the same time. This was crucial: the ability to distribute patronage and redistribute largesse could make or break a politician.[28] Most commodities purchased by the urban poor in Salnave's system came from the United States. The sale of cheap durable cloth, preserved foods, soap, and tobacco enlarged the commerce that Seward wanted to extend. U.S. diplomats on the scene shared their European colleagues' distaste for Salnave and his familiarity with the lower classes, but they recognized his importance to Yankee interests.[29]

Salnave also demonstrated his shrewdness regarding questions of territoriality and neutrality. He let the Môle St. Nicolas issue stand but arranged for other officials to approach Europeans with alternative proposals. In 1868 a Haitian functionary allegedly told the French that guaranteeing Haitian neutrality would give Europeans clear access to the Pacific and remove the United States as an obstacle to their advance. Discussing a possible neutralization convention with Americans, he reversed the argument.[30] In any case, it was to Haiti's interest to encourage U.S. involvement. A multiplicity of players improved the odds for Port-au-Prince in an era still characterized by a lively European colonialism.

Before 1898 Spain was the most troublesome extrahemispheric power in the region. It had traditionally involved itself in the colonization and recolonization of the eastern part of Española and had quarreled with Haiti over Santo Domingo since the Haitian revolution.[31] Many West Indians held Spain's tardiness in abolishing slavery responsible for retarding Afro-Cuban progress. Finally, as the premier Caribbean nationalists, Haitians readily identified with traditional Cuban patriotism and desires for autonomy.

During Cuba's Ten Years War against Spain (1868–79), Haitians followed with interest the career of Cuban nationalist Antonio Maceo. General Maceo, a black man, had attracted widespread attention for his military exploits. Maceo in 1879 visited Port-au-Prince but left abruptly after the Spanish consul's peremptory demand for his arrest.[32] During the war, Madrid worked out a quid pro quo with Port-au-Prince that exchanged official Haitian support of Spanish counterinsurgency for security against Haitian partisans' filibustering from Spanish colonial soil. This arrangement suited President Michel Domingue but not his successor, Boisrond-Canal. Tensions between the two countries continued.[33] Haiti maintained an official neutrality during the Cuban-Spanish conflict. Spain kept Cuban residents in Haiti under surveillance, intercepted all insurgencies mounted from Haitian shores, and applied pressure on the black republic to police all potential subversives.[34]

Spain's relative freedom of action indicated its comparatively secure position. It remained in control of Cuba and Puerto Rico, and could have reconquered the Dominican Republic. The Caribbean could not be termed an "American lake" in the 1860s and 1870s. France ruled Martinique, Guadeloupe, Guyane, and several smaller islands. Britain dominated Jamaica, Barbados, Trinidad, and many other dependencies. The Netherlands and Denmark also had colonies. The United States alone had no possessions. The Central American and Caribbean republics comprised its major trading partners, aside from Cuba. The principal U.S. advantage was its proximity to the region and its ability to supply it cheaply and efficiently with basic provisions.

The 1880s witnessed a revival of Seward's call for commercial expansion, accompanied by a growing clamor for a larger navy, more bases, and government support for an isthmian canal. This agitation stemmed from a burgeoning U.S. economy battling the effects of recurrent depressions and searching for markets for both agricultural and industrial products. Practical and ideological considerations barred the development of a noncontiguous formal empire, but policymakers did not rule out the prospect of client-patron relations with dependent states. Secretary of State James G. Blaine (1881; 1889–92) favored uniting hemispheric trade under U.S. aegis. Blaine saw no practical way to do this without a more vigorous Latin American policy.[35]

The State Department advocated commercial and infrastructural changes that integrated all the Western Hemisphere economies save Canada's. This would include a uniform gold standard, common customs conventions, and inter-American highway and rail systems. Washington also carried forward Seward's bilateral reciprocity treaties with most favored nation clauses. Such arrangements, which tended to exclude third parties, made handy instruments for conquering Latin American markets, which a large merchant marine backed by a modern navy would guarantee. The stage was thus set for new involvements. Years before Alfred Thayer Mahan's 1890 publication of the navalist classic *The Influence of Sea Power upon History, 1660–1773*, the United States had already enlarged its naval appropriations budget.[36]

War provided the means for the United States to accelerate these advances, especially in the Caribbean. Washington followed the declaration of war against Spain with admonitions to the Haitian government and its nationals to refrain from profiteering (a Caribbean practice since time immemorial) and to observe perfect neutrality. Haiti could offer no prizes for sale in its harbors, nor could these ports be havens of refuge. No privateers could fit out or recruit there, nor would the United States tolerate demonstrations on the part of private citizens. Haiti agreed to these conditions. Given its inability to defend itself from attack by either power, neutrality remained its best recourse. Public and official sentiment leaned, furthermore, toward the United States, as it had historically played no role in insular interventions. In 1871 Washington had rejected an opportunity to annex Santo Domingo and did not even express serious interest in naval stations on Haitian or Dominican soil.

The "splendid little war" with Spain, perhaps the most painless in U.S. history, lasted only three months. The United States defeated Spain in July 1898 but continued to occupy the island at the end of September, assuming the role of "protector" of Cuban aspirations. Cuban nationalists began a guerrilla campaign of national liberation. They wanted independence, not a new colonial master. The U.S. public's desire for commercial expansion clashed with its fears of overextending the natural domain of native institutions. Racial fears also played a part in the reluctance to assume an openly imperialist role. The United States consequently neither disengaged from Cuba nor proclaimed the intention of remaining there permanently.

The unwillingness to release Cuba made Haitians uneasy. While they welcomed the Spanish withdrawal from the Caribbean, they quickly observed that an energetic new power was ready to take advantage of whatever opportunities presented themselves. Latin American countries, the Port-au-Prince *Le Matin* opined, must now make the necessary reforms to ensure their political stability, economic independence, and, consequently, continued autonomy.[37]

4   Trade and Culture

An export-oriented agricultural colony, Saint-Domingue imported a substantial proportion of what it needed, instead of diverting valuable land to raising provisions. It paid for these commodities, directly and indirectly, with sugar and coffee, the mainstay of its wealth. Merchants trading with Saint-Domingue consequently developed a strong interest in these crops. After independence, coffee became the major preoccupation of both growers and traders.

Goods that merchants brought to Haiti constituted the other axis of commercial attention. These products, and those who provided them, linked Haiti to its Western trading partners. A powerful merchant community continued to influence events in Haiti as agents of metropolitan economic and commercial power throughout the twentieth century. Located almost exclusively in the port cities, this group played a major role in shaping the black republic's relations with such states as France, Germany, Britain, and the United States.[1]

The mercantile class included members of the traditional Haitian bourgeoisie and descendents of the black and mulatto freedmen who obtained land and capital after the expropriation of white colonists during the revolutionary era. Some entered the import-export trade on their own account, and others served as brokers for foreign concerns. The merchant sector found moral support in the widespread belief that the freedmen's acquisition of "habits of civilization," such as wearing shoes, would accelerate their modernization and social development. The small bourgeoisie helped to create a consumer culture in Haiti patterned on the cultural tastes of the developed Western countries.[2]

The expulsion of the French had given native purveyors an edge in conducting the commerce of the country, but they did not remain alone in exploiting the market. In 1843 the government permitted the influx of larger numbers of foreign traders. The tiny community of merchants from Britain and the Hanseatic states grew slowly and steadily in the nineteenth century. Persons from Caribbean countries, the Middle East, France, and a variety of other European states, gradually swelled their ranks. The need to control foreign residents soon became a strategic one. Aliens and native merchants had to be isolated from political matters, as their allegiances could undermine the state's interests. At the same time, a foreign identity could prove advantageous to a businessman. It preserved the essential brokering character of transactions with nationals and gave the outsider some protection from the strictures of local law and politics. In time, the combined merchant class came to constitute an independent, powerful urban group. In 1880 U.S. minister John M. Langston characterized it as "the most important and influential element in the social life of Haiti."[3]

The trading communities also sheltered a population whose national identity could not always be precisely fixed. The term Creole generally described these people of uncertain citizenship, born in the Caribbean or U.S. Gulf ports. This group included those involved in patterns of circular migration between Haiti, Cuba, and New Orleans; individuals born in Jamaica, St. Thomas, Martinique, Guadeloupe, or the Turks and Caicos Islands who had emigrated to Haiti; and persons of Jewish origin from the Dominican Republic and Curaçao. In an era of lax passport control, when the thousands of tiny Caribbean ports and coves were, at best, casually patrolled, nationality could be a matter of temporary convenience.[4]

A salient characteristic of this transnational group was its high frequency of racial and cultural intermixture. Natives of a region where the predominant language and religion might vary widely from island to island, many individuals were multilingual and, at least, bicultural. Their cosmopolitanism proved an asset to business activity. Foreign values and ideas acquired in time a legitimacy increasingly associated with wealth, class privilege, education, the use of French and other European languages, foreign travel, and light skin color. In contrast, an unequivocally Haitian identity rooted in agrarian life, the Haitian language, and uncompromisingly native customs persisted. The tension between these seeming opposites profoundly affected the debate in Haiti on such diverse subjects as language, politics, race relations, and culture.[5]

The high value assigned to European physical features and culture strengthened a desire for exogamy among the bourgeoisie that reinforced slavery era prejudices against dark-skinned people. "Improving the race" through genetic selection for Caucasian phenotypes reflected a parallel concern with socioeconomic mobility. Against the rural, illiterate, pagan black peasant was counterpoised the urbane and civilized mixed-blood whose Western manners could match those of any European. Alliances with foreigners could also be politically valuable and economically profitable. A foreign passport might ensure one's protection from the whims of arbitrary local officials, and a strategic marriage might facilitate the development of important business contacts.[6]

Numerous elements in Haitian culture conspired to make the family, and for upper-class groups, marriage, cornerstones of community life. The ancestor worship characteristic of African religions and Vodun, the Catholic emphasis on the family bond, and chronic political violence and instability gave kinship overarching significance as the one protective and continuous social institution. Family networks helped to incorporate the bourgeoisie into the metropolitan market system.[7]

All things being equal, the intimate cultural and commercial connection of the Haitian upper classes to the West should have facilitated modernization and development in the black republic. It did not, nor did the indigenous bourgeoisie succeed in preserving its place. Aliens largely supplanted natives in the import-export sector, in major retailing enterprises, and in banking and finance by 1900. Haitian policymakers had long been sensitive to the implications of a trade that outsiders controlled. In the course of the nineteenth century, they wrote laws to regulate foreign nationals' penetration of commerce. Aliens had to purchase trading licenses and pay taxes on expatriate employees. They could buy cash crops only through Haitian middlemen and were generally barred from petty retail activity. Legislation restricted foreign commercial activity to the coastal cities.[8] Efforts to enforce these rules were sporadic. Even if enforcement had been rigorous, however, changing world conditions made it increasingly difficult for small, independent businessmen to operate profitably and efficiently.

The Caribbean region consisted of many islands, some densely settled. The short distances between ports of call prolonged the use of sailing vessels long after the oceanic trade had abandoned them. Steamships, when they finally appeared, precipitated some commercial changes. Faster speeds meant that orders could be filled more quickly without the huge bulk shipments characteristic of earlier eras. The opportunity to rapidly send and receive smaller cargoes lessened the dependence of individual traders and modest firms on the large importers and distributors. By 1900, many retailers had begun the direct importation of goods themselves.[9] On the face of it, this should have enhanced opportunities for small traders to participate, since they could cut out middlemen. In reality, it chiefly benefited those who could trade in volume and ensure foreign suppliers a steady market. The better capitalized foreign commercial houses, which were often branches of overseas trading companies, often prevailed over local establishments in this milieu.[10]

Declining world agricultural prices in the late nineteenth century also adversely affected the Haitian economy. Coffee, the principal export, met considerable competition from Latin America and colonial Africa and Asia. The metropolitan countries privileged growers in their empires, and Haiti's competitor, the mammoth producer Brazil, strongly influenced the market to its own benefit. Coffee had bought time for Haiti in its early years, but could not subsidize its development after 1890. Many native merchants whose credit and liquidity had depended upon strong tropical commodity prices went under during the depression years of the fin de siècle.[11]

Foreign companies replaced defunct Haitian firms, and they offered greatly enlarged competition from 1890 to 1914. During this epoch, the most powerful European states had established political and economic control over vast regions of the globe. They rivaled each other in their efforts to dominate the remaining sovereign states of the tropics. The United States joined them in the Western Hemisphere. As the United States industrialized, it grew increasingly jealous of what it regarded as its regional prerogatives. Many observers predicted that such small, weak countries as Haiti would ultimately lose their independence. Haitian statesmen came to rely even more extensively on a policy they were long familiar with—that of playing the superpowers off against each other. Entrepreneurs could not separate the new trade rivalries from politics. Reciprocal or clientelistic relationships with influential people became a prerequisite for business success. Aliens from powerful countries found their citizenship a growing asset.

Thoughtful Haitians worried about the pressure exerted on the country by private foreign interests and foreign governments. They shared the Latin American fear of losing control over their resources and of compromising their national sovereignty. Yet Haiti's problem did not rest entirely on penetration from abroad. To a large degree, Haitians had adopted attitudes and behaviors that made cultural and psychological infiltration possible. A Eurocentric worldview permeated the national leadership, not only officials but the intelligentsia and urbanites of various classes. Kinship linkages bound many at the top to a foreign outlook and foreign interests.[12]

Chronic political instability in Haiti (as in other Latin American countries) also helped destroy the basis of business prosperity. Internal conflict wrecked infrastructure, undermined confidence in national firms, and, even in peacetime, diverted the energies of those most likely to engage in commerce. Economic and political uncertainties led members of the upper classes to forsake the risks attendant upon business ventures and enter the professions which they used as a springboard to civil service sinecures.[13] If the current leadership proved hostile to their interests, constraints on opportunity in Haiti gave them a powerful motive to subvert the existing order. Foreign and native observers alike criticized educated Haitians for preferring politics over entrepreneurship, and for crowding into law or medicine instead of diversifying their vocational choices. Uncertainties in Haitian political and economic life conditioned their behavior.

The narrow choices available to scions of the Haitian bourgeoisie, and the growing prestige of foreigners, were linked to a process that also involved the economic and cultural depletion of the provincial towns. The demise of the sugar estates early in the nineteenth century had drawn erstwhile free colored planters away from the rural areas. Abandoning agriculture, they settled in such cities as Port-de-Paix, St. Marc, and Gonaïves and turned to trade and business. By the early 1900s the bourgeoisie was on the move again. Its retreat from commerce synchronized with its departure from these provincial seaports, which sank into quaint torpor as their leading citizens established Port-au-Prince addresses. Their removal to the capital swelled the population and wealth of that center, increased its political importance, and began a centralizing process that the U.S. protectorate and dictator François Duvalier would later continue.[14]

City life put the Haitian intelligentsia in touch with mainstream intellectual currents. The subsequent exchange of ideas, commodities, and cultural artifacts was not, however, equal. Wealth, whiteness, and urbanity, all associated with progress, left little room for the articulation of an indigenous Haitian ideal. In any event, such an elaboration would prove a difficult task, further compounded by linguistic and religious disparities. The devaluation of things Haitian was a critical consequence of the failure to address this cultural problem. The bourgeoisie's retreat into the asylum of ambiguous nationality reflected the political and pecuniary advantages of identification with foreigners. It also illustrated a deeply experienced form of psychological and cultural estrangement that often took the form of denial. This denial characteristically discounted the significance of nationality and race and sought transnational alliances on the basis of class. Those so strongly drawn to Europe as to deprecate their Haitian identity did not, however, have a transcendent ideology in mind. They were not internationalists. Worldliness rather than idealism described these sophisticates, whose outlook rested on a fundamental individualism.[15] The development of such a perspective in a country as self-consciously nationalistic as Haiti owes much to its mercantile history. Maritime trade outlasted the plantations and chattel slavery. Tensions that developed between the emerging Haitian state and foreign merchants and powers in the nineteenth century persisted, and the creation of a strong association in the popular mind between consumerism and progress advanced a Eurocentric worldview.[16]

Foreigners also experienced a sense of alienation in Haiti. Many could lay no firm emotional claim on a fatherland. Certain expatriates had no clear nationality. Others, while descended from families respected in the islands, might be itinerant. These individuals could use kinship networks to set themselves up in trade and settle in areas that seemed promising.[17] Nationality was thus a convenience that facilitated business pursuits. By 1900, the increased importance of recognizing and adopting a nationality became identified with the policy objectives of specific countries. The patriotic tie bound subjects to the states to whom they professed allegiance. It enhanced the social prestige that merchants enjoyed in such a dependent country as Haiti. At the same time it enjoined on the recipients of privileged status the obligation to represent the particular interests of their homeland or its government.[18]

Herein lay the source of the conflict between urbanites on the one hand, and those with roots in an indigenous, particularistic Haiti, on the other. The dynamic tension between cosmopolitanism and nationalism contributed to political unrest and helped precipitate the twenty-year U.S. occupation that began in 1915. Before that event, often referred to by Haitians as a *fatalité historique,* a term with providential connotations, the contradictions in Haitian life engaged two generations of polemicists. These critics tried, often with a sense of urgency, to unravel the tangled skein of their country's political and cultural institutions.

Cultural fragmentation marked the black republic throughout its history. Artifacts of the colonial era given new life in the present—the divisions between black and mulatto, peasant and urbanite, Creole speaker and Francophone, illiterate and literate, cultist and Catholic—underlined a fundamental tension in Haitian society. It is easy to exaggerate these differences, however. "Black" and "mulatto" are social constructions rather than biological facts. The Haitian population, like that of any part of the Western Hemisphere where there has been African admixture, spans a continuum of somatic traits. A black or mulatto ascription, therefore, rested on more complex considerations than that of color alone. Racially mixed persons constituted a principally urban population as early as the 1830s, but many also maintained rural properties. Country people might have client relations with town dwellers, contacts that resulted from market networks, or the employment of relatives in urban areas. The use of the French language separated the educated and westernized elements from the bulk of the population, but Creole never lost its place as a lingua franca. Similarly, a continuity of customs and folk belief linked the more privileged classes to the peasant majority.

These bonds gave cohesion to the society but did not prevent conflict. French and Creole elements in the culture led many observers to unduly emphasize color consciousness in attempts to explain social strife. As class and color affiliations were never identical, however, color often confused rather than clarified the situation. It provided a ripe field, moreover, for deliberate exploitation, as politicians often used prejudice to gain support.[19] Culture, however, an often overlooked and underestimated factor, is also salient.

Popular Creoledom created a rich oral literature. Its secular preoccupation was with the patterns and meaning of agrarian life, which it mirrored. The Creole tradition looked inward. The French tradition looked outward across the Atlantic, and generated written texts. Those who wrote in French attempted to join Haiti to the concerns of a larger world community. Over the course of the nineteenth century, the sheer magnitude of the educated strata's literary production marginalized the illiterate Haitian majority. The intelligentsia wrote fiction, poetry, legal and philosophic tracts, polemical pamphlets, and scholarly monographs on the physical and social sciences. It maintained a trenchant and prolific, if ephemeral, journalism. This literature was ignored for many generations. To outside observers, the stark poverty of everyday Haitian existence and the tragedy of despotism tarnished the elegant productions and intellectual brilliance of the cognoscenti. Beside the brutal realities of life, their works seemed to crumble into irrelevance. The contrast between the high tone of the clubs and lyceums where bourgeois thinkers delineated their ideas, and the squalor of the urban slum and rural commune were not lost on detractors.

Haitian intellectuals of the nineteenth century were unfortunate enough to inhabit a universe that perceived as outlandish the idea that erudite blacks could nurture a tradition of research, teaching, and publication. Haitians might believe their intellectualism erased the stigma of mental inferiority that racist enemies had imposed, but to their critics this merely proved the case against them. By the turn of the century, the vogue of industrial education for nonwhite peoples had overtaken the Anglo-Saxon world. Many firmly believed that people of color fared best as docile workers in economies directed by paternalistic whites. That conviction, popularized by the Afro-American educator Booker T. Washington, handsomely complemented an agenda of imperialist conquest, for it provided a rationale for victory as well as a means of usefully exploiting the vanquished. Industrial schools for black Americans and American Indians appeared, with programs designed specifically for use in colonial Africa soon to follow.[20] The Francophone community, to which educated Haitians belonged, did not accept industrial pedagogy or its underlying philosophy. Haitians thus contradicted white American views of black people in an era when U.S. prestige was rapidly growing in the Caribbean region. These predilections and the language and culture barrier condemned the vast Haitian literature to oblivion in the United States.

The inability to appreciate the polemical literature meant that Americans never realized that Haitian writers were addressing questions of the most profound character. Haiti numbered among the few non-European nations in the nineteenth century with intellectuals conscious enough to seriously undertake the study of underdevelopment in an emerging state. Haitians grappled with the implications of their country's weak economy, social conflicts, and political fragmentation long before such problems became universally recognized. Many also challenged the twin ideologies of white supremacy and imperialism that solidified in the course of the century, and they analyzed the deleterious effects that these systems continued to have on Haiti. As

an insurgent literature produced by a tiny group of blacks and mulattoes in a small backward country, the Haitians' critiques found no
audience in the outside world.

At home, however, in the realm of domestic policy, a literature
of self-criticism emerged that the literate took very seriously. Its origins lay in the same processes that brought major change to all of
Latin America in the late 1800s. Even the peasant societies of Central
America had begun to experience the shock waves created by North
American capital penetration in railroad construction and commercial
agriculture. The Spanish-speaking Caribbean republics, Cuba and the
Dominican Republic, began a transition that sharpened local attacks
on imperialism and further solidified a nationalist consciousness. Haiti
proscribed foreign capital and avoided the dislocations attendant on
intensive exploitation, but it also failed to benefit from modernization.
In attempts to confront social and economic deterioration, writers returned to the indigenous polemic tradition to argue for the adoption
of badly needed reforms.[21]

Agricultural stagnation in the context of a declining ecological resource base preoccupied nineteenth-century writers. No Haitian government had been able to make or encourage any substantive social or
economic investment in farming. Administrations instead depended
on the agrarian sector for revenues while simultaneously delivering
benefits primarily to urban constituents.[22] Social conservatism underlined the parasitic policies of the state. Conservatism was not the
exclusive preserve of peasants—to whom suspicion of innovation
and low levels of productivity are generally attributed—but was also
shared by the rural and urban gentry alike. Both groups had a stake
in the maintenance of the social and political status quo.

The hierarchical society in which many took comfort came at the
price of poverty and agricultural backwardness. Writing in 1873,
Demesvar Delorme questioned the priorities that had always forced
development to defer to politics, even during epochs of relative stability. Haitian leaders should realize, he asserted, that rural prosperity
would create the security that many governments had tried to establish through force of arms. Delorme's proposed reforms included the

introduction of new cash crops, encouragement of modest technology, and a state program to repair and maintain roads. As minister of agriculture, Delorme initiated a system of cash prizes for model exhibits at state-sponsored fairs, and tried to introduce coffee decorticating machines from Brazil.[23]

Delorme took a dim view of reform proposals that did not focus on agriculture as the basis for change. He insisted that monetary innovations, for example, or redrafting customs regimes, were useless unless policymakers addressed the underlying agrarian problem. Without larger quantities of valuable exports, trade would continue to be meager and, consequently, government revenues insufficient. He similarly thought industrialization premature. Construction of simple roads and bridges and the establishment of rural enterprises such as fisheries, sugar refineries, and dyeworks were all Haiti needed until greater prosperity yielded the capital required for more sophisticated industries and infrastructure.[24]

Writing nearly a decade later in 1882, Edmond Paul also scored the state for its failure to improve and maintain roads or encourage modern farming. Primitive techniques not only ensured both indigence and social inequality but weakened the government.[25] Delorme and Paul took comparable approaches because they believed the solution to the agricultural dilemma rested on modernization. They stressed education, incentives, and state responsibility for providing a minimum infrastructure.

Neither of these two critics greatly emphasized the dearth of capital. Not until the establishment of the French-owned National Bank of Haiti (which lent money to the government for ordinary operating expenses but did not provide credits for development projects) did Haitian commentators evince a full awareness of the possibilities inherent in loans. While Paul saw an agricultural credit bank as a valuable tool, he apparently assumed that such a bank would be a public institution. Encouraging the activity of foreign private investors raised sensitive political questions.

In the interest of preventing the engrossment of the country by peaceful means, the Haitian constitution prohibited foreign ownership of real estate. The stricture had only modest impact, for resident aliens evaded this law by registering property in the names of Haitian spouses or children. The legislation did not prevent expatriates who were already present from enriching themselves, but it did deter the ingress of new foreign investment in significant quantity. Another polemicist of the era, Anténor Firmin, protested the ban on foreign ownership. Firmin suggested lessening restrictions on foreign investment on the grounds that the law was outmoded and the need for capital dire enough to warrant unprecedented efforts to attract it.[26]

Discussions of agricultural development became increasingly rare by the turn of the century. Worldwide depression, competition from larger, more efficient producers, and the seeming resistance of Haitian political institutions to change undoubtedly discouraged optimists. Léon Audain worried about the increasing cultural divergence of rural and urban Haiti, but most commentators began seeking other reasons for Haiti's failures and suggesting other remedies for its social ills.[27]

Some turned their attention to the global rise of white supremacy. Anténor Firmin and Hannibal Price attacked the new sociological racism that had accompanied the advent of European colonial power in Asia and Africa, and the expansion of the United States. Firmin's *De l'égalité des races humaines* (1885) and *La réhabilitation de la race noire* (1900), written by Price, challenged standard Western historiography. These works depicted blacks in general and Haitians in particular as victims of the slave trade and the plantation. Blacks' contributions to modern civilization would in time equal those that they had made in the classical age. The black renaissance awaited a revival of the Christian spirit and the application of modern science to the social problems caused by centuries of oppression.[28] Others turned to the problem of racism as expressed in internal strife between blacks and mulattoes in Haiti. In *Haïti, vivra-t-elle?* (1905) Alcius Charmant commented on politicians' opportunistic manipulation of caste prejudice and the demagogic use of black heroes to disguise the continued preponderance of a small black and mulatto elite. In Charmant's Haiti, color consciousness poisoned the springs of national life while perpetuating existing power relations.[29]

Not all Haitians subscribed to the doctrine of racial equality that motivated Charmant. Léon Audain, in *Le mal d'Haïti, ses causes et son traitement* (1908), tacitly endorsed the notion that whites are superior to mulattoes, and mulattoes better than blacks. Audain shared the popular turn-of-the-century conception of national character. Anglo-Saxons and Germans were held to be cold, rational, and enterprising. Romanticism, emotionalism, and a poetic sensibility characterized the inhabitants of the Latin states and explained their political instability.[30] If national character lay at the bottom of Haiti's chronic problems, as Audain believed, only exceptional and powerful intervention could alter present conditions.

The theme of race and nationality also emerged in discussions of the Japanese phenomenon. Japan, a nonwhite nation, had raised itself from feudal isolation to great-power status in less than fifty years. It had embraced western science while preserving its own unique culture. Its conquests in the Russo-Japanese War of 1904–5 climaxed its debut on the stage of world history. Charmant, like blacks in other parts of the world, saw Japan as the living refutation of racist doctrine. Léon Audain shared this view. Audain sought a Meiji Restoration for Haiti, a program of vigorous reform supervised by a potent dictator.[31]

Few Haitian writers expressed a preference for a thoroughgoing democracy. Most believed that their society required some measure of authoritarianism. Audain, for example, endorsed the principle of "enlightened" elite rule, and Frédéric Marcelin, author of *Au gré du souvenir*, published in 1913, sought a president, possibly a militarist, with extraordinary power. Conservatives like Audain and Marcelin wanted modernization without social upheaval. Fearful of revolution and the lower classes, they yearned for a charismatic leader supported by an efficient corps of technocratic administrators.[32]

The anxieties that commentators expressed could not be separated from the consequences of chronic national debility. Even if Haiti remained a closed society, it would not stay immune to great-power machinations. Western Europe and the United States had become increasingly involved in Caribbean affairs. The cultural and intellectual climate of the times militated against the continued sovereignty of peoples of color, and the thinnest rationale could serve as an excuse for intervention, or even conquest.

Realizing this threat, Firmin undertook an extensive review of Haitian foreign policy in M. *Roosevelt, président des Etats-Unis et la République d'Haïti* (1905). As the title suggests, the work focused on Haiti's relations with its northern neighbor. While deploring U.S. racism, Firmin applauded Yankee ingenuity. He understood Washington's intolerance of political turbulence and suggested that Haitians' fears of the United States resulted from their refusal to make needed political reforms. An appreciation of the Monroe Doctrine, he believed, would go a long way toward ending friction between the two nations. Firmin's book, written partly to assuage Americans' suspicions that he was a dangerous radical and secure their acquiescence in any insurgent activities he might undertake to become president of Haiti, did not win their good will.[33]

Firmin did not base his views, however, solely on the likely biases of North Americans. He maintained a lifelong interest in the Caribbean. Firmin's *Lettres de Saint Thomas* (1910), outlined ideas for a West Indian federation; endorsed the nationalist struggles of Cubans and Puerto Ricans; discussed the possibilities of regional integration through systematic research and central planning; and endorsed the creation of institutions and the integration of disparate legal codes.[34] Politically and economically competent Caribbean republics, Firmin believed, could serve as a bulwark against imperialist aggression.

Few polemicists shared Firmin's range of interests. They looked inward to discover the sources of the nation's difficulties. Most of them readily identified the political deficiencies that led to civil wars, poverty, repression, and the failure to deal successfully with foreign adversaries. These writers saw the emulation of European society as a way to address the problems of underdevelopment. They did not, unfortunately, derive from Europe the lesson of the consequences of tyranny. The intelligentsia could never reconcile an admiration for democratic institutions with the absence of these in Haiti. Yet Haiti was already politicized in an important way. Its history of struggle, which had worldwide significance, was ingrained in the popular con-

sciousness, and its leadership class knew the rhetoric of liberal republicanism. These traditions could have been marshaled in the service
of popular democracy. Instead, they were used to advance despotism
and oligarchic rule.

Ironically, foreigners gave little credence to the one Haitian who
proposed moral and rational solutions to Haitian problems in the context of Western and, specifically, North American beliefs about orderly
processes of change. Despite his laudatory writings on the United
States and France, Americans and Europeans considered Firmin radi-
cally anti-imperialist. He corresponded with nationalists throughout
the Caribbean, deftly foiled the U.S. Navy in its attempt to gain special
privileges in Haiti, and proposed financial reforms that strictly regulated foreign enterprise.[35] In contemporary perspective, Firmin's ideas
seem moderate. He wished to increase rather than prohibit foreign
capital penetration. He favored the creation of a more efficient state
that could readily guarantee the stable business climate that imperialists desired. Firmin opposed state terrorism, militarism, corruption,
and waste. Why did this scholar of high integrity prove so unworthy
of metropolitan endorsement?

Relations between Firmin and representatives of the great powers
remained outwardly cordial throughout his lifetime. He continued
to be received in foreign offices and legations, but he never reaped
the benefits of great-power support. The New York *Herald* covered a
June 1908 visit by Firmin to the U.S. State Department. Firmin had
come seeking sympathy, officials allegedly told the press. "It was admitted that General Firmin went away without obtaining what he
wanted," the *Herald* reported. Official Washington thought him a professional revolutionist whose supposed friendship and admiration for
the United States cloaked a determined opportunism.[36]

Similar concerns dictated the policy of Britain and other states. The
Foreign Office held suspicions of U.S. motives in Haiti, but Britain's
tiny interests in that country only warranted cooperation with the suppression of revolution. British colonies were not to be used as bases to
launch an attack on the Haitian government. In 1908 Jamaican authorities detained some Haitian partisans in Kingston.[37] The association

made between Haitian insurgency and Caribbean unrest transcended events on Española alone. Negrophobes and imperialists also sought to connect the racial tensions troubling Cuba and Jamaica in the early twentieth century to a pan-Caribbean black agitation. Their sensitivities attest to the existence of a growing political consciousness among black colonial subjects all over the region. The Cuban government fearfully banned early newsreels depicting black American boxer Jack Johnson's victories over white opponents, lest they incite the same violence experienced in the United States. In Havana's uneasy mind, Firmin, like Johnson, was ideologically linked somehow to the Cuban Partido de Color, and related to a violent Afro-Cuban uprising in 1912. Cuba refused Firminists entry in its ports.[38]

Internal reasons also account for the defeat of reform in the black republic. Firmin's supporters could not withstand the widespread authoritarian mentality the bourgeoisie fostered. Relatively young members of the educated class endorsed Firmin, but they lacked significant influence. Established elites, fearing attacks on their vested interests, presented a well-entrenched and formidable front against his ideas.[39]

Affluent expatriates ranked prominently among those who opposed substantive change in Haiti, but it would be simplistic to suppose that they merely represented their home governments. Local foreigners' interests never harmonized completely with their countries of origin. Merchant-bankers, quick to be patriotic if doing so would advance their own position in a particular situation, realized that loyalties too narrowly construed could hamper efforts to trade across a wide spectrum of crosscutting affiliations. Similarly, the foreign offices supported their resident subjects when national prestige or commercial gain seemed to require it. Occasionally they failed to back up their own citizens or sometimes assisted persons of other nationalities if the latter maintained ties to important home enterprises.[40]

The veritable expatriate industry of damage claims against the state tarnished many countries' relations with Haiti during the late nineteenth century. Correspondence about these claims filled reams of paper and comprised a great part of the daily discussions between envoys and Haitian foreign ministry officials. Demands for reparations generally stemmed from casualties expatriates suffered as a result of revolution and civil strife. If a major power represented diplomatically in Port-au-Prince supported the claims, the Haitian government would sooner or later have to pay, even if the damages were sustained during a prior administration. Aliens thus joined the ranks of other parasites who subsisted from the diminishing coffers of the national treasury.[41]

Comparable patterns of behavior and attitudes were observable in the financial world. International lenders rarely let chauvinism stand in the way of profits. The behavior of the merchant-bankers who owned Haiti's private banks paralleled on a smaller scale that of their international counterparts. Many of these individuals, freed by their *rentier* life-styles to be true cosmopolites, lived in Britain, Germany, or the United States. They claimed citizenship and allegiances on both sides of the Atlantic, and engaged in considerable private diplomacy. This contributed in government circles and among the upper urban strata to a softening of nationalist opposition to transnational business and political activity.[42]

The universally worsening opinion of Haiti at the turn of the century facilitated the increasing stridency of conservative elite discourse. Throughout its existence the country had been confronted by racist hostility that assumed cultural and ideological as well as political contours. During the imperialist age, the growing popularity of travel literature further abetted the process of denigrating Haiti. The subjective character of the genre allowed writers considerable freedom to invent. If the subject was Haiti, a long tradition already existed that detailed voodoo, cannibalism, political brutality, picturesque landscapes, and quaint customs. The moral of the story was usually the incapacity of blacks to govern themselves. Repetition proved the most potent weapon in the arsenal of malicious writers. Over the course of time, authors began to repeat anecdotes related by previous scribes, and to present these as personal experiences. Gossip and legends, given weight and force through habit, ascended to tradition and legitimacy. Their endurance, longevity, and omnipresence attest to their ideological utility in a racist and imperialist world system.[43]

Vodun, understood in the West as voodoo, struck deep subterra- nean chords in the psyche, but travel accounts did not stop at provok- ing a sense of horror at the bizarre. They also promoted the social Dar- winist belief that Haitians, like all inferior peoples, were degenerating and would one day vanish entirely, unless, happily for them, they fell under the aegis of benevolent white rulers. The notion of racial decay as applied to peoples of color served to rationalize and justify the extermination of Amerindian and Australasian populations in the late nineteenth century. The often expressed view that the number of Haitian mulattoes, "the civilising element," was declining lowered the country's standing in racist estimations. The disappearance of white genetic material in the Haitian population meant the gradual end of western influence there and the biological and cultural ascendency of Africa. Foreign rule would soon follow, because powerful white states would not tolerate the supposedly inevitable eruption of savagery at- tendant upon this eventuality. Soon there would be no black sovereign peoples. Races that could not withstand the onslaught of moderniza- tion and profit from civilization's blessings, social Darwinists believed, would stagnate and ultimately be annihilated.[44]

5   The End of an Era

Though they deny it, for the people of the United States, national identity has often been inseparable from racial or ethnic identity. An anti-imperialism based on racial exclusion foreclosed the possibility of annexing nonwhite countries or even retaining them as formal colonies. The U.S. government accordingly rejected charges of imperialism even as it aggressively pursued markets, influence, and informal domination of small Caribbean states. The turn-of-the-century enthusiasm for commercial expansion did not rest on the idea of trade among equals. Yet, as the nation sought an undeniably imperialist role, its leaders professed beliefs in international friendship and equality.

These apparent contradictions provided the administration of William B. McKinley an opportunity to make some policy innovations and build a national foreign affairs consensus. Control over the territories won from Spain in the Caribbean and the Pacific had to be established without colonial annexation, for public opinion strongly opposed the creation of an empire. Cuba gained nominal independence but languished as a client state under the Platt Amendment of 1902. Neither Puerto Rico, without a revolutionary army in 1898, nor sparsely settled Guam could offer much resistance to their de facto colonial status. The legal interpretation of Puerto Rico as a conquest precluded application of the Northwest Territory Ordinance of 1787 as well as certain constitutional privileges. The United States thus acquired a new domain but disallowed citizenship for its residents. In the Philippines, the U.S. Army quelled a native insurgency on the grounds that no indigenous government could keep Manila and its dependencies out of the hands of possible aggressors. In an act of questionable legality, Washington imposed sovereignty on the islands and rationalized this as a temporary expedient. The Supreme Court meanwhile challenged the validity of the Spanish acquisitions. Its rulings on the so-called Insular Cases upheld congressional jurisdiction over unincorporated territories and defined Puerto Rico as such.[1]

Political conditions in the Dominican Republic soon gave the United States an opportunity to shore up its new position as a colonial power in the region. U.S. shipping companies and banks competed with French and German interests in Santo Domingo, where foreign indebtedness raised fears that Europeans could unduly influence the politically unstable country through gunboat diplomacy. In 1904 revolution created an opportunity for President Theodore Roosevelt to refine U.S. Caribbean policy. Until then, Roosevelt had viewed the Monroe Doctrine primarily as an opportunity for free trade in Latin America. European interventions to collect on delinquent accounts or punish breaches of decorum had not disturbed him. The Dominican situation and its implications, however, led him to seriously consider the forceful exclusion of Europeans from the Caribbean republics and unilateral U.S. patrol of the area.[2]

Roosevelt chose instead a less drastic option. Customs receipts provided the principal source of Dominican state revenue. Roosevelt put the customs houses under receivership and scheduled debt payments to foreign lenders through U.S. officials. He justified this action on grounds that Dominican volatility threatened U.S. security. This so-called Roosevelt Corollary rested on the conviction that the United States must uphold law and order in the Caribbean to deprive extra-hemispheric states of an excuse to meddle in regional affairs. Roosevelt recognized that he had revised the Monroe Doctrine. That long-standing policy, originally pronounced to facilitate the Latin American revolutionary process, now served to hinder it.[3]

Roosevelt's action in the Dominican Republic related to more general beliefs that he held about race and culture. The declining white American birth rate figured among Roosevelt's concerns as did the continued vitality of the white race, for the president saw all others as patently inferior. The "gooks" and "dagoes" of whom he sometimes spoke were perpetually childlike and unruly beings whose inability to achieve prosperous and stable societies reflected their secondary place on the evolutionary ladder. As immigrants to the United States, they crowded and befouled the cities, disseminated anarchism, and increased the crime rate. For individuals of Roosevelt's persuasion, moreover, order constituted the heart of civilization, and fundamental notions of order lay at the core of U.S. foreign policy in the Caribbean. This perspective saw only disorder in the history of Latin states deprived of the Anglo-American heritage of constitutional rule and encumbered by absolutism and tyranny.[4]

The Roosevelt Corollary was a response to the perceived need to regulate Caribbean affairs. During the Roosevelt era financial insolvency exacerbated crises in such states as the Dominican Republic and Venezuela. Inability to govern effectively resulted in poverty and economic stagnation, political unrest, and, most dangerously from the North American perspective, incursions by foreign powers seeking to collect debts or broaden their spheres of influence. Roosevelt's position that the United States would act as an arbiter in disputes between Latin and European states served as a holding action. It did not address the chronic problems in Latin America that created favorable conditions for great powers seeking opportunities.

Roosevelt's successor, William Howard Taft, similarly regarded the Caribbean republics as politically immature. He believed that providing the material resources to make administration effective would alleviate some of their difficulties. Dollar Diplomacy, a policy associated with the Taft administration, put U.S. bankers in touch with debtor governments. The State Department facilitated contacts between the few large U.S. banks that could do overseas business in the 1910–13 period and the cash-short republics that wished to contract loans. The banking community showed little enthusiasm for extending credits to unstable regimes unless Washington extended explicit guarantees. It most frequently demanded the imposition of U.S.-administered customs receiverships or international consortiums. When the federal government proved unwilling to undertake responsibilities of this kind, the banks then insisted on steep interest payments from recipients.[5]

Loans defrayed the operating expenses of governments and consolidated debts. If these countries could regularly meet their obligations and maintain fully functioning administrations, U.S. officials reasoned, they would no longer attract revolutionaries, foreign speculators, and adventurers. They could then peacefully pursue the economic development that would put them permanently out of the reach of foreign and domestic subversion. They would cease to be a problem in the "backyard" of the United States.

Haiti in 1910 received a multilateral loan that owed as much to Washington's new policy as to the efforts of its traditionally European creditors to maintain their positions in the black republic. Haiti's constant need for credit furnished the context for the transaction. A tradition of revolutionary succession aggravated the situation. Insurgents borrowed money from resident foreign merchant-bankers to pay for their military campaigns. Once they acceded to the presidency, the heavily discounted loan became a matter of state. Creditors could then demand attachments in the form of special customs exemptions or other favors. Their privileged position gave them considerable influence, but not as much as the United States feared.[6]

Washington policymakers had defined an arbitral role for the United States through the Roosevelt Corollary. Before 1910 U.S. banks could not rival European financial institutions for credit markets in Latin America. Consequently, North American capital simply participated as part of larger syndicates. A 1904 loan to Mexico, for example, included, among others, such banks as the international firm Speyer (all branches); a Sephardic bank in Amsterdam; the French firm Lazard frères; the New York lenders Guaranty Trust, Mutual Life, National City Bank, and banks in Chicago, Philadelphia, and Boston.[7]

Drafting a transnational loan to Haiti in 1910 was in many respects a matter of preserving national influence in a global atmosphere of rapidly mounting commercial and financial rivalry while facilitating the transaction. U.S. capital clearly had to be included in any consortium, given the State Department's predilections and capacity to disrupt arrangements it disliked. A new loan would also have to satisfy the Quai d'Orsay. The French viewed the Bank of Haiti as their principal diplomatic instrument, despite its obvious deficiencies and Haitian President Nord Alexis's repudiation of it in 1905.[8] The French bond market, where Haitian securities were floated, would also have to consent to any arrangement.

All elements of the financial and diplomatic community agreed that a Haitian loan should include a reorganization of the Bank of Haiti and that U.S. bankers should participate in extending credits. Accord, however, did not extend far beyond those basics. Neither France nor Germany relished the prospect of expanding the U.S. role in Haiti. Washington itself feared that the bank loan and reorganization would reduce its clout with Haitian officials. The U.S. minister in Haiti, Henry Watson Furniss, accordingly began undermining European efforts to install a plan that would multilateralize control of Haitian finances through a tripartite French, German, and U.S. commission. Haitians disliked the infringement on sovereignty that the commission entailed, and the State Department believed that the body would also limit Washington's options. It characterized the loan terms as too onerous for Haiti to undertake.[9]

In September 1910 the Haitian legislature convened in extraordinary session to consider two loan and bank contract proposals. The first, endorsed by the German minister to Haiti, outlined a plan in which French, German, and German-American lenders would provide capital in a proportion of 2:1:1, guaranteed by a customs regime. The second proposal, made by Speyer and Company and approved by the U.S. minister, did not call for customs control and proved more popular with Haitians. Interestingly, no one ever questioned the role of Paris as the natural market for Haitian securities. France's place would be secure no matter which version of the plan officials ultimately accepted. The contest opposed the United States to Germany, with Britain supporting U.S. inclusion. Both sides offered large bribes to Haitian lawmakers to secure passage of their respective plans. The German-sponsored project succeeded in both chambers after the customs regime clause was deleted. Only the stormy protests of Washington and London prevented its actual enactment.[10] Once the contract's proponents agreed to increase U.S. participation to fifty percent, Washington dropped its objections. It did so despite its knowledge that the new Bank of the Republic of Haiti did not substantially differ in organization from its predecessor, which had been universally regarded as inadequate. Whatever the weakness of the financial instrument per se, the United States had achieved what it desired: increased leverage in Haitian affairs.[11]

U.S. influence in Haiti grew even stronger as a result of a rail concession initiated by New York subway builder James P. MacDonald and financed by the National City Bank. Plans to situate commercial banana plantations along the right-of-way accompanied MacDonald's project to construct a Haitian national railroad linking Port-au-Prince and Cap-Haïtien. The MacDonald group purchased approval of the project from the government of President Antoine Simon despite bitter opposition from the population of northern Haiti, where the plantations would be located.[12] MacDonald, who wanted to integrate Haiti into the U.S. economy, was soon pushed out of the project by his lender, National City Bank. A City Bank vice-president, Roger Farnham, then became president of the National Railroad of Haiti.

For Haiti, U.S. policy from Roosevelt to Taft moved from a distant, admonitory posture to one that grew more interventionist and intolerant of competition from other major countries. The State Department nevertheless refrained from explicit actions in the black republic. It instead permitted national corporations, particularly those associated with National City Bank, to take initiatives, and supported them over the protests of Haitians, and, increasingly, over the objections of U.S. diplomatic and consular personnel.

Woodrow Wilson's election in 1912 broke the long-standing Republican monopoly on the White House. While Wilson's victory owed much to his association with social and economic reform, including an antagonism to the abuses of big business and high finance, National City Bank remained preeminent in Haiti during his two-term administration. The explanation for this apparent inconsistency rests with Wilson's decision to aid U.S. overseas banking in order to penetrate foreign markets and stimulate trade. Lending money to Latin American governments would not only give rulers the security they needed to remain in power, but would also free them from reliance on European creditors. Like Roosevelt and Taft before him, Wilson thought that Latin American insurgency often resulted from outside agitation.[13]

Wilson firmly believed that parliamentarianism and a well-articulated legal system constituted the highest forms of government. In his view, radicalism and revolutionary succession in the hemisphere demonstrated the political backwardness of nations that needed a period of instruction and political wardship before they could be genuinely self-governing. A tense international climate reinforced the impression that political violence in the region harmed U.S. interests.[14]

Wilson articulated his Latin American policy in 1913 at a meeting of the Southern Commercial Congress in Mobile, Alabama. As South American delegates listened, Wilson likened the ordeal of financial exploitation suffered by less developed countries to that experienced by the United States in the nineteenth century, when its weakness made it a target for European imperialist schemes. This common experience, Wilson said, nurtured a sense of solidarity between the United States and its sister republics and led North Americans to repudiate any program of territorial aggrandizement at the expense of their neighbors.[15]

The Mobile Address conveniently ignored U.S. aggression against Mexico in the 1840s and, while it alluded to the democratic objectives of the Mexican Revolution of 1910, made no reference to Wilson's interference in Mexican affairs. Wilson scored the European powers for the harshness of the loans they concluded with American states, but did not refer to the exploitative character of the Haitian loan that the U.S. government had approved.[16] In essence, Wilson's policy was one of guaranteeing the safety of North American interests in Latin America and forestalling revolutionary insurgency. He shared with his predecessors the belief that this could best be done through the universal recognition of U.S. hegemony in the region, which, as delineated by the Roosevelt Corollary, would allow Washington to mediate political disputes and impose short-term military solutions when needed and, as outlined by Dollar Diplomacy, through overseeing the finances of client states.

The outbreak of war in Europe enhanced the salience of a sec-

ondary theme in U.S. Caribbean policy. Jealousy of foreign intervention remained a motif, and long before the United States entered
World War I, Washington officials expressed trepidation over Germany's growing role in the independent republics' import-export sector. Traders from Hanseatic cities had also made substantial inroads
in the British colonies and became the principal carriers of European
goods to the region. Observers typically exaggerated the threat Germans posed to U.S. concerns. Keenly sensitive to the advantages
given German businessmen by state support; superior education; and,
above all, elaborate, efficient, and highly integrated methods of organization, stateside commentators contributed to the illusion that Germany was surpassing the United States in business development in
its very backyard.[17]

For Haitians, France rather than Germany ranked second to the
United States in the import market. France purchased the bulk of Haitian coffee, but even so, its most popular products, chiefly articles
of bourgeois consumption, could not displace the North American
staples trade, which catered to the peasant majority. French and U.S.
commerce in Haiti were complementary rather than competitive. German exports more closely resembled North American in the realm of
manufactured goods but could not best the U.S. advantage in supplying Haiti with basic food and textiles. These facts, gleaned from
the statistics of the period, were familiar to contemporaries, which
indicates that the anti-German clamor had an origin and purpose im-
bedded in issues other than trade rivalry.[18]

Trade nevertheless served as a convenient cover for great-power
conflicts in Haiti, particularly as it remained the only important medium of international exchange in that country. The multinational consortium that chartered the National Bank of the Republic of Haiti in
1910 rapidly became a Franco-American enterprise devoted chiefly
to collecting the inflated Haitian debt. No genuine finance capitalism existed in Haiti. Local laws restricting investment and barring
the ownership of real estate by foreigners had stunted the development of industry and corporate agriculture. Commerce provided the
only conventional avenue through which metropolitan states' national

objectives could be achieved, and it thereby became a matter of contention. State Department officials were gradually convinced that the
United States had to prevent interlopers from engrossing Haiti politically through its increasingly institutionalized pattern of subsidized
coups d'état.

Despite overwhelming ideological, political, and economic pressures, Haiti had managed to hold on to its precarious independence.
Cultural resistance played an important role. An abiding fidelity to
the indigenous culture had always characterized most of the population, who were socialized to little else. Educated groups, usually more
ambivalent, nevertheless included a substantial number of traditionalists. As early as 1910 certain members of the elite revived the *calinda*
and *maxixe*, dances of Congo origin that had formerly embarrassed
them. During the same decade, young urbanites found it chic to pre-
tend ignorance of French and pass themselves off as Creole speakers
exclusively.[19]

This behavior related in part to the pressure that Haitians felt from
imperialist encroachment and subsequent military occupation during
the World War I decade, when the crimes and folly of the great empires
aroused anticolonial resentments all over the world. The era of expansion that crested with the partition of Africa in the 1880s ushered
in a host of ideologies that supported the major powers' opportunism. Positivism, social Darwinism, and eugenicism were ideological
instruments employed to dissect and reintegrate the new world order.
The imperialist age also witnessed the maturation of anthropology,
sociology, geography, and such specialties as African and Oriental
studies. These fields helped account for the vast array of newly recognized peoples and cultures and justified the systems of social and
political exploitation to which they were subjected.[20]

No sooner had the "civilizing mission" attained unquestioned authority than its antithesis appeared. Using the colonized world as a
backdrop, art and literature began to probe the European Self and
to recognize it in the supposedly barbaric Other. Joseph Conrad's
white adventurers mirrored in fiction the relapses into savagery of
the real-life mercenaries and rogues of colonial experience. For the

astute reader, the jungles and deserts of Asia and Africa mapped the landscapes of the Western psyche. This process of self-discovery via the colonized societies continued into the twentieth century. Picasso's study of African sculpture led him to innovative uses of space in his own work. Freud's forays into the unconscious broke open the door that Westerners always assumed sealed them off from the supposed disorder of "savage" peoples.[21]

Events in Haiti from 1913 to 1915 seemed to verify the worst Western opinions. Haitian presidential politics, always essentially personalist, came to be dominated by regional strongmen heading private armies recruited from the peasantry. These peasant mercenaries, called *cacos*, based their partisanship on traditional kinship, godfather connections and other clientelistic relations (*compèragé*), and regional loyalties. Less frequently, they were purely mercenary. The reward for supporting particular candidates, aside from sporadic remuneration, included the right to pillage cities and towns that fell prey to revolutionary struggles and to loot the homes and properties of their patron's adversaries. Presidential candidates paid their *cacos* with monies advanced to them by supporters, who might include wealthy Haitians as well as foreign merchant-bankers. After succeeding to the National Palace, the victor disbanded his troops, who, unless kept loyal by patronage, were free to render their assistance to a successor. Cacoism was both an effect and a cause of rural insecurity and central government debility.[22]

After the presidency of Nord Alexis, 1902–8, Haiti witnessed a succession of short-lived presidential regimes, all of which arose through force and all of which ended prematurely. The U.S. Navy became a familiar fixture off Haitian waters. In 1915 President Vilbrun Guillaume Sam tried to break the cycle and gain needed time to consolidate his rule by jailing as many political adversaries as possible, and in some cases, taking their relatives as hostages. His police nevertheless failed to detect a plot to storm the National Palace which took place on 27 July 1915 in the wee hours of the morning.[23]

Routed from the palace, Sam sought asylum in the French legation, from where he sent orders to the prison to have all political prisoners and hostages executed. Working with speed and ferocity, jailors shot, stabbed, and bludgeoned 167 people to death. The military commander of the prison then escaped to the Dominican consulate. When the insurrectionists, including relatives of the hostages, arrived and witnessed the carnage, they pursued the prison official to the consulate and shot him. Hours later, they invaded the French legation and dragged Sam out onto the street where he was clubbed and stabbed to death. Infuriated mobs then hacked his body to pieces and dragged them through Port-au-Prince suspended from ropes and chains. These events were witnessed by telescope aboard a flagship portentously named the U.S.S. *Washington*, which lay off Port-au-Prince. The diplomatic corps as a body asked its commander, Rear Admiral William B. Caperton, to occupy the city.[24] Caperton thus began a U.S. military presence that endured for twenty years.

The invasion of the French legation led the United States to take preemptive action against an anticipated French naval demonstration. Washington requested that France not deploy ships and promised to safeguard French interests. President Wilson asked Josephus Daniels, secretary of the navy, to cooperate with Secretary of State Robert Lansing in placating the European powers so that they would permit unilateral U.S. occupation of Port-au-Prince. Wilson also determined to neutralize European influence by preventing Haiti from repaying loans formerly contracted to finance revolutions. These decisions, made on 31 July and 4 August respectively, indicate that Wilson was clear on at least this aspect of U.S. policy at an early date.[25]

By late November, Lansing had elaborated a Caribbean policy that definitively articulated broad U.S. goals in Haiti. It derived from ideas that Lansing developed in June 1914 when he opposed the alienation of Caribbean national territory. At the time, he defined inappropriate European influence as that which contained an element of permanence, and he distinguished between the interests of the United States, which greatly concerned him, and Pan-Americanism, to which he was indifferent.[26] Lansing elaborated on these themes in a November statement, tailored to fit Caribbean conditions more closely. European powers formerly extended their political control in the Caribbean through conquest, occupation, or cession of unattached territory, Lansing argued. More recently, European capitalists, by financing revolutions and corrupting governments, had brought weak American states to submission. This practice could be as grave a menace to U.S. interests as the traditional methods of domination, he believed, and only the advent of "stable and honest" rule in the Caribbean could end it.[27]

A letter from Lansing to Wilson regarding Mexico further reveals how the secretary of state's views on the Caribbean islands differed from his opinions on correct ways to proceed on the American continents. Lansing cited the dangerous deterioration of Mexican-American relations in mid-1916. He thought the United States should steer clear of using the term "intervention" in describing any invasion of that country. Intervention, Lansing explained, implies interference in another nation's internal affairs, humiliation in case of defeat, and unpleasantness in subsequent relations with other Latin American states. To his mind, intervention "suggests a definite purpose to 'clean up' the country, which would bind us to certain accomplishments which circumstances might make extremely difficult or inadvisable." At the same time, "it would impose conditions upon us which might be found to be serious constraints as the situation develops."[28] None of these second thoughts appeared to be of equal weight as far as Haiti was concerned, however; the United States would "clean up the country" but foresaw neither unusual difficulties in achieving its aims nor limitations in the options it could exercise.

U.S. policy in Haiti appeared improvised, but the fundamental underlying ideas and assumptions were well developed by the end of 1915. The chief work of the latter half of that year consisted of tactical decisions of an immediate nature, aimed at the subjection of all elements that posed obstacles to Washington's reform plans. Militarily, the occupation proved more ambitious than any previous U.S. interventions since the Spanish-American War. Most operations in the Western Hemisphere had been police actions only. They lasted long enough to restore quiet in coastal towns where foreigners maintained residences and other property. The Haitian occupation, however, attested to the growing technical maturity of the U.S. Marine Corps, which expanded rapidly during the 1902–17 era.

Through joint maneuvers with the Navy, the Marine Corps emphasized techniques devised expressly for insular campaigns, which the establishment in 1910 of a special training school for amphibious warfare further improved.[29] In spite of its ubiquity and the eccentricities of its personnel, the Marine Corps in Haiti remained an arm of policy rather than its source. That the State Department relied so heavily on a military solution to its problems with Haiti reveals more about its policymaking than about the positive or negative qualities of the instruments that Washington officials chose to utilize. By opting for a military solution to the problem, they indicated their disposition to contain rather than dissipate the sources of Haitian discontent.

The first priority was to disarm all presidential candidates and disband the *cacos*. To Rear Admiral Caperton, head of the U.S. military forces, the answer to guerrilla depredations lay in offering peasant mercenaries settled work and providing adequate and permanent security in the countryside.[30] Caperton amnestied and rewarded those who turned in their rifles. He carried out this program through former insurgents who profited by lending their assistance to this scheme. Aside from sharing in the bounty, they boosted their own position among their erstwhile confederates by being in a position to disburse funds, whatever their origin. They also benefited from the opportunity to make contacts with other mercenary leaders and consolidate friendships with those who might aid them in future struggles. Their supposed cooperation with the foreign invaders vividly illustrates the continuing divergence between U.S. and Haitian perspectives and objectives. The Yankees thought that *caco* leaders, in surrendering, had acknowledged defeat. For the Haitian politicos, however, the old regime was merely suspended, not destroyed, by the intervention. They could use the United States—a temporary interloper—to further their own ends. As a result, *caco* generals pressed for increasingly greater rewards. The consequent stalemate in the disarmament program led Caperton to proclaim martial law within the zone of effective U.S. occupation.[31]

Martial law facilitated the capture of many more guerrillas, as the Marines held a technological advantage. The *cacos'* realization of their military inadequacies led them to accept an armistice on 29 September 1915. The Americans paid the Haitian soldiers for their rifles and added promises of future employment with the projected rural police force or with the National Railroad. Outside the occupation zone, however, insurgency continued. Some rebel bands, more devoted to brigandage than politics, held sway on the Dominican frontier. They raided U.S.-owned sugar estates on the eastern side and held livestock for ransom. Caperton called for strong action to deal with this problem and initiated a search-and-destroy campaign in late autumn of 1915.[32] In several swift forays, the Marines systematically destroyed guerrilla camps in the North. By 19 November Caperton reported the total pacification of a vast section of the country. He hoped that serious revolutionary activity was now a thing of the past.[33]

Secretary Daniels nevertheless worried about the high Haitian casualty rate. He suggested that future operations be confined to patrols rather than to maneuvers so as to spare life on both sides. Caperton defended his policies by citing the pressing need to end northern banditry. He denied that the *cacos* had political motives and presented the campaign as a police action against bandits. As the Haitian army no longer existed and the new constabulary had just begun, the admiral saw little alternative to deploying U.S. troops. He remained sensitive to the numbers of people killed, which led him to minimize the casualty rate in his reports.[34] Haitian accounts and the private statements of certain U.S. participants in the "pacification" effort tend to corroborate the view that casualties were higher than officially reported.[35]

If some Haitians experienced relief when the first Marines landed in July 1915, their sentiments soured by early 1916. U.S. authorities imposed a 9:00 p.m. curfew on Port-au-Prince, and any person at large after that hour could be shot on sight. Heavy patrols cruised the Bel Air and Warf Herb neighborhoods, which they considered dangerous nests of *caco* infiltration. Nevertheless, more Marines had chamber pots emptied on their heads as they passed under darkened windows than died in sniper attacks.[36] Caperton argued strongly for the maintenance in Haiti of a force that in March 1916 equalled seventeen hundred. He claimed that reduction in troop size would compromise U.S. prestige and control, especially as the new Haitian constabulary, called the Gendarmerie, was neither adequately trained and supervised, nor reliable.[37]

Marine Major Smedley D. Butler, an outspoken racist but an efficient officer, headed the Gendarmerie and staffed its officer ranks with Marine enlisted men. An unselfconscious chauvinist, he brought to his job an open, cavalier paternalism. "We [Marine officers] were imbued with the fact that we were trustees of a huge estate that belonged to minors. That was my viewpoint," he later told a Senate committee investigating the occupation. An incident that occurred during U.S. Assistant Secretary of the Navy Franklin D. Roosevelt's official visit illustrates Butler's conduct in Haiti and attitude toward Haitians. As Frank Friedel relates it, "When the President of Haiti started to climb into his official limousine ahead of [Roosevelt], Smedley Butler . . . seized President Dartiguenave's coat collar and started to pull him back, but Roosevelt stepped aside and insisted that the Haitian should take precedence."[38]

After the initial defeat of the *cacos* in 1915 and 1916, Butler's imperiousness and the back-up presence of U.S. troops quelled insurrection for three years. Peace did not endure, however, and new fighting erupted as a result of the pacification policies. Washington believed that Port-au-Prince's poor access to the interior had contributed to the success of past insurgencies. Officials planned to construct a national road network with press-ganged peasant labor. Rural Haitians would build the road as a tax-like obligation similar to that entailed on peasants in prerevolutionary France, the so-called *corvée*. The *corvée* had been briefly employed in Haiti by King Christophe and others, but had fallen into disuse early in the nineteenth century because of peasant resistance. The revival of forced labor for road building was supposed to benefit the country commercially by securing good overland communications for markets, but the primary reason for the roads was strategic. Many of the most expensive routes crossed rugged, sparsely inhabited terrain and had little economic value. By the end of 1918 enough of them had been completed to answer military needs.[39] At first peasants seemed willing to labor on roads in their own localities, but abuses of the voluntary system soon appeared. Foremen carried workers far from their homes, fed and housed them poorly, and subjected them to physical brutality. The Marine Corps recognized the problem as early as 1916, and over the next three years phased the program out. Repression nevertheless continued in the form of petty harassment and intimidation by Haitian police appointed under the occupation government.[40]

The regime coupled attacks on popular rural insurgency with an interest in eliminating subversive domestic influences among urban Haitians. The desire to make cooperation with Europeans less attractive to Haiti was related to the hope of tieing the black republic more closely to the U.S. market.[41] The political control that the armed forces and intelligence services of the United States imposed on Haiti fostered the growth of U.S. overseas banking, specifically that of the National City Bank of New York.

Merchants provided commercial banking services for much of Latin America. The mercantile system performed adequately in most countries and often obviated the need for foreign branch banking. In Haiti, however, U.S. actions against French and German nationals had neutralized merchant power. The successor to the merchant-bankers formerly dominant in that country would be a U.S. bank prepared to render the necessary overseas services. No bank at the time could play this role more readily than National City Bank, then in a highly expansive phase of its history.[42]

In 1915 National City Bank's president, Frank A. Vanderlip, riding a crest of euphoria, described the institution's position as "almost absurdly strong." The bank planned a public relations conference on South American affairs to be held in Washington in the spring. Vanderlip assigned several senior officers to study selected Latin American countries with respect to government finances, investment needs, infrastructure, political conditions, and existing banks.[43] National City Bank already possessed such information on Haiti, thanks to the efforts of its vice-president, Roger Farnham, also president of the National Railroad of Haiti. It further elaborated its Haitian policies when it added a new vice-president to its personnel roster: Francis M. Huntington Wilson, formerly assistant secretary of state in the Taft administration.

Huntington Wilson had been directly concerned with Haitian affairs, and in a 1916 article for the *Annals of the American Academy of Social and Political Science*, he delineated a diplomat's view of the political aspect of foreign banking, which encapsulated to a considerable degree the National City Bank position and accordingly clarified its posture in Haiti. Huntington Wilson quickly dismissed idealism in economic foreign policymaking. The advantages a nation derives from overseas investments have nothing to do with service to humanity, he argued. The decision to protect a foreign investment and the degree of commitment, Wilson believed, should be based on the investment's value to the national interest of the creditor state.[44] Wilson defined two broad areas of advantage that policymakers should consider before committing the government to guaranteeing investments abroad: the political and the economic. Political advantage inhered in investments that fortified U.S. influence in such fundamental spheres of interest as Latin America. The United States should also maintain a strong position in those areas where good diplomatic relations fostered trade development, as in China. Arrangements that strengthened U.S. friendships with the great powers also had merit. Wilson prescribed investment in countries with profitable markets and in areas "where it is wise to preempt a dawning development."[45]

Economic advantages reciprocated the political. They included the establishment of permanent markets accompanied by peacekeeping and stabilization efforts; investments that underwrote free trade; investments that cemented friendships with "natural allies" like England; and business propositions needed to get a Yankee foot in the door of a developing economy, where the United States might quickly beat rivals. Far-off countries like Persia or Manchuria might not be worth the trouble of penetrating, but the United States could sweep its own backyard clear of competitors without interfering with colonial possessions.[46]

World War I helped make Wilson's aggressive tone possible. U.S. investors could now buy out the European interests in Haiti. The severity of dislocation for Haitians would be offset by the short-term relief the war had brought to certain sectors of the economy, such as logwood production. When Germany cut off synthetic dye exports, the Allies fell back on natural dyewoods from their dependencies and client states. Other tropical resources also supplied Western needs. War stimulated Haitian emigration to the cane fields of Cuba and the Dominican Republic, as those countries accelerated sugar production to meet the increased demand. During fiscal 1915, twenty thousand Haitians departed from the port of Aux Cayes to Cuban mills.[47]

The war boom proved ephemeral and did not address the need for a long-term plan to put Haiti on a sound economic footing. Aside from expunging foreign influence and managing government finances rationally and sparingly, the United States had no clear idea as to how Haitian resources could best be developed. Even with regard to fiscal policy, the Wilson administration moved slowly to set the treaty provisions in motion. One of its major difficulties involved locating the appropriate talent pool from the mass of those who, while perhaps "deserving Democrats," often knew little of foreign policy and colonial administration. Late in 1915 Woodrow Wilson communicated to Lansing his dissatisfaction with the candidates for the financial adviser position. None of them possessed "sufficiently large calibre" for the job, and the president knew none of them personally.[48] Just as Huntington Wilson had outlined a grand agenda for U.S. capital that he was not sure it could accomplish, Woodrow Wilson's mission in Haiti suffered from a peculiar lack of readiness.

Sam's assassination and the violation of two foreign legations and a consulate prompted the decision to land Marines in 1915. The landing had far-reaching implications for the trading community and the role it played in Haitian life. The literature on the occupation suggests that U.S. authorities successfully eradicated extrahemispheric challenges to their hegemony in Haiti and in the process eliminated the resident alien commercial networks, replacing them with stateside firms. This was not the case. The United States did not want to eliminate foreign traders in Haiti; it preferred instead to reorient them toward U.S. export and capital markets. The very presence of foreign merchants could usefully disguise the fact and impact of U.S. domination and help perpetuate the illusion of an open door to free trade. Nationality thus continued to serve a pragmatic purpose. The Germans were the only merchants who could not be assimilated into the Pax Americana in Haiti, for their country had ambitions of its own, and after April 1917 these clearly conflicted with the U.S. agenda.

Washington pursued a policy of displacing German interests whenever and however possible. After the war, this policy continued in an effort to ensure that the Germans never regained their former position. Occupation authorities began deporting leading German nationals from Haiti. Some of those expelled had lived there for as long as twenty years and had established families. The deportations broke up homes and affected many who had not been in any way responsible for the war. Realizing this, the Haitian government proved reluctant to cooperate in the expulsion effort. German influence ultimately could not be totally expunged. In August 1921, treaty officials took German property out of sequestration and lifted the ban against certain prominent businessmen. The merchant-bankers quietly reclaimed their holdings. By October, $2 million in cash, buildings, real estate and wholesale commodities had been restored. The Hamburg-American Line also resumed operations.[49]

The history of the Haitian-American Sugar Company (HASCO) provides an example of how the more heavily capitalized and critically important ventures were "cleansed" of German capital. German-owned HASCO controlled the public utilities in Port-au-Prince and Cap-Haïtien in 1917. It staffed its enterprises with German personnel. The advent of the U.S. occupation brought attention to HASCO's activities. Military authorities believed that Americans should control such a strategic enterprise in the event of a war between the United States and Germany. They also claimed to be dissatisfied with the sugar company's record, regarding it as more of a promotional and speculative concern than a serious effort to launch commercial agriculture in the island republic. The United States therefore forced HASCO to fire its German employees and tried to have all stock transferred from German control. Despite State Department objections, a 15 percent German participation persisted. The president of the Haytian-American Corporation, of which HASCO was a subsidiary, complained of the ongoing anti-German prejudice in the U.S. government, a bias that long outlasted the war. Washington officials practiced a policy of calculated obstruction, he asserted, which injured the interests of Haiti as well as those of the sugar outfit. Through the course of the 1920s, HASCO wrangled with treaty officials over duty-free imports and supposed buck-passing between Haitian and American officials concerning the company's prerogatives.[50]

Other firms fared the same, as the treaty regime made diligent efforts to root out German management and securities ownership in all U.S. corporations doing business in Haiti. In 1916 New York and Chicago banking interests with Cuban sugar connections acquired the Haytian American Corporation, but Germans retained some stock ownership. The Haytian American Corporation continued to assure Washington that German interests had been retired, but they had not, and remained a source of conflict between the company and Haitian and U.S. officials.[51]

The occupation regime never dismantled the German import-export sector. It feared the depressive effects on Haitian commerce, especially in the southern part of the country. Germans had cash on hand, an essential ingredient in coffee brokerage. During the hostilities, the War Trade Board allowed German brokers to purchase Haitian cotton, for which they paid high prices. Occupation authorities nevertheless looked forward to the day when Berlin could be totally eradicated as a factor in the Haitian economy.[52] In the meantime, North Americans would set about trying to recast Haiti in their own image.

6   Under the Gun

In 1915 the United States began a military occupation of Haiti that lasted two decades. Citing widespread violence, anarchy, and imminent danger to foreigners' lives and property, the federal government ordered Marines landed at Port-au-Prince. The Haitian protectorate was unprecedented in its duration, the racism that characterized U.S. behavior in the black republic, and the brutality associated with pacification efforts. Political reorganization rapidly proceeded during the late summer of 1915, despite the uncertainty of President Woodrow Wilson and the State Department as to how to proceed. Many policies that lasted throughout the occupation took shape during these early months. These included the exclusion of European interference in Haitian internal affairs as well as the prohibition of any extrahemispheric exercise of naval power there.

The occupation brought to fruition a process begun years before. Long before the humiliating encounters between Marine officers and Haitian presidents, aliens dictated terms to Haitian leaders. Foreign battleships trained guns on Haitian shore installations before many Yankee veterans of the *caco* wars were born. The depression induced by the military regime's financial policies had its precedent in prior manipulations by expatriate financiers. Finally, the devaluation of Haitian culture by Protestant, positivist, and dogmatic North Americans recalled an age of imperialism that was rapidly becoming obsolete in other parts of the world.

After peace had been restored to Port-au-Prince following Sam's assassination, the U.S. Navy and State Department, through their field representative, Rear Admiral William B. Caperton, cast about for a suitable Haitian president to accept the terms they planned to dictate. Few volunteers could be found. Their choice finally settled on a willing candidate, Sudre Dartiguenave, president of the Haitian senate. The legislature duly held elections, this time under the duress, as Hans Schmidt points out, of the U.S. Marines rather than the *caco* armies of the past. Dartiguenave's election was soon followed by the promulgation of a Haitian-American treaty, passed without comment by the U.S. Senate in February 1916, which "legalized" the occupation. Its provisions included financial oversight by U.S. officials, the establishment of a native constabulary with Marine officers, federal supervision of public works, and the settlement of all foreign claims. Clearly the new government would boast scant local support.[1]

Haitian nationalists greeted the occupation with revulsion. Peasant insurgents mobilized in 1915 to repel the invaders. They were led by a handful of militant leaders, some of them educated, like Charlemagne Péralte, who as commander of Léogâne under the Sam government, had refused to surrender control of his district to the Marines. Outgunned, however, peasant guerrillas signed an armistice in September. Having ended armed resistance for the time being, occupation officials then went to work on the Haitian constitution. The traditional refusal to allow foreign ownership of land, embedded in the constitution of 1889, was then in effect. Foreign powers had long resented this clause, and development experts considered it a cause of the dearth of available investment capital. The Haitian legislature's refusal to approve a document drafted in the State Department in 1917 led to the twelve-year suspension of that body, effected dramatically by a U.S. Marine officer under President Dartiguenave's orders. A "popular" plebiscite in which less than 5 percent of the electorate participated approved the U.S.-endorsed constitution.[2]

Many other U.S. policies proved unpopular, such as the revival of the *corvée*, forced labor, which required peasants to work on road gangs away from their homes under armed supervision with nominal pay and inadequate food and lodging. Foreign guns also safeguarded a national bank that operated only for aliens' benefit. Handsome salaries for imported bureaucrats drained the Haitian treasury, while indigenous functionaries received less remuneration for the same work. Newly arrived U.S. personnel insisted on racial segregation and introduced it into hotels, restaurants, and clubs. Curfews, press censorship, and intensive surveillance made Haitian dissidence risky.[3]

These conditions and the failure to improve the local economy led to the resurgence of *cacoism* in 1919. Many of those who had deplored the guerrillas three years previously and assisted in routing them now saw them as heroes. Independent bands attacked foreign installations in the countryside, and especially targeted the properties of the Haitian-American Sugar Company and its clients. A thousand men massed in the frontier district of Hinche, under Péralte's command, and in Lascahobas. Raids on Port-au-Prince involved assassinations of selected prominent citizens, looting, and the capture of hostages for ransom. U.S. authorities realized that collusion between the *cacos* and urban residents facilitated these activities.[4]

The occupation forces responded by launching counterinsurgency strikes. Marines razed settlements and shot those believed to be rebels and bandits. Military officials acknowledged the deaths of over three thousand persons in these conflicts. Soldiers also assaulted and harassed urban residents. Abuse took on a particularly racial character. Marines tightened security in Port-au-Prince while initiating a new rural campaign. The *caco* war of 1919–20 was vicious and hard fought. Near Croix-de-Bouquets, just minutes by motor from Port-au-Prince, insurgents killed four Haitian civil engineers, whom they considered collaborators. In the North, Péralte's band seized a machine gun and ammunition drums from a downed U.S. reconnaissance plane and shot a crew member.[5]

Resistance centered in the departments of the North and the Artibonite, but numerous Haitians and foreigners in other parts of the country supplied financial and moral support for the movement. Rumors of Zamorist assistance for Péralte disturbed occupation authorities. In October 1917, Charlemagne Péralte, by now publicly associated with the spirit of revolt, led his brothers and sixty others in an attack on the U.S. commander of Hinche, his own hometown. Péralte was sentenced to five years at hard labor after the group's eventual capture. He escaped from prison and retreated to the mountains where he reunited with his comrades.[6]

The organization of a native constabulary to maintain a sadly lacking law and order had been one of the occupation's first projects in

Haiti. The responsibility of confronting rebels would ultimately fall to the so-called Gendarmerie d'Haïti. U.S. military and civilian officials saw this unit primarily as a peacekeeping force, not an army. They recruited men who would have been *cacos* before 1915. The Marines planned to sell the old weapons that the guerrillas had surrendered to a stateside department store for retail as wall trophies, and they ordered new uniforms for the Gendarmerie.[7]

The Gendarmerie was not ready for a counterinsurgency campaign, however, and proved ineffective in the field. The U.S. military thus had to run the program directly, which it did with ruthless success. Marine Corps General Lewis B. "Chesty" Puller, a veteran of the Haiti campaign, pioneered the use of bombers and personally flew "dozens" of missions. The Marines used bush landing strips cut by prisoners of war for these early "search and destroy" missions. They could not accurately distinguish guerrillas from noncombatant peasants, and many Haitians suffered. Harry Franck, an American journalist who followed the Gendarmerie during the *caco* war, preferred treks in the countryside to life in town. "There is so much to be seen and heard in gendarmerie company," he declared. "If one chances to 'pop off' a *caco*, there is not even the trouble of explaining, for one's companions will do that in their laconic report to headquarters."[8]

After the pacification campaign of 1919–20, greater attention turned to "Haitianizing" the Gendarmerie and extending its powers, especially over public works, but it never overcame general opposition. It proved more successful in the intelligence realm. Until 1920 the organization relied on information from paid or intimidated informants. Thereafter, a small detective squad, consisting primarily of local leaders (*chefs de quartier*) supplied needed information. These men drew no salary but enjoyed favors. A criminal investigation and identification bureau, headed by a French civilian, organized the *chefs'* espionage activities. The regular constabulary fully incorporated the spy ring in 1927.[9]

Complaints persisted about Gendarmerie conduct, especially in rural areas, and the outfit's repressive responses to those witnessing brutalities or offering criticism of officers' behavior. As gendarmes were recruited from the same social groups as the former *cacos*, U.S. Consul Damon Woods suggested, greed and ignorance led them to expect support for breaches of good conduct. Thefts from and assaults upon peasants comprised the most frequent grievances. The Gendarmerie was also accused of favoritism in its operations and of using anti-Vodun campaigns to settle officers' personal grudges.[10]

The occupation regime had succeeded in creating a single military organization that controlled the entire country and yet subordinated itself to civilian control. For the moment, the Gendarmerie remained apart from national politics, but U.S. reforms did not alter the traditionally predatory relationship between the Haitian armed forces and the largely peasant community. The North American presence checked large-scale abuses of power during the 1920s. In spite of the violence that punctuated this decade, U.S. officials concerned themselves less with Gendarmerie abuses in Haiti than with political fallout abroad. They wished to keep Haiti out of the news.

The protectorate struck a critical blow against Haitian resistance when Marines finally located and killed Péralte in October 1919. A captain, supposedly in black face, stole into his camp and assassinated him. Péralte's chief lieutenant, Benoit Battraville, continued the struggle until May 1920, when he too was slain. When *caco* leaders died or surrendered, the event was heavily publicized in an effort to discourage further revolt. The Marines photographed Péralte's body on a litter of boards as if he had been crucified, and then buried him in concrete, allegedly to deter subsequent use of the corpse for superstitious purposes. The famous photograph of Péralte on the "cross" confirmed his pure martyrdom, and by the late twentieth century Haitians regarded this patriot as a major figure in their history.[11]

Military experts judged the "bandit suppression" work complete by mid-June 1920. Rumors about the war had drifted back to the United States, where they incited mounting criticism from Republican sources anxious to discredit the Democrats and from civil rights and peace advocates. Only after the most flagrant offenses had occurred, and the presidential election of 1920 had passed, did the U.S. Senate begin its investigation into the occupation. Subcommittee hearings chaired

by Republican Senator Medill McCormick of Illinois also probed conditions in the Dominican Republic, similarly occupied from 1916 to
1924.[12] The Senate hearings provided the incentive for an improved
administration of the protectorate and an end to the worst abuses.
The senators called for continued occupation, but with control vested
in a high commissioner. This functionary would possess diplomatic
powers, answer to the State Department, and supervise an elaborate
bureaucratic network.

The commission served Haiti as a shadow government that left the
client state with little exclusive jurisdiction. The individual selected as
high commissioner was John B. Russell of Georgia, a Marine officer
and former judge advocate of the Navy. Russell had also served as brigade commander during the early years of the occupation. Russell's
appointment demonstrated policymakers' belief that Haiti needed the
discipline that a southern militarist could provide.

Bureaucratization was not only an end in itself, but a demonstration
of the need to gain time to make permanent changes. Haiti required
modernization if the occupation was to be justified and continuing
peace ensured. Development questions could not be separated from
strategic concerns. Military authorities, for example, attributed their
counterinsurgency successes to the roads built under their auspices.
Road-building policy clearly reflected the regime's priorities. Paved
routes spanned areas without markets in a country that used animal,
not motorized, transport. They gave rise to a new system of coast-
bound trucking, but their continued upkeep required additional expenditure. The eventual deterioration of many of the roads indicated
in part that Haiti could not afford them.[13] Other plans included clinic
construction and agricultural and medical services. In most cases,
these projects were undertaken without sufficient thought as to how
Haitians could sustain them after the protectorate expired. They relied
excessively on technical expertise from North Americans who gained
their tropical experience in dependencies rather than sovereign states
and who brought a determined moralism to their tasks. The missionary tone with which U.S. officials subsequently clothed the occupation
surfaced less than a fortnight after the sailors and marines landed

in 1915. William Jennings Bryan had assured Solon Ménos, the Haitian minister in Washington, that Haiti had nothing to fear from U.S. intervention. On the contrary, "The intelligent Haitians should feel gratified that it was the United States rather than some other power whose motives might not be as unselfish as ours." [14]

True to Bryan's words, official occupation rhetoric had a veneer of the same Progressivism that characterized domestic reform during the same era. The underlying philosophy in both instances pinpointed efficiency and competence as the elements necessary to ensure good government. During this period, many U.S. municipalities opted for city managers rather than mayors, believing that trained administrators would rise above the tawdry seductions of politics. On the national level, the federal government assumed certain regulatory functions, designed to make the political economy function more smoothly. The realization of justice and social stability, Progressives felt, would stem from prudent management. Similar solutions to political problems, they believed, could aid foreign countries. [15]

During the mid-1920s, Ulysses B. Weatherly, an Indiana University sociologist, worked out a Progressive rationale for the Haitian occupation. Describing it as "an experiment in pragmatism," he wrote: "Before the people can really be free there must be an elaborate process of building; there must be constructed the material equipment through which society may function, and there must be developed the intelligence and the civic spirit which are absolutely essential in a democracy. The impossibilists argue that it is better that a nation be allowed to work out these results for itself, even at the expense of waste, muddling, and violence. The pragmatists insist that intelligent guidance from without may sometimes accelerate the process of national growth and save much of the waste." [16]

This reasoning explains the technocratic character of the administration that the United States imposed on Haiti once it solved the problem of establishing military control. The regime could coexist with racist thinking, as the U.S. case had already demonstrated. The old civilizing mission of the nineteenth century, clad in Progressive trappings, remained intact. Paternalism was its most benign expression, and its most malevolent manifestation was the overt racism associated frequently with members of the military establishment.

Colonel Littleton W. T. Waller, who arrived shortly after the occupation began, exemplified the latter tendency. Though more flamboyant than others, Waller resembled them in his assumption that he "knew the nigger and how to handle him." He believed that cultural differences among blacks made little difference and, in any case, blacks had to yield to white domination. The Haitians "are niggers in spite of the thin varnish of education and refinement," he claimed. "Down in their hearts they are just the same happy, idle, irresponsible people we know of." [17]

The State Department expressed a more sophisticated variant of this prejudice. Certain officials, convinced that only vocational training suited blacks, consulted Thomas Jesse Jones, a noted purveyor of that philosophy, on Haitian prospects. Jones worked with the Phelps-Stokes Fund, a foundation that systematically undermined those independent educational institutions that refused to endorse its narrow definition of education for blacks.[18] The choice of Jones suggests that State Department officials tended to see Haiti primarily as a repository of cheap labor.

Technical advisers turned their attention to Haiti's chronic poverty, which Wilsonians believed made it vulnerable to revolution. Officials relied on the wisdom of select foreign bankers to analyze problems peculiar to the local economy. One of these, Domenick Scarpa, a National Bank of the Republic of Haiti (BNRH) vice-president, wrote a July 1916 report on the Haitian economy. Scarpa disingenuously suggested that real rehabilitation lay beyond the capacity of both the bank and occupation officialdom. His report is significant because of its breadth, his knowledge and authority, and the influential policy recommendations he made.

Scarpa pointed to the dual currency usage in Haiti. Foreign traders and members of the bourgeoisie were paid in dollars; gourdes were reserved for financial transactions with "the home trade." Gourdes slowly moved to the countryside during the harvest and returned to the cities during the "dead season," when peasants had no cash. This

seasonal flow accounted for much of the fluctuation in the rate of exchange once the occupation regime curbed merchant-banker speculation.[19] Haiti's currency was a fiat money based on government decree
rather than on a gold or silver standard. Exceeding the limits of its
supply elasticity would prove disastrous. Haiti did not have industry
or even a varied agricultural economy. Its one-crop dependency created urgent, short-term demands for cash. Interest rates could not be
used to regulate the money supply because high risk-high rate conditions made lending impractical, as did the unstable rate of exchange.[20]

These conditions had long encouraged the development of speculative enterprises, Scarpa suggested, and discouraged the growth of
businesses that would enhance the public welfare. A gold gourde or
the exclusive use of U.S. currency could not help matters, for gold
would simply drift back to the metropolitan centers as a result of
Haiti's financial obligations and import dependency. Dollars would
follow suit and raise the cost of real wages and production. Scarpa
regarded this as an undesirable effect, for the conviction that Haiti's
best hope resided in low wages had already become a truism by that
time. Wages would naturally rise, according to conventional wisdom,
once the Americans began to develop the country.[21]

The banker expressed enthusiasm about the anticipated progress.
"*All* is still to be made in Haiti. . . . With cheap labor we may well
hope to recoup the many, many years that have been wasted." Scarpa
regarded the low standard of living and depressed income structure
as Haiti's only asset in the struggle for development. "Put labor on
the level of what it costs in Cuba or Porto Rico—and what will be
the chances remaining for Haity [sic]?" Scarpa endorsed the maintenance of the gourde/dollar exchange rate at 5:1, a more liberal tariff
convention, the abolition of export taxes, tax holidays for pioneering
corporations, and port improvements.[22] His ideas helped create an
enduring legacy. Fiscal austerity, permanently depressed living conditions, favored status for foreign investors, and low wages remained
the cornerstones of financial policy to the present time.

On the face of it, occupation policies sought to maximize the possibility of foreign investment. In reality, a combination of opposition

from U.S. critics, partiality and suspicion on the part of treaty officials, and internal resistance stymied industrial development plans.
Many U.S. firms refused to invest in Haiti without strong guarantees.
As a result, corporate interest in the black republic flickered. The Sinclair Oil Company could not agree with President Louis Borno on the
government share of any oil it found. Borno sanctioned an explora-
tory concession, but Sinclair rejected his terms and left the country.
The United States Geological Survey's research found Haitian min-
eral reserves commercially meager, and Texaco and Standard Oil of
New Jersey, which had "prowled around," gave "it up as a bad job"
by 1929.[23]

Rubber concerns also inspected Haiti in the 1920s. Firestone expressed interest, as did Goodrich, whose representative thought the
peasants would make satisfactory estate workers and regarded the
proximity of Haiti to the United States as a decided advantage. Goodrich wanted to use old plantations as cultivation sites, though this
meant dispossessing squatters who extracted logwood and grew small
crops there.[24] Liberia's success as a rubber colony and the onslaught of
the Great Depression prevented the full-scale development of Haitian
rubber cultivation during the epoch.

Despite these problems, U.S. officials did not lack a policy toward
corporate enterprise. They simply played favorites. The activities of
firms already in the field were just as questionable as new ventures
that the State Department routinely rejected; the justification that the
former were upheld because they predated the intervention and represented prior commitments does not explain why radical modification
in their contracts could not have been made. On the contrary, the
State Department backed these concessions, going so far as to block
the development of other corporate initiatives in so doing.[25]

The record with regard to agriculture was similarly disappointing.
Few of the expatriate technicians understood peasants' economic behavior, which they often dismissed as simply ignorant. Coffee, logwood, and sisal, all important exports, grew semiwild. Cultivators
carelessly prepared these commodities for market because it did not
pay them to handle them better. Speculators stood between the pro-

ducers and the buyers, taking their percentage as well as the export tax out of the transaction. The resulting price did not warrant the expenditure of greater labor costs in processing the products.[26]

Few experts comprehended these economies. Most continued to pursue schemes to instruct Haitians in techniques and behaviors that were not necessarily appropriate to their circumstances. Occasionally, perceptive scientists made constructive suggestions but found their advice sometimes ignored. One botanist, for example, argued strongly for a program of afforestation. The high commissioner viewed his study as too pessimistic and had it suppressed. The man lost the job to a candidate who had more "tact."[27]

With a few exceptions, corporate plantations made little headway, but indigenous labor lost none of its appeal to entrepreneurs elsewhere. Cheap Haitian labor had long attracted sugar producers in Cuba and the Dominican Republic. Those workers who wanted more than the meager wages and one cupful of rice and bean hash per day provided by local companies had to emigrate. Labor joined coffee and other commodities as a significant export during the occupation years, and labor management provided a source of income for the Haitian bourgeoisie.[28] The major recruiter in Aux Cayes made enough money from what was popularly called the "slave trade" to invest in freight facilities, ice plants, and movie theaters. Consuls regarded Cuba as a sinecure and regularly cheated the Haitian government out of remittances due on each worker disembarked there. In 1919–20, of the $29,181 Port-au-Prince should have received, consuls sent it $1,984.30.[29]

Both Haitian and U.S. officials expressed concern over the exodus. They did not plan to give away what they considered Haiti's most valuable asset, its cheap labor, and remittances were then too small to significantly affect the economy. The high commissioner, himself a native of the Black Belt in the United States, approved of agricultural companies. He believed that the peasants needed to become habituated to wage labor and steady work, a striking contrast to their small-plot gardening experience. Russell wanted the United Fruit Company to set up plantations in Haiti but could not persuade the firm to locate there. United Fruit contented itself with recruiting Haitian workers for its operations elsewhere in the region.[30]

In the course of the 1920s, venture capitalists initiated schemes to grow cotton, pineapples, and other products. Most did not succeed. In some instances speculative companies never intended to plant. In other cases, they fell prey to poor management. Uncertainties related to land and water use hampered commercial agriculture. Haiti was no El Dorado. Its people had developed the fruitful Cul-de-Sac plain as much as the current water supply and technology permitted. Irrigation could reclaim some land, especially in the Artibonite Valley, long the focus of pipe dreams about internal improvements. The politics of water rights indefinitely delayed a mammoth irrigation project organized by a U.S. congressman.[31] Other attempts to alter Haitian agriculture included a progressive land tax on state property payable by tenants and squatters. The tax's many adversaries argued that the rates, given the earning potential of the average peasant, were too high. They pointed to the possibility of the tax leading to evictions and to the high cost of collecting the revenues. This proposal, made law in August 1924, faced considerable U.S. and Haitian opposition and was never enforced.[32]

Historic legislation against alien real estate ownership had limited foreign plantation development, and peasant tenure continued to characterize national agriculture. A small group of wealthy landholders sought foreign investment during the occupation era. Help came first from HASCO, which contracted for cane from gentlemen planters and advanced them credit. A few members of the landed gentry became HASCO agents.[33] The U.S. government, unlike the plantation companies, backed away from a close association with the landowning class. President Calvin Coolidge, in a rare pronouncement on Haiti, advised Secretary of State Frank Kellogg on the imprudence of developing latifundia. He preferred that the "natives" keep the land. General Russell agreed. Despite his fondness for plantations, he ascribed Haitian backwardness to the state's retaining land that should be in private hands. Russell endorsed land grants by prescription in order to assure political tranquility.[34]

The absence of sufficiently large individual estates further blocked the emergence of full-scale corporate agriculture on a contractual basis. Even after the abolition of the law forbidding foreign tenure, the problem of aggregating enough land to plant efficiently remained. A firm like HASCO could not drastically alter the pattern of smallholding in the Cul-de-Sac, where it maintained installations. It could and did, however, compete with petty cultivators and distillers.[35] In 1928 officials launched a cadastral survey to help establish clear titles. This involved the aerial photography of land in the Artibonite and other parts of the country. They stored the negatives in a warehouse belonging to the Public Works Administration. Considerable fear existed in Haiti that the survey would lead to widespread evictions and the conversion of the peasantry into a landless proletariat. It is also probable that title registration would revive old feuds. That uneasiness temporarily abated when someone broke into the warehouse and set fire to the films.[36]

After the demise of the cadastral survey, Washington settled on prescriptive rights as the next best option. No one wanted to repeat the Dominican experience, where the expansion of sugar and lumber operations had dispossessed large numbers of rural people. Despite this apparent resolve, several plantation companies managed to acquire state lands for leasing during the 1920s. The Haytian-American Development Corporation held fourteen thousand acres in 1929, on which it planted sisal. The Haitian Agricultural Corporation had twenty-two hundred. HASCO, in addition to 630 acres leased from the state, owned twenty-four thousand as a pre-1915 concessionaire.[37]

In 1930 the National Union, a Haitian organization that concerned itself with land questions, assailed the Haytian-American Development Corporation's sisal project. It accused the company of destroying houses and food supplies in various localities where sisal competed with provision crops and livestock for acreage. Petty government officials staffed company stores that kept peasants in debt peonage. Laborers' money went abroad in payment for imported food while locally owned shops lost custom. The Haytian-American Develop-

ment Corporation had diverted a stream for its exclusive use in the
Fort Liberté commune and had even taken its workers to the polls
under military supervision so that each one could vote more than once
for laws favorable to foreign interests.[38]

Sisal cultivation drew particular criticism because of Financial Adviser W. W. Cumberland's private interest in this crop. Cumberland
came to Haiti in 1923 and began his company with an initial stake
of $1 million. He boasted in his memoirs that he had made the com-
pany operational without paying out any graft but did not attribute his
success to his position. Cumberland planted only on barren land, he
declared, because he did not want to purchase cheap real estate from
Haitians and then watch them drink up the profits and become pau-
pers.[39] The Cumberland experience prompted the State Department
to ban private enterprise for treaty officials. Cumberland insisted that
he took no active part in the sisal enterprise while an official, and
he rationalized his business as in Haiti's interest. Lesser employees
tried in vain to fight Washington's order through fruitless appeals to
congressional friends.[40]

The occupation also sought to stifle foreign businesses that lay
outside the U.S. orbit. Officials regarded Germany as their greatest
challenger, but also acted quickly when they perceived Britain and
France evincing growing independence. After World War I, for example, the British briefly attempted to regain their lost momentum in
the Caribbean. The Royal Bank of Canada, headed by an energetic
manager believed hostile to the occupation, was one of their agencies in Haiti.[41] Secretary of State Charles Evans Hughes endorsed a
competitive policy aimed at curtailing the Canadian bank's ambitions.
Fears that it would purchase French-held shares of the National Bank
of the Republic of Haiti (BNRH) led the State Department to increase
its vocal support of the National City Bank.[42]

Washington also fended off French complaints about arbitrary and
bureaucratic mismanagement of the Haitian customs service. In drafts
addressed to the French ambassador and German chargé in the U.S.
capital, the State Department pointedly declared that no other nations
would be invited to participate in reform of Haitian tariff regulations.

The note for the French ambassador was not as curt as that addressed to Chargé von Haimhauser, but the message remained unambiguous. It also made clear that tariff policy in Haiti derived from Washington, and not from the high commissioner's office.[43]

Wartime restrictions on foreign businessmen mirrored the aggressiveness with which the United States supplanted European control in the Caribbean. The Webb-Pomerene Act of 1918 and the Edge Act of 1919 allowed corporations to form overseas trusts and cartels to facilitate trade.[44] Expatriates who endorsed the occupation usually prospered, for vocal support of the United States helped their businesses. The protectorate gradually loosened the foreign community's steadfast identification with European metropoles by using the carrot-and-stick method. The carrot represented law and order and the stable, if chronically depressed, economy that firm control ensured; the stick symbolized the threat of financial ruin and political reprisal against those who criticized or charted an independent course. If aliens accepted the discipline imposed on them, that is, the current reality of life in Haiti, they need not suffer unduly.[45] The new order transcended the old struggle between Haitians and foreigners for control of the export-import sector. The North American presence meant that both Haitians and foreigners had to accommodate themselves to the designs of new masters.

In the United States, cartelization was associated simultaneously with trade restriction and creative innovation. Overseas, the call to patriotism dulled the contradiction. In Haiti, the desire to eliminate supposedly subversive European influences supported the goals of U.S. corporate growth. Yet the peculiar circumstances of the occupation forced Washington to internationalize the instruments of this expansion. To preserve the appearance of equitable treatment, some of the existing business organizations, with their European personnel, had to be tolerated and drawn into U.S. financial and commercial networks. Francis M. Huntington Wilson, former assistant secretary of state and National City Bank vice-president, had already thought this out long before the United States went to war. "Good men from small countries without political significance in world politics already make their influence felt as employees of foreign governments and as merchants in foreign countries," he wrote. "The war may set free many more men and send them about the world to work for their own interests, for the country they most believe in, and perhaps ultimately for an adopted country. International commerce must have its courtiers and the good will of all such men should also be reckoned with. They spread friendship or prejudice against us. Many of them are importers and will push our goods or someone else's according to the manner in which we deal with them." [46]

Europeans in Haiti formed part of Wilson's *comprador* class. Some, without strong allegiances to a fatherland, could be incorporated into New York or Chicago-centered business communities. Syrio-Lebanese already oriented themselves toward the United States. The task was now to assimilate the Europeans, many of whom would lose nothing in the process. The only losers (aside from Haitians) would be the continental metropoles.

The use of the European commercial community as manufacturers' representatives substantially assisted the growth of U.S. influence and the increased consumption of North American commodities. Before the occupation, most merchants, if they were agents at all, represented commission houses. Now many had authority to exhibit and sell specific well-known product lines. Brand names became important. Haitians, British subjects, Syrians, and Danes sold Studebakers, Scott Tissue, and Gold Medal Flour. By 1919 a third of the importers, exporters, and retailers in Port-au-Prince represented manufacturers, including some French brands. At least two businessmen did this exclusively. The renovated Armour Building in the dock area was one of the most elaborate showrooms in Port-au-Prince. With an experienced traveling salesman as manager, the company sold meat, soap, and fertilizer from this branch house. [47] U.S. enterprises also helped finance European concerns in Haiti.

Over 87 percent of the firms listed in the *Blue Book of Haiti*, a 1920 business directory, had begun operations before 1915. Of those established during the occupation, 43 percent belonged to Haitians and 22 percent to Syrians. Some of this new Haitian enterprise represented

German property held in trust, but the Syrian share reflected the growing prosperity of that group. The impression of diversity conveyed by the *Blue Book* disguised the continued domination of aliens. The foreign business that sprang up during the occupation totaled 56 percent of all new firms.[48] During this period, a few Haitians acquired important manufacturers' agencies. They had already experienced the foreign domination of their commerce. The current process was now one of unilateralization: the orientation of trade toward a single center, the United States.[49]

Plans to remake the black republic came undone on the reefs of the Great Depression. By the late 1920s most statesmen recognized that the Western Hemisphere's economic problems were structural. As a raw materials exporting region affected by the global slump in commodity prices and European financial failure, Latin America could not be altered through military intervention and the appointment of North American proxy officials. Neither could those expedients prevent the widespread defaults on government loans characteristic of the period. As Robert N. Seidel put it, "The depression proved to internationalist Progressives that their schemes for progress and development stood and fell, ultimately, according to the actions of economic laws which, unlike civil or corporate law, could not be easily amended." [50] Reformers could not fit Haitians into a framework made in the United States and wasted phenomenal sums of money in their attempts to do so. By the end of the decade, policymakers were uncertain that developing countries could absorb any "intelligent guidance," and Washington knew it lacked the capability to endow its less fortunate neighbors.[51]

The drive to normalize Haitian-American relations during the Hoover administration represented a repudiation of fifteen years of military rule. In 1930 the State Department raised the rank of its chief officer in Haiti to ambassador and sent the Latin Americanist scholar Dana G. Munro to fill that post. Munro did not blatantly exercise the dictatorial authority characteristic of General John Russell's High Commission, but his powers exceeded those of an ambassador. Late in 1931, for example, he ordered a moratorium on the payment of Haitian official salaries, including that of President Sténio Vincent, because he disapproved of certain appointments Vincent had made.[52]

An incident in 1929 at the agricultural training college at Damien precipitated an essential change in the direction and operation of the protectorate. Until 1929 the Haitian government had supplied scholarships totaling $10,000 to Damien students. Many recipients, members of the bourgeoisie, would not perform actual farm tasks, such as feeding livestock. These young men instead subcontracted such jobs to rural youths while they confined themselves to academic studies. In an attempt to halt this practice, the government began withholding 20 percent of the bursaries in order to support poorer students who had no qualms about dirtying their hands. The elite students objected strenuously and went on strike. They won the cooperation of law and medical students, who struck in sympathy with them and organized student demonstrations all over the country.[53]

Attempts to further enlarge the strike failed until 4 December, when the firing of an employee precipitated a walkout in the Port-au-Prince customs house. Other persons left their places of work and crowds gathered in the city. After a declaration of martial law, the Gendarmerie restored order. On 6 December, however, peasant sugar producers in the Aux Cayes area, already aggrieved by taxes, protested the competition levied against them by HASCO's nine-thousand-gallon-per-diem-capacity still. HASCO produced 40 percent of all the alcohol consumed in Haiti. Small distillers, unable to duplicate the corporation's economies, lowered the prices they paid to growers. Poor coffee prices also contributed to rural dissatisfaction. Coffee would become even more expensive to produce if occupation officials enforced the new standardization proposals currently under consideration.[54]

Fifteen hundred peasants went to Aux Cayes on 6 December to present their complaints to the authorities. They encountered a small detachment of twenty U.S. Marines who, unnerved by the size of the crowd confronting them, opened fire. They killed twenty-five persons and wounded seventy-five others. Despite the obvious economic root of popular discontent, U.S. officials persisted in attributing the agitation to the subversive activities of nationalists.[55]

Officials tried to suppress details of the Aux Cayes incident, but news reached the United States and banner headlines appeared. Opinion had changed dramatically since the *caco* war in 1919. The public had tired of U.S. policy in Haiti, and many now conceded that fifteen years of control had yielded too little significant change to warrant extension. Aux Cayes prompted President Hoover to appoint a commission of inquiry and a second commission assigned to review Haitian education. Black American educators, led by Robert R. Moton, president of Tuskegee Institute, staffed the education commission. They were expected to approve the system of "industrial education" in the Booker T. Washington mode that had led to the Damien conflict. They did not. During the 1920s, serious rebellions erupted on black American college campuses as students and faculty alike challenged the utilitarian Tuskegee philosophy and its concomitant focus on political acquiescence and abstention from protest. Washington's death in 1915 began a process that conservatives could not control. By 1919 Tuskegee Institute itself offered an education far more liberal than any had dreamed of earlier in the century. The Moton report on Haitian education contested the separation of agricultural and industrial training from the remaining curriculum and censured the Haitian government for failing to provide general public education. Its findings may also have been influenced by the racial discrimination that the group suffered at the hands of the U.S. Navy, which, intent on enforcing Jim Crow regulations, left it temporarily stranded.[56]

The commission of inquiry was a five-member, all-white group headed by former New Jersey Governor Cameron Forbes.[57] It did not call for the withdrawal of the Marines and showed little enthusiasm for the nationalist movement, whose ubiquitous, planned demonstrations, Forbes believed, lacked spontaneity, sincerity, and mass support. Most thoughtful Haitians wanted the United States to stay because they had no confidence in their own ability to govern. Forbes advocated a continued, if less visible, Marine presence.[58]

The commission of inquiry criticized Woodrow Wilson's original staffing of the treaty regime and noted its shortage of experienced colonialists. Forbes disliked the antidemocratic manner in which client presidents had been imposed on the country and "kept in by the bayonets of our own troops." He nevertheless sympathized with the current Haitian president, Louis Borno, and felt that he had a "right to feel sore" at the High Commission's undermining of his position. The Forbes Commission endorsed some important changes in the regime's structure. It called for the abolition of the High Commission, the resumption of presidential and legislative elections, and the restoration of normal diplomatic relations.[59]

The Hoover administration accepted these recommendations and began a phased disengagement and normalization. Hoover and Stimson planned a general revision of U.S. policy toward Latin America to end the expensive interventions thought particularly burdensome in a time of economic depression. The new approach substituted indigenous armed forces for U.S. troops. North American officers trained these national guards, perceived as police rather than an army, just as they did in the Dominican Republic and Nicaragua.[60] The Good Neighbor policy stressed cooperation rather than coercion, and in Haiti, it cleared Sténio Vincent's path to the presidency in 1930. Vincent had a reputation as a militant and outspoken critic of the treaty regime. Reinstatement of representative government resulted in the selection of a legislature some Americans considered radical and nationalist.

The Hoover administration reached an agreement to gradually terminate the occupation before Franklin D. Roosevelt became president of the United States in 1933. A new treaty abrogated all functions of the protectorate except those relating to financial administration, alienation of land, the avoidance of entangling alliances, and law and order. These exceptions were, of course, among the most essential aspects of government. By 31 December 1934, the constabulary, renamed in 1928 the Garde d'Haïti, would be completely Haitianized and the Marines withdrawn. Provisions were made for continuing fiscal oversight by Americans.[61] The United States had neither changed nor reformed Haitian politics but inadvertently strengthened and assured the survival of many of its worst features.

7 *Le Vogue Nègre*

Fundamental changes in U.S. society made their mark on the character of the Haitian protectorate. The decline of scientific racism and the emergence of politically significant black urban communities played an important role in creating the climate for ending the occupation. The Marine landing in the summer of 1915 had made little initial impression on blacks. Like that of most Americans, their attention focused primarily on the war in Europe, and they at first ignored the Haitians' plight. Booker T. Washington believed Haitians to be a backward people in need of discipline and enlightenment. Unimpressed by the refinement of its upper class, Washington attributed the black republic's stagnation and violence to its neglect of sound industrial education. A handful of intellectuals glorified Haiti's revolutionary past and the unique culture of its people, but most Afro-Americans saw the occupation as a logical consequence of Haiti's political failures.[1]

But these assessments changed after World War I. The decreasing popularity of accommodationism, the renewed interest in civil rights, and the rediscovery of black nationalism softened Afro-American opinion. Well-known racial leaders and organizations led the way in responding to the Haitian controversy, which, once well publicized, drew ordinary black citizens' attention to racial injustices in the Caribbean nation. They wrote to the State Department, the black press, and to the president; they attempted to use their leverage as Republican voters and agitated for participation in policymaking that affected Haiti.[2]

The 1920s was a decade of unrest among colonized peoples and national minorities all over the world. Their struggles ranged from mild attempts at reforming the imperialist systems to nationalist protest, trade union organizing, and communism. In Haiti, the treaty regime scrutinized every ideology that might challenge the status quo.

121

U.S. authorities did not worry about bolshevism, a doctrine that found little initial acceptance among the elite and remained inaccessible to the illiterate and largely rural popular masses. Fearful of the leveling impact of Leninism, the upper classes were no more prepared than the Americans to see peasants empowered.

Attention turned to Garveyism, for the Jamaican-born Pan-Africanist Marcus Garvey had a following among Haiti's blacks, but not its mulattoes. Garveyism thus reinforced the perceived ancient divisions in Haitian society rather than providing an instrument for national unification and resistance to oppression. It was nevertheless an anti-imperialist racial movement, regarded as deeply subversive by the European and North American guardians of empire. U.S. officials shared information with the British government about Garvey and other black dissidents.[3]

In 1919 the State Department sent the Colonial Office a confidential report on black radicalism in America and its impact in the Caribbean. The investigative branch of the U.S. Justice Department, under J. Edgar Hoover's aegis, launched an inquiry into the activities of the Universal Negro Improvement Association (UNIA). Fearing the effects of anticolonial thought and race consciousness on island populations, the British widely proscribed the Garveyite organ *Negro World* in their colonies. They abstracted intelligence on UNIA ventures, and conducted surveillance of the organization's international activities. Garveyism met a cold reception at best in official colonial circles.[4]

Garveyites had begun operations in Haiti by late spring 1920. John Russell, then a colonel and the brigade commander, reported the existence in Port-au-Prince of a company called the Negro Factories Corporation. This group was the commercial arm of the UNIA. Russell noted the corporation's connection with the UNIA's Black Star Line, which had recently sent a ship to the Haitian capital. The line's avowed purpose was to bypass the major carriers and establish direct trade among black importers, exporters, and producers in Africa and the diaspora. The Black Star Line's stock sold in Port-au-Prince at five dollars a share, and large crowds warmly welcomed its steamer, the *Yarmouth*, when it arrived in port. Russell commented that Haitians of "not the best" reputation were associated with the enterprise and cautioned that they should be carefully watched. Given Russell's perspective, these bad reputations doubtless had something to do with nationalist proclivities.[5]

In mid-October 1924, several Port-au-Prince newspapers carried a press release of UNIA origin citing the last Sunday in the month as "Haitian Independence Day," to be commemorated by blacks throughout the world. The opposition paper *Le Nouvelliste* suggested that two minutes of silence at noon be devoted to prayer throughout the republic. On 26 October, the Sunday in question, a demonstration took place in the Haitian capital, planned, as Russell noted, "by the Black Party, which consists of the black politicians of Port-au-Prince but does not include the peasant class." One of the banners in the procession that made the rounds from the cathedral to the Dessalines statue and then to Belair proclaimed: "Vive la Negro Improvement Society." Another declared, *"À bas l'Occupation, Vive Haïti."* [6]

The client government and its sympathizers joined U.S. officials in opposing Garveyism. In 1924 *Les Annales capoises* (a progovernment paper published in Cap-Haïtien) discredited the synchronized 26 October demonstrations in Port-au-Prince and Cap-Haïtien, noting that in the latter city, only two hundred out of an urban population of twenty-two thousand had attended.[7] A report on Garveyism prepared by U.S. Consul Winthrop Scott in 1923 indicated the limits of the movement's penetration in the country. Scott interviewed what he believed to be a cross section of Capois and found that mulattoes mistrusted Garvey's racial politics. The Jamaican had strongly condemned their privileged position in the Caribbean and the United States, and his appeal to color recalled Haiti's own traditions. "Colored people" also knew the checkered history of the Garvey movement and believed it disreputable.[8]

Haiti's persistently upheld separatism also undermined Garveyite efforts to promote an international brand of black solidarity. Haitians did not constitute an oppressed minority, nor were they, a sovereign people, particularly susceptible to the call to redeem Africa. Illiterate and parochial, most Haitians possessed little authentic knowledge of foreign blacks. Russell reported an absence of peasant representation in the Garvey movement. Only urban elements appeared to be genuinely aware of the existence and significance of a larger diaspora.[9]

Certain cultural and class differences, however, separated the Garvey movement even from that part of the Haitian population that could most readily absorb its ideas. An *Annales capoises* editorial of 30 October 1924 made some of the distinctions explicit. It deplored those opposition leaders "who boast of being the intellectual and social *elite* of the country and place themselves under the orders of the workman who does not possess as they that beautiful Latin culture, that civilization of which we are so proud and which distinguishes us from all the other negroes in the world. It is an absurdity to ally ourselves with a foreigner who has not been able to accomplish anything in his own country[,] for the purpose of combatting a man, a president, who by his character is one of the most representative of Haitians."[10]

Les Annales capoises sneered at Garveyism's working class and petty bourgeois origins and composition. It claimed that while such upper-middle-class activist-intellectuals as W. E. B. Du Bois and James Weldon Johnson could be taken seriously, Marcus Garvey and his organization represented only "the backwash of Jamaican workmen immigrated to New York since the war." They could have no influence in Washington, and it was there, "not at 135th Street in Harlem," that the question of the occupation would be settled.[11]

The scorn that the newspaper evinced for Garvey acknowledged in oblique fashion the long-standing Jamaican community in Haiti. These proletarians were no longer subjects of the crown. Though culturally assimilated in Haiti, they did not enjoy high status in their adopted country. Widespread advocacy of Garveyism would have increased their influence and promoted yet another foreign group that had until then been successfully subdued. Perceptive Haitians also realized that the UNIA did not countenance exploitation of blacks by blacks, a fact fortuitously revealed in a letter written by a Haitian UNIA official about Liberian corruption. It seemed that the fraternal equality that Garveyites advocated did not suit defenders of the status quo in either hemisphere.[12]

Despite establishment opposition, some Haitian nationalists continued to make contact with the Garvey movement in the early 1920s. The UNIA also maintained links with Haitians abroad. It organized laborers in the cane fields and fruit plantations of Central America and the Caribbean. In Cuba, it was the only organization concerned with the welfare of migrant Haitian and Jamaican sugar workers. The Cuban branch eventually became almost a shadow consulate for these laborers and was second in membership size only to the UNIA in the United States.[13]

The U.S. branch also maintained direct ties with the UNIA in Haiti. In 1925 the Reverend Auguste Albert, Cap-Haïtien distributor of *Negro World*, went to New York City to further the association's work. Albert planned to preach at certain Harlem churches and meet with local leaders, as he hoped that evidence of black American support would influence policymakers in Washington. Authorities made no attempt to bar Albert from the United States, believing that as neither an anarchist nor a communist, the pastor could not legitimately be denied a visa. Refusal to admit him would be more politically harmful than allowing him free entry.[14] As Garveyism appealed primarily to a small, urban group in Haiti, occupation officials saw no need to repress it vigorously.

Black consciousness remained problematic because of the divided character of Haitian leadership. Conflicts attributed to differences between blacks and mulattoes indicated tensions that long antedated the advent of Garvey who, if nothing else, was a consummate modernizer. In establishing small businesses, freight companies, and cultural organizations, he intended to unite the diverse cultures of the black diaspora and create transformative institutions and industries. Garveyism cared little for regional and national particularisms, particularly if they stood in the way of a larger unity. As a consequence most Haitians, in their insistence on their uniqueness and exclusivity, did not warmly embrace it.[15]

White American opposition to Garveyism was essentially a political response to black nationalism. The deeper aversion to Haitian culture per se had cultural and psychological roots. The age-old association of

Haiti with African cults and magic made the black republic abhorrent to many Westerners. A significant number of Haiti's few champions also deplored its indigenous customs. They saw them as obstacles in the path of civilization as they perceived it. By the 1920s, however, a very different foreign reaction to Haitian institutions had emerged. Those who found worth in native traditions began to make their influence felt.

The changing viewpoint derived from World War I, which profoundly shook the faith of Europeans and many Americans in the traditional values of their societies. Hundreds of Americans exiled themselves to Europe, where they joined compatriots F. Scott Fitzgerald and Ernest Hemingway and other members of the Lost Generation. Disillusionment with convention and a fascination with the "primitive" and exotic augmented the international vogue for African and Asian civilizations in the 1920s. The growing respectability of nonracist theories and cultural relativism in the social sciences abetted the trend.[16]

The most pronounced North American expression of the new interest in blacks was the Harlem Renaissance and the attendant exploits of Afro-American expatriates in Europe. Continued U.S. military presence in Haiti delayed a widespread public reevaluation of black culture. A literature of protest and self-criticism, however, had developed during the years of the protectorate. Represented by such works as Léon Laleau's Le choc, and Jean Price-Mars' La vocation de l'élite, it was a reactive nationalist literature concerned chiefly with opposition to direct foreign domination. Only after the Americans departed with their delusions of a civilizing mission fulfilled could free rein be given to a Haitian sensibility rooted in an Afro-Caribbean identity.[17]

The ebullient mood of the 1920s was followed by the somewhat chastened atmosphere of the depressed 1930s. The emergence of négritude literature in Haiti corresponded roughly with the appropriation of surrealism and the deconstruction of colonialism in other Francophone literatures by such pioneers as the Martinican, Aimé Césaire, who utilized Haitian themes; the Guadeloupian Léon Damas; and the Senegalese Léopold Senghor. In Haiti, Carl Brouard, Jacques

Roumain, Normil Sylvain, and others transcended the romantic traditions of local color and insisted on "authenticity" in their poetry and
prose as they made war on convention and cultural imperialism.[18]

The United States, by means of military occupation and growing
economic domination of Haiti, now substituted for France as the resented metropole. The French writer André Breton, widely regarded
as the founder of French surrealism, came to Haiti to travel and lecture
in 1946 under official French auspices. He encouraged Haitian literary
activity. Ironically, repudiation of imperialism in the French language
was now deflected to the United States, with the assistance of one of
the world's sturdiest—if temporarily enfeebled—colonial powers.[19]

The literati's identification of the French language and culture (as
opposed to Creole) with an anti-American stance was not the only
paradox that confronted Haiti during the 1940s. Négritude, which had
arisen as a meditation upon centuries of oppression and a celebration
of black life, came to justify social and political stagnation and conservative elite hegemony. The notion of an ineluctable racial essence
presented as impervious to, and indifferent to, innovation made this
possible. Romantic views of peasants as children of nature excused
their exclusion from political participation while simultaneously legiti-
mating the idea of Haiti as a cultural museum whose ancient dust
could not be undisturbed by the winds of change.

The North American perception of Haiti had meanwhile under-
gone subtle change. Scorn, exaggeration, and outright falsification
still abounded in U.S. travel literature during the late 1920s and early
1930s, but the Haitian characters in some of these treatments increasingly assumed human proportions. Even Marine Corps officers' mem-
oirs began to depict Haitians as complex, multidimensional personalities, but a lurid style and the stubborn racism with which the best
were loath to part continued to taint works of this genre.[20]

Haitians hotly criticized these portrayals of their country. A great
deal of bitterness accompanied the appearance of John H. Craige's
Cannibal Cousins. Haitians correctly identified this literature with a less
polite side of the international *vogue nègre*. While some whites who
appreciated black art, music, and culture were motivated by a refined

esthetic sensibility, others simply enjoyed the sensationalism of exploring a socially forbidden realm. As Josephine Baker had discovered in Paris, the latest tropical nightclub revue had more "sex appeal" and yielded more profit than the studied creations of the Harlem Renaissance's painters, poets, and playwrights. Evocation of voodoo drums, orgies, and sorcery sold books. The U.S. film industry also got into the act. During the 1930s, the films *White Zombie* and *Emperor Jones* aroused the wrath of Haitian filmgoers. These movies portrayed black "natives" in stereotyped Hollywood fashion, and critics pressured film distributors to withdraw them from circulation in Haiti.[21]

While zombies in greasepaint flickered across the silver screen in the United States, anthropologists began systematic field investigations in Haiti. Melville Herskovits (1895–1963) provided anthropological and historical evidence for the continuity and linkages of black religions and cultures in the diaspora. Anthropology came to recognize the complexity of Haitian society as a result of the work of Boas, Herskovits, and Zora Neale Hurston.[22] A new appreciation for Haitian culture further underlined the bifurcation between those who considered themselves part of a larger Francophone world, and those who identified more closely with Creole traditions. The Haiti of négritude, anthropological investigation, and tourist adventure was not the country of the bourgeoisie, a class that remained ambivalent toward the new emphasis on local traditions.

U.S. policymakers had neither bolstered a Haitian middle class independent of the civil service nor wooed the existing bourgeoisie with guarantees. They accepted elite claims to power, but did very little, both during and after the occupation, to ensure that its economic position, and therefore its permanence, would last. The upper class, though cultured and refined, failed to meet Yankee standards. Criticism of the corruption and arrogance of this group was commonplace, but such faults did not deter U.S. cooperation with oligarchies in other Latin American countries. Why was Haiti the exception?

Anglo-American disdain for mulattoes, a product of a bipolar conception of race, played a part in white American distrust of the Haitian bourgeoisie. Underlying the hostility to mixed bloods was a deep-seated belief that such persons, as links between the races, endangered the established order in what should be a rigidly color-defined world. White Americans who were none too thoroughly schooled in their own cultural traditions greatly resented mulatto claims to Francophone culture. The European connection, moreover, raised sensitive political questions. Could continental sophistication be separated from the hegemonic ambitions of France and Germany?

Mulattoes thus constituted a multiple challenge, which could only be met by impugning their personal worth. The conspicuous failures of the Haitian bourgeoisie as a leadership class greatly assisted this denial, but the terms of rejection had more to do with what "Negroes" were supposed to be. The Haitian upper classes included persons of purely African phenotype who were culturally "mulatto" in that they too had assimilated European values and attitudes and often encountered the hostility of North Americans for not affirming traditional stereotypes. Their critics mourned a lost world where blacks knew their place and did not boast frock coats and Sorbonne doctorates.[23]

Before and during the occupation, popular media commonly depicted Haiti as a barbarous land with little hope of redemption, save through a civilizing mission. Mass market literature and films emphasized lurid and sensational elements in its culture. By the late 1930s, however, a major evolution in public perceptions of Haiti was under way.[24] The attitude of urban, educated Haitians toward indigenous traditions also experienced gradual change, as some began to see value in folklore, music, the Creole language, and Vodun. Sténio Vincent had advocated using peasant culture, of which many urbanites were ashamed, as a lure to tourist development well before the beginning of World War II. Vincent's interest in exploiting this theme suggests a realization that international opinion was moving away from crude racism and that Western visitors might now enjoy what had previously repelled them. Renewed interest in Vodun coincided with the emergence in other Latin American republics of *indigenismo*, a literary and artistic movement that probed and celebrated popular folk cultures. This trend harmonized with a long-standing tradition of romanticizing the peasantry. In any case, the enclave nature of tourist resorts would not seriously disturb an upper class that had never claimed much public space.[25]

In the early 1940s writer and critic Jacques Roumain directed the Port-au-Prince municipal government's ethnological museum, which included a collection of Vodun artifacts. The museum represented an intellectual retort to the massive campaign against Vodun launched during the same years by Roman Catholic clergy. The Church's "anti-superstition" campaign appeared only to sharpen the fascination with the Afro-Haitian cults, which now blossomed on canvas in paintings by Hector Hyppolite, Wilson Bigaud, and Castera Bazile; while the poetry of Carl Brouard, Jean Brierre, and Normil Sylvain celebrated peasant culture in general. Voodoo became the focus of numerous dramatic events in nightclubs and theaters that drew a considerable foreign audience. Attempts were nevertheless made to purge some elements of Haitian culture of their popular character and render them suitable for elite consumption. Port-au-Prince officials often banned the sometimes obscene *rara* bands, for example, until the 1950s. Wishing to present a well-groomed image to visitors, the government also revived an old law that required peasants to wear shoes on trips to the capital.[26]

In the United States, the new priority given to Haitian culture noticeably affected Afro-Americans as the first stirrings of the civil rights movement were felt internationally. In *Haiti and the United States*, J. Michael Dash wrote extensively of the collegial relations between Haitian and Afro-American intellectuals. Scholarly and cultural exchanges between the two groups began during the U.S. occupation and continued through the World War II era. These intellectual communities shared an interest in African cultures of the diaspora and in race relations. In some respects, acts of recognition or friendship toward black Americans constituted an oblique rebuke to Washington. In the eyes of some, however, President Elie Lescot's use of the collaboration to conceal color caste discrimination in Haiti tarnished it. The work of such Afro-American writers as Rayford Logan, Langston Hughes, and Mercer Cook nevertheless increased Haiti's visibility in the United States and introduced it to a wider audience.[27]

The black republic's popularity with the Afro-American intelligentsia survived the fall of Lescot, and such luminaries as Walter White,
secretary of the NAACP, and Mary McLeod Bethune, president of the
National Council of Negro Women, were state guests during Dumarsais Estimé's presidency. The Association for the Study of Negro Life
and History later organized a Haitian tour sponsored by Langston
Hughes, Rayford Logan, and others. Social news of Haitian individuals and events appeared in the black popular press more frequently
between 1949 and 1956 than ever before or after.[28]

Race relations played another, somewhat different role in helping
to revise perceptions of Haiti and create a tourist trade. Many of the
visitors drawn to the country in the early 1950s were liberal whites
intimidated by the approaching race-relations storm in the United
States. From their own perspective, their sympathetic interest in Haiti
illustrated their lack of prejudice. Selden Rodman contrasted the hospitality he, a white man, enjoyed in Haiti with the ill-treatment generally accorded blacks in the United States. Herbert Gold indicated
that this hospitality even extended to the failure to hold culpable foreigners accountable in fatal automobile accidents. Liberal guilt, then,
contributed another factor to the changed atmosphere.[29]

Haiti became the haunt of the chic international traveler and drew
an impressive list of celebrity guests. Visitors in the 1940s and 1950s
had varied motives. Among the North American cognoscenti, Haiti's
appeal related to a general revolt against the perceived materialism
and conformity of U.S. life. At home, this sentiment expressed itself in
the fascination with such cultural phenomena as the expatriate artist
and writer, the bohemian, and the bebop musician. Some visitors to
Haiti attempted to identify what they saw as a raw, elemental energy.
For Gold: "In the rank, oily harbor of Port-au-Prince, glistening black
boys dived for coins, snatching at the glint of silver, seeming to turn
like playful dolphins for the pleasure of the tour ships. The smoke
of charcoal fires lay over the white heap of a city built on hills like
Naples, Haifa, and San Francisco. The lizards played up walls and
across ceilings, darting after flies. Beyond the port, the town was
sleepily insomniac, drinking coffee and rum-coca to stay awake, but

to see it as a tourist was to see frantic commerce and subtle sexual gaming, a struggle to stay alive and feel vivid in the heat."[30]

Gold gave voice to what would later be termed "ethnic tourism," a form of expression in which "the tourist endeavors to make contact with a different reality, manifest in undomesticated nature, in relics from the past, or in the behavior of culturally distinctive strangers."[31] Rodman, long an aficionado of the black republic, tried to capture "what it [is] that we are all seeking and that we find in Haiti." For him, it was the "basic simplicity" of life there. In lauding "the independence and spiritual stability [of] the peasant," Rodman wondered, "in the final analysis, of what importance is economic well-being? Does specific caloric intake have anything to do with peace of mind? Do modern means of communication really contribute to the understanding of people among themselves? Are plumbing, grocery stores, bank accounts, and double-entry bookkeeping necessary for a good life? What is happiness?"[32] Rodman's view reflected that of a small coterie of artists and writers whose full stomachs allowed them to take a rather cavalier attitude toward the privation they saw around them. Others nevertheless took up their search for authenticity, lured not so much by the attractions of Haiti itself as by the need to identify with the tastes of the smart set.

Haitian tourism existed in embryo in the late 1930s. In 1938 the West Indies and Central America drew approximately $33 million or about 20 percent of the U.S. tourist dollar. The prospect of bringing Haiti into a regional industry in the late 1930s induced Port-au-Prince to establish a National Tourist Office headed by the president of the Haitian Chamber of Commerce. The U.S. State Department also made a survey of tourist possibilities in Haiti, with special attention to hotels. Officials interviewed U.S. businessmen with extensive interests in the Latin American travel and entertainment industries. Those consulted included W. R. Grace and Company, Nelson Rockefeller, and Juan Trippe of Pan American Airways. The major railroads, airlines, and shipping firms did not want to expand operations in Haiti, a country that offered few of the amenities that lured pleasure seekers to Cuba, for example. The State Department decided to delay any effort to press the Export-Import Bank for funds to develop tourism there.[33]

The nascent Cuban, Panamanian, Puerto Rican, and Virgin Island resorts served as models for a prospective Haitian travel industry, whose initial success would depend on planners' ability to coordinate cruise ship movements with shore facilities. This would be no easy task, as, historically, the demands of freight service dominated regional shipping.[34] Some resorts were operated by transport companies, such as the Queen's Park Hotel in Port-of-Spain, Trinidad, owned by Pan American Airways, and the Hotel Tivoli in Balboa, Canal Zone, run by the Panama Railroad Company. War in Europe had severely reduced passenger traffic, and the State Department could expect little improvement until the advent of better transport service. The underdevelopment of Haitian tourism formed part of the country's general paucity of infrastructure. The Haitian government nevertheless interested itself in the possibilities that tourism might offer. President Vincent wanted to attract American visitors of "the better class" and offered to amend a law to facilitate casino gambling should the hotel industry think it advisable.[35]

The U.S. fiscal representative suggested the formation of a corporation whose directorate would include representatives of shipping lines, banks, travel agencies, advertising agencies, and hotels. These would organize subsidiaries in each of the American republics. Where local financing was available, the larger holding company would control management only. The company would invest in areas where local capital proved inadequate. This plan, if fully executed, could have standardized hotel administration throughout Latin America to conform to North American tastes. It also echoed the sentiment expressed by hotel entrepreneur Conrad Hilton, who clearly understood the cultural implications of replicating Hilton hotels throughout the world. "Each of our hotels is a little America," he once declared.[36]

Haiti would earn some foreign exchange within the confines of a travel industry thoroughly dominated by stateside investors and consumers. The task of acculturation that Marines with bayonets failed to accomplish would be undertaken by tourists with cameras. The same top-priority bondholders whose prerogatives edged social spending out of the official Haitian budget could further perpetuate indebtedness through judicious investment in hotels, nightclubs, and resorts. Ultimately, tourism proved premature because of major carriers' disinterest. The State Department decided to delay any effort to press the Export-Import Bank for development funds, and nothing was done until after World War II.[37]

Official U.S. interest in Haitian tourism between 1934 and 1941 did not therefore signal any innovation in perceptions of Haiti, but instead represented a continuation of conventional guidelines. The Hoover-Roosevelt Good Neighbor policy—the peaceful pursuit of conflict resolution between the United States and the Latin American republics—softened but did not alter the harsh contours of Haitian-American relations. The White House and the State Department obliged Haiti to place debt service above allocating funds for national development, and political and economic orientation toward Washington before European friendships.

The Estimé administration planned a national exposition in December 1949 to salute Haitian art and culture. It had several hotels built to accommodate anticipated visitors, and authorities cleared a slum to erect the Cité de l'Exposition. Gate receipts from the exposition were low, but the event gave Haiti an unprecedented amount of international publicity. The profound social and cultural changes of the postwar period greatly facilitated the project. Increased prosperity and leisure in the United States after the austerities of the depression and World War II, the growing efficiency of air travel, and the popularity of the Caribbean locale accompanied Haiti's debut as a choice site. Cheaper and more frequent flights enabled larger numbers of visitors to arrive. The chief beneficiary of these changes, Pan American Airways, carried 90 percent of all tourists to Haiti. Organized crime, associated with the hotel and resort industry in South Florida and Cuba, also appeared in Haiti during the late 1940s.[38]

The tourist boom could not have taken place without some infrastructure in place. It also had awaited revised policies on the part of the U.S. government. Yet a successful Haitian tourism in the late 1930s and early 1940s required a change in Haiti's image. However consistent the fundamental policy objectives of the United States during and after the occupation years, the propaganda needs of a would-be tourist Mecca are not the same as those of a military protectorate. Continued occupation of Haiti had required rationalization on the grounds of present danger, as well as the putative primitiveness and incompetence of the natives, qualities hardly reassuring to fastidious vacationers. Removing these ascriptions by substituting Haitianization for a permanent U.S. military presence was the first prerequisite to altering perceptions of Haiti. By 1942 the U.S. legation itself was contemplating official sponsorship of events having to do with Haitian history and traditions. Examination of the official correspondence for 1940–44 reveals a substantial increase in documents concerned with social and cultural matters. The 1940s witnessed the establishment of the Haitian-American Institute, and nongovernmental institutions and foundations also began to show interest in Haitian society and problems. The Carnegie Endowment for Peace studied the feasibility of restoring La Ferrière, King Henri Christophe's fortress near Cap-Haïtien.[39]

After World War II, a vogue for "Haitian" resort clothes erupted on the New York fashion scene. This was attendant on the "discovery" of Haiti. Leading U.S. department stores, such as New York's Lord and Taylor, Carson's in Chicago, and Bullock's in Los Angeles, began marketing the fad in "Haitian" sportswear, perfume, millinery, and jewelry. Travel magazines promoted the country, and, indeed, aside from Guantanamo-based U.S. Navy personnel taking shore leave, the first substantial U.S. tourist immigration during the 1950s consisted of comparatively sophisticated urban consumers.[40]

Changing attitudes toward beauty had fostered a tourist industry designed to attract the middle-income vacationer, rather than the wealthy traveler of yore. For white women, bronzed skin had once signified that the bearer habitually labored in the hot sun. When women's sports came into vogue in the 1890s and gradually ushered in the acceptability of a somewhat darker complexion, pallor became the hallmark of unhealthy female industrial workers. The rich, moreover, were accustomed to sunbathing on the Riviera. The relaxation of dress after World War I and the rise of nudism and other health fads created a new recreational culture based on beaches and resorts.[41]

A spate of Hollywood films set in tropical locales in the 1940s and 1950s—typically starring such actresses as Carmen Miranda, Rita Moreno, Delores Del Rio, and Rita Hayworth—broke with tradition in their tacit portrayal of leading ladies as mestizas or mulatas. While the "Chiquita Banana" stereotype marked no great breakthrough on the race relations front, Latin and Caribbean settings, because they could be detached in the viewer's mind from the troubled U.S. racial scene, offered more social space to present people of color favorably. For this reason, the 1956 film *Island in the Sun* could treat interracial sex, a taboo subject in a North American milieu.[42]

The island romance genre even provided some roles for actresses and dancers who actually were of African descent. Carmen De Lavallade and Dorothy Dandridge played slave girls in historical potboilers about piracy and the slave trade. On the dance stage, Katherine Dunham, Pearl Primus, and their troupes familiarized U.S. audiences with basic principles and themes of African, Caribbean, and specifically Haitian choreography. These developments facilitated the transformation of Haitians from superstitious and bestial blacks inhabiting a dangerous, hostile land, to good-hearted, if unschooled, citizens of a picturesque country. Their blackness, no longer seen as menacing, simply underscored the gentle exoticism of the place and provided one more color to its charming kaleidoscope.[43]

Promoters of the romantic Haiti established a travel industry that did little to spread the benefits of tourist revenues but instead reinforced cleavages between the city and the countryside. In the realm of ideas, the mystique glorified the apparent stoicism of the peasants and celebrated their abstention from politics in the name of admiring their "independence and spiritual stability." In spite of poverty, leftist insurgencies appeared distant from the popular mass consciousness, and except to visitors already sensitized to racial antagonisms, the ongoing color conflict in Haiti seemed quaintly remote.[44]

On the surface, it appeared that North American writing on Haiti had turned away completely from the perspective characteristic of the occupation epoch. In some ways, however, the new approach was more insidious. An earlier generation believed that it could impose reform ideas on an alien population. The new generation did not believe that any change was desirable or necessary. The liberalism of the cold war era, stripped of efficacy by political repression, expressed itself most freely in the cultural realm and abandoned the political. Matters of taste and esthetics came to prevail over substantive issues of power because the North American intelligentsia had abandoned pursuit of the latter. In such a milieu the fine sensibilities that one might develop in the area of music or art, for example, could readily coexist with the greatest callousness toward the palpable suffering of those whose culture was under consideration.

Haiti's golden age of tourism, which lasted for perhaps seven years, coincided with a period in U.S. history when liberals saw themselves as centrists rather than as radical reformers of society. As such, they had no interest in class consciousness or "redistributive social change," but rather in rule shared among business, labor, and political elites. They therefore had little real difficulty with the Haitian politics of the era.[45] In his book *The Vital Center*, Arthur M. Schlesinger, Jr., defined U.S. liberalism as a considered appreciation of the best strains of both conservative and radical thought. As one scholar noted, "It was all too easy to move from [Schlesinger's] qualified acceptance of the conservative tradition to uncritical adulation of it. . . . it was only a short step from the salutary perspective of the vital center to the superficialities of the 'New Conservatism' in the 1950s."[46]

This intellectual climate provided the backdrop for the emergence in 1957 of a dictatorship harsher than any regime Haiti had experienced since colonial times. It set the stage for a perspective on Latin American conditions that was so uncompromising that almost any efforts to undermine the status quo in the black republic were regarded as subversive of hemispheric peace and stability. The effects of this evolution in thinking, however, were not immediately realized. The transition occurred during fairly flush times for Haiti, an epoch when its reputation as a darkly menacing land yielded to a new representation as a beguiling picture book island. This was, nevertheless, the face that Haiti chose to show to the outside world. Gentle breezes wafting from the sea, lively tropical revues, and the tinkle of ice in glasses of planter's punch could not entirely disguise the ongoing tensions in Haitian society and, despite the growing number of concerts, expositions, and benefits sponsored by the U.S. embassy, the deeper conflicts between the sister republics.

8   Island Neighbors

Haiti emerged from the occupation only to slide into the middle of a world depression. It had an expensive plant to maintain but few resources with which to do so. Over the objections of a militant legislature, President Sténio Vincent reached an agreement with the State Department in 1933 that extended U.S. control over Haitian finances to protect foreign bondholders' interests. The National City Bank sold the National Bank of the Republic of Haiti (BNRH) to Haiti in 1935. Though endowed with a mixed directorate, the National Bank remained under U.S. supervision until 1947, the date of retirement of the 1922 loan.[1] The Executive Accord of 1933 abolished the office of financial adviser and replaced it with a fiscal representative, whose more restricted powers were limited to customs collection, oversight of the Haitian internal revenue agency, budget inspection to ensure that expenditures did not exceed receipts, and control over debt-servicing accounts. Like the financial adviser, the fiscal representative would be a U.S. citizen, and a former adviser, Sidney De la Rue, easily slipped into the new position.[2]

Anticipating a new cycle of foreign intrigue, officials discouraged European lenders, but did not eagerly facilitate additional U.S. aid in 1934–35. Only anxiety about undesirable aliens gaining influence prompted the federal government to consider helping Haiti get a loan and relaxing its hard line on negotiations with France.[3] Haitian attempts to secure French credits nevertheless failed. In the closed trading climate of the 1930s, the French equatorial colonies could match independent producers of tropical commodities. Unable to improve the quality of its coffee, Haiti slipped from its preferred place in the French market. Its relations with France cooled during the occupation years, especially after Paris presented it with a list of imports for which it demanded special treatment. The Haitians, bound by most-favored-nation agreements with other states and unwilling to forego needed revenues, refused the terms. France would not finance credits unless it could enjoy the same control as the United States did over Haitian customs and internal revenue receipts. The Franco-Haitian treaty finally collapsed in May 1935 when Paris suddenly demanded payment in gold of the balance of the 1910 loan.[4] Global depression conditions and the defaults of other Latin American states continued to make credits generally unavailable.

Port-au-Prince then turned to U.S. bankers in hopes of securing funds that would be free of federal supervision. Talks with the president of Chase Manhattan Bank, National City Bank, the Morgan group, and smaller banks proved fruitless. The devaluation of the dollar, to which the gourde was pegged, made long-term dollar loans unacceptable to financiers. Supposedly chastened, the Haitians capitulated. "It was not until they reluctantly abandoned the belief that they could get a loan without the assistance of the American government," a U.S. functionary wrote, that "there [was] any change in their attitude toward the United States, its citizens and officials. Once the Haitians understood that no foreign country would interest itself in a loan," and that no bank would touch them "except and unless the American government indicated its interest in one way or another, was there a radical change in Haitian policy."[5]

Breaking with its history of open intervention, the United States would henceforth play a subtler hand in Haiti, not unlike that played by France and Germany in the past. It based this change on its recognition that outright intervention would accomplish nothing, rather than on a realization that the occupation had been unjust and unproductive.[6] The Hoover administration undertook the withdrawal from Haiti in the same pragmatic spirit that had marked the beginnings of intervention, and many U.S. officials have defended it to the present day.

The indifference with which observers witnessed the Haitian government desperately searching for funds in the mid-1930s was matched only by claims that native laziness and intractability caused the subsequent decay of the roads and public works. According to such assertions, had the Haitians only better marshaled their meager internal revenues, the occupation infrastructure would have survived.[7] Public works maintenance necessitated continuing and increasing outlays of foreign exchange, however, and these had always been at a premium. In short, foreign control cost considerable money. From the salary of the North American president of the National Railroad to officialdom's varied duty-free imports, Haiti exported its state revenues.

The occupation did bequeath one lasting legacy: a professional armed force with modern weapons—the Gendarmerie, later called the Garde d'Haïti. As in the Dominican Republic, Cuba, and Nicaragua, U.S. military officers trained indigenous personnel to staff and operate a national guard. Washington intended these units to be police forces and provided them with light weapons. As such, they were to have no role in governance, and efforts were made to instill in them a professional rather than political ethic. These outfits nevertheless tended to absorb the milieu around them. In every instance, the effect of U.S. tutelage had been superficial. It had not altered the political culture of the recipient country. A militia could be employed by an ambitious individual to advance personally, and in Cuba dictator Fulgencio Batista rose to power as a result of his control of the national police. In the Dominican Republic Rafael Leonidas Trujillo, Jr., ascended through the ranks of the National Guard; and in Nicaragua, Anastasio Somoza García also used his country's militia to achieve total control of the state.[8]

Washington had viewed the pre-1915 army of Haiti as a relic of a barbarous past. It therefore took great pains to distance the subsequent Garde d'Haïti from politics. President Vincent, whose terms of office extended from 1930 to 1940, also wished to neutralize the Garde and eliminate any challenge to his own authority. He accordingly divided it, leaving the Garde proper under the control of its commandant, and created a palace guard led by another powerful officer.[9]

In spite of these precautions, interested observers doubted that the Garde would abstain indefinitely from politics. By 1936 its Marine-imposed discipline had relaxed, and class, color, and personal antagonisms began to surface in response to matters of power and promotion. The State Department viewed military efficiency in Haiti as less important than the maintenance of law and order, which required national police. The U.S. embassy kept a watchful eye on leading personalities within the organization, and Washington officials pressed for a continuing advisory presence in order to perpetuate U.S. influence on the Garde. The desire to prevent the emergence of another Caribbean generalissimo was genuine.[10] The national government's persistent deficiencies, however, continued to promote the politicization of the Garde. Many of those faults were directly associated with one man—President Sténio Vincent.

A former mayor of Port-au-Prince, Vincent came to the presidency identified with a nationalist agenda. He presided over the occupation's conclusion and prolonged his tenure through personal association with nationalist politics. By early 1937 the excitement over restored sovereignty had abated, and Vincent needed new victories to proclaim and money to distribute. He wanted to press forward with plans for a low-income housing project in the capital. A flood in Port-au-Prince and the return from Cuba of migrant workers placed additional strains on the weak economy.[11]

Few Haitians who did not benefit personally from Vincent's rule approved of it. Vincent met the mounting discontent with repression. Labor leaders, dissident intellectuals, journalists and others went to prison for criticizing the regime or describing living conditions in Haiti. Foreign liberals who had once applauded Vincent now deplored him. Walter White, secretary of the NAACP, who had protested Marine brutalities during the occupation, declared that Vincent "practically admitted to me that he did not want the marines or American financial control entirely ended." The U.S. presence lent a stability that perpetuated his control. Vincent consequently had little difficulty in assenting to the Montevideo accord of 7 August 1933, which set a date for Marine withdrawal but left U.S. authority over Haitian finances intact.[12]

This agreement did not please those who wanted all U.S. intervention in Haitian affairs terminated. Vincent's detractors at home and abroad dunned him for his part in the matter. These included members of his team who had political ambitions of their own. One leading critic, Elie Lescot, served as Haitian minister to Washington. The aspiring Lescot presented himself as avidly pro-American in contrast to Vincent. He simultaneously courted, and was rewarded by, Dominican dictator Rafael Trujillo.[13] The Washington-Ciudad Trujillo axis gave Lescot enough leverage to bargain with Vincent over the presidency, an office that the increasingly unpopular Vincent would have to relinquish in the forthcoming elections.

A pledge from Lescot to guarantee Vincent's personal safety and the security of his property once the former assumed office led Vincent to have all presidential candidates save Lescot arrested. Vincent also nominated Lescot senator of the republic, an office which allowed him to participate in the senatorial debate over the succession while keeping his diplomatic status in Washington. Vincent and Lescot jointly chose the prospective deputies in the upcoming April 1941 elections, and Vincent agreed to ensure that the Garde supported his successor. Vincent, meanwhile, met secretly with key army brass to urge the nomination of a military officer for the presidency, but they failed to agree on a candidate. Vincent's maneuvering suggests how important the Garde had become as early as 1940.[14]

The incumbent president was ultimately thrown back on Lescot, whose Trujillo connections made him unpopular in Haiti. Beginning in 1937, Lescot had written a series of self-incriminating letters to "*El Benefactor,*" which acknowledged his own role as an anti-Vincent conspirator and indicated that he had accepted Trujillo's money. The prudent Dominican kept this correspondence. During his tour of duty as Haitian minister to the United States, Lescot misappropriated some state funds, for which Vincent demanded immediate reimbursement. Lescot then had to borrow from Trujillo. Trujillo retained the Haitian's letter of entreaty. To make matters worse, Lescot failed to "launder" the loan and sent it to Port-au-Prince as it was—a draft on Ciudad Trujillo made out to himself.[15] Under the circumstances, an endorsement from Vincent would not improve the low esteem in which the Haitian public held Lescot. Predictably, Lescot waited until only twelve days before the election to declare his candidacy so as not to give any opposition a chance to form. With Vincent's help, the Haitian legislature duly elected Lescot president on 15 April 1941.[16]

President Lescot proved no populist. Haitians, he believed, were too backward for democratic institutions, and he viewed the national legislature as an unnecessary expense. Washington discouraged his plan to abolish it and install a twenty-one-member council of state because it would alienate U.S. public opinion.[17] Yet Lescot soon fulfilled his wish to cripple the chambers. World War II gave him the excuse he needed to declare Haiti a belligerent and assume extraordinary powers for the duration of the conflict. His staunch espousal of the Allied cause and U.S. disinclination to interfere with Haiti while at war with major powers, assisted him in this enterprise. Lescot also strengthened the Garde's hand by allowing military tribunals to judge those accused of common civil infractions.[18]

The State Department hailed these innovations as the "prompt and drastic action" necessary to guarantee "national security" following recent Axis torpedo attacks in the Caribbean Sea and mysterious fires in Haitian cane fields.[19] The promise of largesse made potential adversaries temporarily accept Lescot's maneuvers. Washington rewarded his anti-Axis zeal with a promise to buy the Haitian cotton crop as long as the war lasted; a credit for the National Bank of the Republic of Haiti from the Export-Import Bank to strengthen the gourde; joint public and private sector exploitation of sisal; and a lend-lease agreement.[20]

U.S. officials did not endorse some of Lescot's more extreme projects. His proposal for two-tiered military conscription—the creation of a modern army out of elements of the educated, light-skinned elite and labor battalions out of the black, illiterate masses—was quietly discouraged. Given U.S. criticism of Japan's forced-labor policies, a client state could hardly be permitted to follow suit. Wartime planners showed greater interest in sending Haitian agricultural laborers to other parts of the Americas to harvest derris plant, wild rubber, and oil nuts, but widespread Latin American opposition to black immigrants aborted that scheme. Even at this date, muted conversations took place about "surplus Haitians" whose home economy could not absorb them and who needed employment outlets in some country other than the overburdened Dominican Republic.[21]

Joblessness and agricultural decline surfaced as problems commanding official attention during the war because of their relation to strategic security and efficient wartime production. Organizing Haitian agriculture for export was risky because of the scarcity of nonessential shipping. Boom-time cash crop production had caused economic and ecological problems in the past, as when, for example, the short-lived World War I–era logwood rush resulted in the felling of many irreplaceable trees.[22] Haiti and the United States nevertheless cooperated on a massive project to grow cryptostegia, a latex producing plant that would help ease the rubber shortage caused by the Allies' lost access to Southeast Asia.

North Americans experienced in agriculture in the tropics and the southern United States headed the Société Haïtienne-Américaine de Développement Agricole (SHADA). Lescot cleared its path in Haiti by decreeing certain strategic zones where the company could rightfully cultivate rubber and sisal. Small properties of one and a half acres or less were exempted in an effort to avoid peasant unrest. SHADA nevertheless held rights to prime land, acreage best suited for food crop production. Each SHADA plantation could also rely on a security force composed of fifty to sixty members of the Garde d'Haïti, for which it ostensibly paid.[23]

SHADA began work in Haiti in 1941, and by the end of the year it had cut 755,942 board feet of lumber from wooded areas in order to plant cryptostegia. In mid-1942 it bought the Cap-Haïtien trunk line of the National Railroad of Haiti, purchased two agricultural companies, and acquired control of a third belonging to the Haitian government. SHADA planned to purchase crops grown by independent farmers and hire what it called "cooperators," or tenant farmers, who would plant on its land and abide by its rules. In March 1943 the corporation employed 69,477 persons. Many of these were drawn away from staple provision production in order to meet the demand for rubber. Food shortages resulted.[24]

Critics of the program, which included the U.S. War Production

Board's rubber director, called attention to SHADA's practice of growing export crops while awaiting the maturity of the rubber plants,
razing houses and gardens on lands it leased, and adjusting its over-
head by laying off Haitian laborers while retaining its well-paid expatriate staff. SHADA's defenders claimed that some of the criticism
was partisan: Republicans wished to overhaul the lend-lease program.
Others doubted that the corporation's activities could account for all
of Haiti's economic ills and attributed food shortages to the persisting
illegal practice of exporting such commodities as rice. Reductions in
food supply directly traceable to SHADA, they argued, were compensated for by the stimulating effect the company's large payroll had on
urban trade and the demand for imports.[25]

Increasing import demand and attracting capital to the cities were
artificial effects that did little to energize Haiti's ailing rural economy.
Cap-Haïtien suffered a 100 percent increase in food prices because
of scarcities that SHADA activities created in the area. U.S. military
intelligence reported growing anti-Americanism in the Artibonite Valley as a result of land expropriations undertaken by the corporation.
State Department officials meanwhile expressed doubt that cryptostegia could continue competing successfully with plantation-grown rubber after the war. Drought and high prices for exported rice created
so grave a situation that the U.S. government ultimately scuttled the
cryptostegia project and solicited funds from the office of the coordinator of inter-American affairs to resettle returning peasants. Coordinator Nelson Rockefeller recommended that technical and financial
aid be provided, but vehement opposition from the office of Wartime
Economic Affairs prevented assistance from reaching peasants. The
project's failure marked a political defeat for Lescot and won him few
allies in rural Haiti.[26]

SHADA and its demise accentuated the chronic problems of poverty
and underdevelopment. A Haitian-American economic commission
studying opportunities for postwar development early in 1944 found
few trade and investment possibilities that seemed workable. Neither
cottonseed oil, utilities, nor simple manufactures for local use would
appeal to investors. Haiti could benefit from cement manufacture,

trucking, and hydroelectric projects, but they were not cost effective. Relatively few persons could find industrial employment in that overwhelmingly agricultural country. The commission suggested tourist development and the introduction of light assembly and handicrafts.[27]

A banana industry had emerged during the occupation. The Standard Fruit and Steamship Company, which for years had employed Haitians on plantations all over the Caribbean, now waded through the paperwork and negotiations necessary to put the small, noncontiguous plots of the Artibonite Valley in banana palms. The capital-intensive cultivation Standard Fruit developed relied heavily on imported insecticides and machinery. Haiti accounted for 10 percent of the firm's global operations in 1939 and exported 1.4 million bunches.[28] The trade suffered from the scarcity of shipping for this highly perishable commodity. By the late summer of 1942, it could locate no transport at all. The Caribbean Area War Shipping Administration suggested that the U.S. government purchase and then destroy the crop. Bananas fell victim to the failure of rational planning, not peasant "conservatism." As they had in the past when cash crop opportunities folded, peasants uprooted their plantings.[29]

The largely foreign, export oriented firms in Haiti had created few options for the educated, urban stratum who formed the primary political constituency and could bring down a regime. Aside from the perennial coffee traders, rarely did members of this group interest themselves in commercial agricultural development. They did not share in the profits made by the big plantation companies. Lescot therefore pressed these corporations to provide management training for Haitians and eventually allow them to assume administrative positions.[30]

Lescot's identification with the interests of both U.S. firms and the urban bourgeoisie led him in 1942 to be compromised by a movement among the French Catholic clergy and its following that launched an assault against Vodun. In an effort billed as "the anti-superstition campaign," priests accompanied by religious mobs sacked temples and burned ritual objects. Cultists were compelled to renounce their faiths. Some writers have seen Lescot's hand in the agitation. The campaign coincided with the cryptostegia project, Remy Bastien argues, and provided a rationale to evict peasants from land desired by SHADA. While the drive did provide a cover for common criminal behavior and may have indirectly benefited the cryptostegia project, evidence suggests that it was an independent attempt by a profoundly conservative, low-paid clergy to regain the leverage that they had lost as a result of Lescot's pro-Americanism and the divided politics of occupied France. Similar abuses of Protestants soon followed the attacks on cultists, prompting Lescot to attend a Protestant church as proof of his own disapproval of religious intolerance.[31] Lescot sought to neutralize the pro-Vichy elements in the Church by encouraging the missionary presence of North American priests and seeking the good offices of such religious leaders as Francis Cardinal Spellman. He also requested and obtained the recall of the papal nuncio, a man who intrigued heavily with Trujillo.[32] The Dominican dictator, fully aware of Lescot's problems, had no intention of continuing his clandestine support of the Haitian unless it proved useful. He planted articles hostile to Lescot in selected periodicals and endorsed the candidacy of the popular soldier Demosthènes Pétrus Calixte.[33]

Lescot's presidency—marred by corruption, the detested cryptostegia project, and a virulent campaign against Vodun—could not survive the restoration of normal international conditions. A student strike that began on 7 January 1946 followed popular revulsion against a continuation of the regime. On 11 January 1946 at 4:00 p.m., Colonel Franck Lavaud of the Garde announced that Lescot was under house arrest and that a junta consisting of himself, Major Antoine Levelt, and Major Paul Magloire had assumed control in Haiti. The military promised elections and the restoration of constitutional rights after abolishing a legislature composed of Lescot's placemen.[34]

The State Department based its support of the junta on the argument that Lescot's forced resignation had left a power vacuum that contentious civilian leaders could not fill. Washington's first inclination was to make recognition contingent on a promise of elections. Due to conflicts among Haitian politicians, however, U.S. officials came to see the military as a source of greatly needed law and order. The militarists themselves exploited this view, and in an effort to acquire legitimacy and arms from the United States, they emphasized the pressures they felt from Trujillo (who abandoned Calixte and recognized the junta within three days of the coup d'état) and from Dominican dissidents attempting to overthrow their dictator.[35]

The junta also proved agreeably conservative on the question of communism, which helped to ingratiate it with Washington policy-makers during the early cold war years. State Department officials considered the growth of Haitian radicalism an offshoot of French influence on the urban elite and believed that radical Marxists shared the glamor associated with French culture. Both the junta and the State Department kept quiet watch over the visits of such French leftists as André Breton. These individuals' positions as intellectuals gave them considerable credibility among the educated classes. The political instability in France itself continued to concern those interested in an anticommunist Haiti during this period.[36]

Citizens who did not like Lescot also opposed the purely military coup d'état. Students whose actions had precipitated the takeover did not immediately support the junta and called for fresh leadership in any provisional government. In the presidential campaign, which elicited the participation of the full Haitian political spectrum, the most popular candidates were affiliated with the Mouvement Ouvrier Paysan (MOP) founded by Daniel Fignolé in 1946. MOP's power rested on the urban slums and on the endorsement of certain intellectuals, workers, and some army personnel.[37]

Fignolé was proud of his charismatic following among the poor people of Port-au-Prince and called their massed power the "steamroller." Fearful of the possibilities of popular mobilization, the junta banned demonstrations and confined candidates to radio programs and public appearances. After a particularly stirring broadcast by Fignolé, the government denied radio access to MOP and often repressed spontaneous protests with brutality. On 12 April 1946, however, some twenty-five hundred slum dwellers converged on the streets near the Legislative Palace to rally for Calixte, who had formed a coalition with MOPists. The legislators were in session at the time, yet the police did not disperse the demonstrators. A U.S. Foreign Service Officer speculated that Paul Magloire, who controlled the police, wanted the lawmakers to feel the full weight of popular indignation and to recognize that a candidate that Magloire himself supported—Dumarsais Estimé—posed a feasible alternative to MOP populism. Indeed, after Estimé's successful election, his supporters subsequently co-opted Fignolé by adding him to the cabinet. Fignolé's acceptance of this deal simultaneously weakened him as an urban leader and sacrificed his following to the new president.[38]

The late 1940s marked a period of extensive labor activism by HASCO, SHADA, and Port-au-Prince dock workers, as well as members of the needle trades, domestics, and drivers. All of these workers wanted better wages and working conditions. Both the junta and the U.S. embassy worried about labor's demands, and Ambassador Orme Wilson communicated to the State Department his desire to see the military government stand up to popular pressure.[39] The junta attempted to do so by establishing a labor union, the Fédération des Travailleurs Haïtiens, to undercut MOPist organizing. Despite this competition, MOP remained a potent force in Haitian politics through 1949 and also served as a vehicle for the expression of black nationalist ideas. MOP organized the sugar workers on HASCO estates in 1948 but suffered some defections as a result of the failure of its general strike. The three-thousand-member organization made the improvement of wages and working conditions the centerpiece of its program. It also endorsed continued friendship with the United States and Cuba while maintaining an official stance of opposition to Trujillo. MOP communicated its political line to the illiterate through song lyrics set to popular music and sung at picnic rallies and similar gatherings.[40]

MOP's success demonstrated that thereafter Haitian politics would have to include classes not formerly represented. Population growth and the U.S. occupation had swelled the numbers of persons living in Port-au-Prince and had stimulated the development of a lower middle class, which now clamored for recognition. While urban elements remained a small percentage of the total population, the aspirations and strategic location in cities of the dissatisfied groups meant that they could no longer be ignored and would have to somehow be accommodated.[41]

An accord was reached through the presidential election of a black man from the Artibonite, Dumarsais Estimé, an educator and attorney. Estimé had a mandate, accorded him by the military junta and popular demand, to establish social peace by ensuring the petty bourgeoisie's share in employment opportunities and its voice in politics. He was also to undertake at least symbolic efforts to alleviate the misery experienced by the urban poor. The rise of popular radicalism necessitated this last measure—MOP's "steamroller" would flatten the upper classes if not contained. Elite elements, business interests, and foreign observers understood this well. While many did not like Estimé's black nationalist image, they recognized the basis of his power and the reasons for the firm support the military accorded him. The old bourgeoisie had not fallen; it was simply asked to share power, perhaps as a temporary expedient. It consequently acquiesced in his presidency as the lesser of several evils.[42]

Estimé sponsored the integration of black, as opposed to mulatto, elements into all areas of public life. The new government, interested in economic development and mild reforms, had no revolutionary pretensions and little to offer most citizens, who remained mired in rural poverty. In foreign policy matters, Estimé did not differ substantially from his predecessor in conforming closely to Washington's expectations. Haiti supported the U.S. position on Korea, for example, and rebuffed efforts at rapprochement initiated by Eastern bloc powers.[43] Yet Estimé did not see eye-to-eye with the United States on the Dominican Republic. As Lescot had discovered, acquiescence in the broad outlines of U.S. diplomacy did not guarantee protection from Trujillo, with whom each Haitian chief of state had had to come to terms. The Dominican problem had deep historical roots. It was a troubled relationship complicated by Washington's differing perspectives on the two countries.

U.S. perceptions of the Haitian bourgeoisie, and especially mulattoes, contrasted sharply with the view of the analogous Dominican class. Historic fears of inundation by Haitians and a desire for identification as a Hispanic nation that was at least mestizo if not white, led the Dominicans to deliberately repress Haitian elements in their society. The white upper class remained endogamous, and Dominicans in general preferred to ascribe somatic traits associated with Africans to Amerindian genes. The Haitian mulatto bourgeoisie by contrast, despite its often fawning embrace of European culture and its disdain for many aspects of indigenous life, never actually denied its African antecedents. Racial, cultural, and ideological conflict, concern about the integrity of national borders, and ultimately, anxiety about foreign domination, lay at the heart of the Haitian-Dominican conflict. It colored the frontier disputes and tensions caused by the eastern migration of Haitian laborers.[44]

The border region developed its own distinctive, mixed culture, linked in some measure by family and clientelistic networks. The so-called *rayanos* of the border, who emerged as a subculture in the nineteenth century, spoke Spanish and Creole and could count kin in both countries. One of Trujillo's most powerful lieutenants, Anselmo Paulino, came from a mixed frontier background and had married a Haitian woman. Estimé himself was related to Trujillo through his cousin, André F. Chevalier, who had served as Haitian minister to the Dominican Republic until shortly before Estimé became president.[45]

As politically important as *rayano* society was, it did not eradicate the Dominicans' longing for membership in a broader Spanish-speaking and Latin American, rather than African and Caribbean, community. Trujillo himself, of mulatto origin, sought to lighten his own appearance and that of the nation. In the 1930s, Undersecretary of State Sumner Welles approved the adoption of a Caucasian national image for the Dominican Republic. He saw it as a counterpoise to the cultural and demographic pressure that Haiti exerted and suggested that Italian or Castilian settlers be brought in to whiten the country.[46]

The mutual hostility between Haiti and the Dominican Republic ironically lowered the cost to the United States of maintaining surveillance and control over them. The presence of the ruthless Trujillo restrained the hubris of Haitian leaders, and Trujillo could be disciplined

if need be. Ultimately, destroying the peasant insurgencies on Española during the respective interventions left little for U.S. military gov-
ernors to do. Realizing that neither the host countries nor taxpayers at
home could sustain the costs of effective colonial occupation during
the Great Depression, U.S. policymakers prescribed disengagement
in the Caribbean republics. They instead fostered the substitution of
indigenous militias whose primary responsibilities were the maintenance of law and order. These police forces soon became politicized
vehicles to carry ambitious leaders and cliques to power. Haiti and
the Dominican Republic had national guard outfits, but because of the
unequal resources available to the respective governments, their size
and strength were unmatched.

The Dominican Republic had received major sugar investments.
The desire to protect the sugar quota further consolidated commercial
relations and friendships between U.S. entrepreneurs and Dominican
businessmen and politicians. The eastern state boasted a higher GNP
and a lower population density than Haiti. It produced more food and
possessed a larger national bourgeoisie, which enjoyed more security
as a dominant class than did its Haitian counterpart. Trujillo's Dominican National Guard was not only capable of repressing disorder
at home but also represented a potential threat to its neighbor. This
situation reversed nineteenth-century conditions, when the sparsely
settled Dominican Republic proved no match for successive Haitian
armies. The Dominican Republic, with the United States, formed one
of the two axes of Haitian foreign policy.[47]

Haitian-Dominican relations were further complicated by Rafael
Trujillo himself, a dictator for almost thirty years. A creature of the
U.S.-sponsored National Guard, Trujillo used the military to form
connections that catapulted him to lasting power. He milked state
industries for his own benefit and even had the four-hundred-year-
old capital, Santo Domingo, renamed for himself. Not satisfied to hold
unquestioned sway over his own compatriots, Trujillo set out to make
himself a regional power. He began with Haiti, seeking to control it
by bribing prominent leaders and functionaries and supporting con-

spiracies against the current administration. Trujillo's aid could never be taken for granted. He often played off Haitian factions against one another.[48]

In 1929 the two island republics signed a treaty to resolve frontier questions. In exchange for more than forty thousand acres of rich land traditionally populated by Haitians, Port-au-Prince received the Étang Saumâtre, a lake that it hoped to develop commercially. In spite of the border agreement, impoverished Haitians continued to enter the Dominican Republic illegally, squatted on arable land, or found employment as agricultural laborers.[49] Early in October 1937, units of the Dominican National Guard, under Trujillo's orders, massacred from fifteen thousand to twenty thousand Haitian migrant workers on the frontier. The murders were carefully planned to coincide with Trujillo-inspired provocations in Port-au-Prince designed to bring down the Vincent government. As early as August 1937, at least one American knew of Rafael Trujillo's plan to exterminate Haitians in the Dominican Republic. Either Sidney De la Rue, fiscal representative to the Haitian government, failed to pass on this intelligence or Washington officials did not take it seriously.[50]

The massacre began on 1 October with the execution of several Haitians on the frontier. On 2 October, Trujillo made a violent anti-Haitian speech. Dominican officials subsequently informed him that an important spy ring in Haiti had collapsed and that his most useful informants had been identified and slain. The dictator then gave the order to kill all resident Haitians. The slaughter began during the night of 2 October and continued for thirty-six hours. A product of contingency planning, soldiers nevertheless made the blood bath look like a spontaneous eruption of popular indignation by dressing as simple peasants and hacking Haitians to death with machetes rather than using bullets. Atrocities occurred as far east as Samaná Bay, but most of the killings took place in the Cibao (the Dominican interior north of the capital) and on the border. One officer, dutifully following orders, allegedly shot the family cook, an aged Haitian woman, in his own kitchen. At Santiago, as many as two thousand persons were decapitated in a town square. In Monte Cristi, bound Haitians were drowned in the bay. Soldiers shot or hacked to death thousands as they fled across the border. Witnesses recalled blood and bodies everywhere. A characteristically flawed pronunciation of *perejil*, the Spanish word for parsley, betrayed Haitians fluent in Spanish who sought to escape death by pretending to be Dominicans. Oddly, no murders took place on any U.S.-owned sugar estates.[51]

A curtain of silence swiftly descended on the two republics that remained unbroken until 10 October, when President Vincent, in a note to Trujillo, professed disbelief that the Dominican government bore any responsibility for the holocaust. Five days later, Haiti and the Dominican Republic signed a secret joint communiqué that reaffirmed their amity. Trujillo's government issued a condemnation of the atrocities and claimed that it was investigating them.[52]

Official U.S. correspondence asserts that envoys living in Haiti knew nothing about the horrendous occurrences until rumors and spontaneous reactions of outrage reached the United States through Santo Domingo. There was no news coverage, supposedly because of the isolation of the area where it had happened. The *New York Times*, for example, carried the story on 21 October, seventeen days after the events took place. Washington expressed no official concern until 7 November. Secretary of State Cordell Hull had been a Trujillo admirer.[53]

Ferdinand Mayer, the U.S. ambassador, did not share this insouciance. For him, the relations between Haiti and the Dominican Republic had reached a point that threatened the Good Neighbor policy in the Caribbean. He saw Dominican aggression as an extension of the growing fascism of the period and compared it to events in Europe. Mayer likened Washington's inaction to Britain's lost opportunity to pressure Germany by condemning the Italian attack on Ethiopia in 1935. Its failure to take a principled stand had led to the present deterioration of the balance of power. Mayer called on the United States to assist Haiti and "put Trujillo in his place."[54]

Afterwards, the State Department, armed with census figures, used the racially mixed character of the Dominican Republic to argue that the attacks had *not* been racially motivated and the U.S. government therefore could not be accused of a racist motivation in its failure to protect Haitian migrants. Whatever the merits of such tortured logic, the claim that the Roosevelt administration was remiss in checking the growth of fascism in Latin America was less easily parried. The massacre had come on the heels of the Italo-Ethiopian War in 1935 and Hitler's ongoing depredations in Europe. Port-au-Prince understood clearly that the United States and the western European powers had allowed these conquests to occur. Concerned Haitians feared that Washington would view a Dominican takeover of Haiti with similar resignation.[55]

Haitian anxiety also rested on the knowledge that Trujillo had considerable influence with U.S. politicians. Representative Hamilton Fish of New York, in 1937 the ranking minority member of the House Foreign Affairs Committee, expressed outrage at the massacre but abruptly reversed his stand after traveling to the Dominican Republic in 1938. The congressman, feted by Trujillo, returned to the United States with a $25,000 campaign contribution. Fish was not the sole beneficiary of *El Benefactor*'s bipartisan generosity. The rhetoric emerging from Ciudad Trujillo further confirmed the murderous thinking of members of the regime. According to Foreign Minister Ortega Frier, the Dominican Republic aimed to populate the frontier with armed settlers, and that "by the year 1940 the world would see a killing of Haitians which would completely overshadow" recent events. This was not mere oratory, for Trujillo continued the border terror even after news leaked out to the world press. Near the town of Capotille, Dominican soldiers summarily executed four Haitians in full public view and forbade the removal of the bodies, which rotted in the sun. As late as 1943 Trujillo had not abandoned his mission of extending "civilization" and development to the frontier, which he was in the process of "dominicanizing."[56]

Mayer believed that a U.S. military mission to Haiti would alleviate the problem of Dominican aggression, curb the dangers of internal instability, and end the arms build-up that the Haitian-Dominican conflict engendered. Vincent had appropriated funds to strengthen the Garde following the Dominican crisis but used the money to fortify the National Palace rather than the hinterland. He thus increased the power of ambitious elements in the Garde. Mayer worried about Vincent's survival and reiterated his concern that U.S. prestige would suffer if he fell and the political situation deteriorated only three years after the end of the occupation. Legation officials remained circumspect, however, and tried to avoid committing themselves when asked by Vincent what the United States would do if Trujillo attacked Haiti. The State Department did not intend this to happen, but the U.S. legation's posture of "the most scrupulous neutrality" could only look like hand washing to anyone seeking a firm commitment.[57]

President Vincent, meanwhile, appeared undisturbed by the massacre. Only public wrath and dissension among some ranking officials, notably the foreign minister, forced him to make a show of indignation to Trujillo. The Haitian and Dominican governments settled on a cash reparation. The negotiations were conducted with the least publicity possible at U.S. Undersecretary of State Sumner Welles's suggestion. Welles realized that the widespread airing of the case in Latin America, or the involvement of other Latin American countries in arbitration, would strengthen Trujillo's adversaries and make his tenure less sustainable.[58]

Vincent's flagging authority in Haiti did not rest solely on his ineffectual response to the Dominican massacre. Mayer, who closely observed Vincent's political evolution, was disturbed by remarks the president made in an 18 December 1938 speech at Aux Cayes. Power to elect heads of state should again be a legislative prerogative, Vincent argued, alluding to a body now thoroughly under his control. He cited the economic distress caused by Haiti's high birth rate and return migration. He called for the reinstitution of forced labor as part of national development programs. Mayer, familiar with Vincent's authoritarian tendencies, believed that he was testing public reaction.[59]

Was Haiti ready for the same type of ironclad dictatorship that characterized its eastern neighbor? The U.S. ambassador did not believe so. Unrest in Haiti was now pervasive, and he noted the "gradually fomenting revolt against the ruling class of mulatto politicians in general, and President Vincent in particular."[60] Popular resentment and the demand for black political representation would not be satisfied until nearly a decade later. The corruption, autocracy, and toadying to Trujillo associated with Vincent continued under the administration of his successor, Elie Lescot. The repayment of a campaign loan from Trujillo comprised one of Lescot's first tasks upon assuming office.[61]

The centennial of Dominican independence from Haitian rule, 1943, unleashed new frontier aggression by the Dominican National Guard, accompanied by hostile letters from Trujillo to his Haitian colleague, perceived as a client or adversary as the occasion dictated. Trujillo organized an assassination attempt against Lescot in 1944. Widely circulated rumors of a plot involved the Dominican consul at the frontier town of Belladère and several Haitians, and Haitian police recovered arms and ammunition wrapped in official Dominican stationery. This did not arouse public opinion, however, because of widespread dissatisfaction with Lescot. Fear of Trujillo led the Haitian government to ask the press not to publicize the conspiracy, and Lescot showed weakness by public denials of what everyone knew had occurred.[62]

The Haitian president certainly enjoyed more rapport with Washington than with Ciudad Trujillo, but this was because of his passivity toward the United States. Lescot had jockeyed himself into power partly as a result of courting the Americans on the one hand and the Dominicans on the other. Washington exacted of him total conformity to the long-range U.S. foreign policy objectives for the Caribbean region. Secretary of State Cordell Hull praised his constant "enthusiastic cooperation and support" for U.S. policies and his steadfast refusal to entertain any sentiment for occupied France. During a New York trip in 1942 Lescot claimed that "of Vichy I know only the water."[63] Only on the subject of race did he get ahead of his patrons. Speeches that he made in 1942 to black American audiences urged them to commit their energies to the war effort and linked antifascism to the struggle against racism. Some officials found even these benign remarks inflammatory and warned Lescot to be cautious in making statements about U.S. race relations.[64]

Lescot's steadfastness did not secure reciprocal fidelity in either the White House or the State Department. President Roosevelt proved a model of cordiality when Lescot paid a state visit in 1943. He deplored the Trujillo dictatorship but let Lescot know that the United States would do nothing to help him. The exigencies of war provided the excuse. Secretary of State Stettinius recalled FDR telling the Haitian that "the situation was very delicate," and things had to be kept "on an even keel."[65]

Even when Lescot later informed Roosevelt about the assassination plot, FDR, after two months' delay, replied that while the report saddened him, he was "gratified" to learn that Lescot would "do nothing to disturb the continental solidarity which is so necessary in the present struggle." State Department officials carefully worded Roosevelt's letter to remove any suggestion that Roosevelt either believed or disbelieved Lescot's claim. The Justice Department shared this equivocality and shrugged off an initial request for an investigation. It later claimed it could find no evidence of Trujillo's involvement in a plot.[66]

On one hand, Washington's disinclination to back up Lescot undoubtedly related to the fact that he could be kept loyal and subservient without support. The demise of his weak presidency would not appreciably affect the fundamental structure of Haitian politics. On the other hand, Trujillo's extensive power in both republics proved a useful adjunct to the pursuit of wartime goals in the Caribbean. The United States might also have regarded secret Dominican surveillance of radical Spanish exiles and Jewish refugees on the island a useful wartime service and wished it to proceed uninterrupted.[67]

Trujillo, fundamentally unchallenged by any power that could harm him, continued to nurture Haitian opposition figures. Some of these relationships remained conspiratorial. Others were overt because of certain dissidents' advertised disaffection. Haitian leaders often turned Trujillo's tactics against him, as when Dominican intelligence operatives uncovered overtures made to Haiti by anti-Trujillo plotters late in 1949. Members of Estimé's government reportedly told would-be insurgents that Haiti could render no military assistance but could offer "certain facilities" should efforts to dislodge Trujillo begin bearing fruit. Estimé denied any knowledge of or personal involvement in this discussion and reaffirmed his official position of nonintervention in Dominican affairs. Trujillo's subsequent mistrust of Estimé found expression in efforts to abort Haitian development projects.[68] When the Haitian government rebuilt the town of Belladère at a cost of $600,000, paving streets, erecting houses and a hotel, and installing electricity and plumbing, Trujillo retaliated by rerouting to Jimaní the commercial Dominican traffic that had customarily come to Belladère from Elías Piñas, thus leaving the newly refurbished Haitian town isolated. Economic destabilization was not Trujillo's only weapon. Just as he had plotted against Lescot, he organized intrigues against Estimé.[69]

One of the most sordid of Trujillo's activities involved a series of fires and assassinations planned for the Haitian capital in 1949 that were to be synchronized with a border raid by a Haitian dissident military officer. The plot included burning the Dominican embassy in Port-au-Prince and killing two officials who, forewarned, had had the luck to escape and make the story public. The destruction of the embassy and the murder of the Dominicans would be Trujillo's excuse to launch a full-scale invasion of Haiti and install an obedient client as head of state. A 1950 investigation of the incident by the Organization of American States showed plain evidence of official Dominican involvement. Clearly Trujillo was a destructive influence in the region.[70]

The Dominican dictator's seeming invincibility encouraged him in adventures against neighboring republics and precipitated a rash of informal anti-Trujillo alliances and filibustering attempts to rid the Dominican Republic of him. These activities led to what one official called a Caribbean "arms race." Haiti sent a representative to Washington to ask for assistance in a naval build-up to match the Dominicans. The Cubans followed suit.[71] In January 1948 Haiti sent a military mission to Venezuela. Haitian-Venezuelan friendship dated back to the days of Pétion. The two powers mutually deplored Trujillo and their perceived victimization by him. While they had no military alliance, and Venezuela did not plan to supply arms to Haiti, Port-au-Prince expected Venezuelan and Cuban support if attacked by the Dominicans. Havana in the late 1940s openly opposed Trujillo. A Cuban delegation made anti-Dominican statements during a good-will visit

to Port-au-Prince in December 1948. One member, a Havana legisla-
tor, unequivocally assured the Haitian foreign minister that he could
count on Cuban aid if Trujillo launched an invasion.[72]

World War II provided the original rationale for continued U.S. in-
dulgence of Trujillo, and the cold war permitted the perpetuation
of rigidities in U.S. foreign policy that prolonged his tenure. Washington strongly disapproved of the Caribbean Legion, a group of
democratic insurgents committed through filibustering to removing
regional dictatorships. Aside from the reflexive opposition to political
change through revolution, the United States also deeply distrusted
some Legion leaders: men like the Dominican Juan Bosch, and others
who were republican veterans of the Spanish Civil War. More was at
stake than principle. Washington, in tolerating dictatorship because of
a presumed need to repress social-democratic insurgents, subverted
stability and heightened local tensions. Matters became even more
grave once the Cuban Revolution challenged traditional Yankee domination. Only the advent of Castroism increased official discomfort
with Trujillo to the breaking point.[73]

The character of Haitian-Dominican diplomacy played a major role
in U.S. relations with Haiti in the early Duvalier years. Some U.S.
policymakers had a troubled conscience about Trujillo but felt that the
commitment to nonintervention put in place by Hoover and Roosevelt
should stand. In the wake of the Haitian tragedy, the State Department put heavy pressure on Trujillo to refrain from seeking office in
1938. He nevertheless remained the power behind the scenes. Once
Washington began to more vigorously reassert its interests in the area,
as exemplified in its successful effort to depose Jacobo Arbenz of
Guatemala, it became more difficult to rationalize Trujillo's continued
presence. Only Fidel Castro's highly visible defiance demonstrated to
the Eisenhower administration the gravity of the situation. Until he
was assassinated in 1961, Trujillo served the United States as an instrument of indirect pressure on Haitian governments. The leverage
that Washington could not exercise for reasons of scruple, the Dominican dictator could unselfconsciously exert. All too often, however, the

innocent paid for this *politique de doublure* with their lives. In the early 1950s an anonymous Haitian businessman summed up the dilemma as he drove a North American passenger through the rutted streets of Port-au-Prince. As his car struck a pothole—in French, a *trou*—he remarked to his companion that Haitians were "caught between two *trous*, *Tru*man and *Tru*jillo."[74]

9   Toward the Third World

The year 1946 inaugurated a period of relative optimism for Haiti, much of it due to the improved credit situation the nation experienced as a dependent economy of the prosperous United States. The following year the Estimé administration retired the 1922 loan by raising an internal bond issue worth up to $10 million. From this, Haiti realized $7.26 million, of which $5 million serviced the debt. The remainder went toward the commemoration of the Port-au-Prince bicentennial and other projects for which Estimé is remembered. The government also succeeded in reducing the size and changing the composition of the BNRH directorate, which had consisted of three Americans and three Haitians. It appointed five Haitians.[1]

Enthusiasm for change, a favorable market for Haitian commodities, and resultant limited prosperity for the urban sector gave Estimé time to begin building the town of Belladère, and the Cité de l'Exposition, near the Port-au-Prince business district. Genuine changes accompanied Estimé's presidency. His regime marked the political maturation of the Haitian middle class and its attempts to displace the old merchant-dominated national bourgeoisie, a process begun over a decade earlier in the British Caribbean and hastened by global depression. Business interests and the mulatto elite still hoped to regain their former influence and remained hostile to Estimé. Only the army could depose him.[2]

The organized political expression of the urban poor, Daniel Fignolé's Mouvement Ouvrier Paysan (MOP), nevertheless remained active. MOP endorsed a policy of courting Cuba and the United States as counterweights to a hostile Dominican Republic and pressed for better wages for laborers. Haiti's only political party with a mass following, MOP espoused the ideological black nationalism that had originally facilitated Estimé's candidacy. Poor people in the capital city continued the tradition of commemorating the fall of Lescot. The U.S.

consul noted that the celebration appeared to have genuine meaning for them. Estimé enjoyed much of his prestige among slum dwellers, but they were also a burden to him. As Finance Minister Gaston Margron informed State Department representatives in a 1946 Washington meeting on Haiti's debt, the urban proletariat and the thirty to forty thousand unemployed "intellectuals" in the cities had to be bought off to avoid disorder.[3]

Estimé's nationalist position on such traditional sore spots as alien ownership of real estate, the expatriate clergy, and foreign participation in the retail sector irked U.S. officials and such U.S. corporations as Standard Fruit, which operated in Haiti. These issues came to the fore in discussions of the proposed 1946 constitution. The collective efforts of the foreign embassies were mobilized to pressure Estimé into abandoning measures that would restrict the privileges accorded foreign capital. Estimé believed that his difficulties with the BNRH owed much to Americans' desire to amend the constitution. Ultimately the Haitian legislature compromised on most of these matters: it did not limit the size of foreign land holdings, it lifted the ban on expatriate clergy, and it allowed aliens to control investments through Haitian managers.[4]

Estimé's ability to move skillfully among a variety of external and domestic interests proved transient, for it could not withstand the effects of an increasingly fragile economy. World prices for coffee and sugar had dropped by the end of 1948. The return of depressed conditions, coupled with rumors of official corruption and allegedly rash state expenditures, did not augur well for the president's survival. No observers more keenly sensed the slightest changes in the Haitian political weather than U.S. resident diplomats. The U.S. embassy assessed Estimé's fortunes as having taken a turn for the worse by December 1948. Aside from the impact of the economic slump, diplomats focused on possible tensions between the president and the army, where certain officers associated with the traditional bourgeoisie appeared restive. The military had helped Estimé into office, and he courted it assiduously. Its loyalties, however, were not assured.[5]

Relations with the Dominican Republic also played an indirect role in the mounting uneasiness. In 1948 six Latin American governments, including the friendly regime of Venezuelan democrat Romulo Betancourt, fell to conservative forces. Nicaraguan dictator Anastasio Somoza, moreover, orchestrated a coup attempt in liberal Costa Rica. The bold Somoza, seen as analogous to Trujillo, and the demonstrated power of the army in these countries could not have been reassuring to the Haitian government. Port-au-Prince moved quickly to reaffirm its relations with Havana as a counterpoise to the loss of Caracas, which might have backed up Haiti in the event of a Dominican invasion. Interestingly, the U.S. State Department did not view the Cuban entente as a healthy sign of Caribbean distaste for dictatorships. Washington instead saw this rapprochement as contrary to its own policy of deterring the formation of regional blocs.[6]

Factors that had originally made Estimé an attractive candidate eventually proved to be his undoing. He had profited from a critical realignment in Haitian politics which, because it challenged the hegemony of the old ruling groups and gave popular expression to both black nationalism and Marxism, proved inherently unstable. Mastering labor had been a government objective since the rise in working class militancy that accompanied Lescot's demise. Estimé tried to defuse the fierce populism of the period by controlling trade union organization, and trying to diffuse the Marxist sophistication of the student movement through distributing scholarships for study abroad. Those awaiting a champion who would restore the old order viewed his balancing act with disapproval.[7]

The conservatives' opportunity arose when Estimé imprudently attempted to change the constitution in order to prolong his term. He was deposed in a bloodless coup staged by the same militarists who had removed Lescot in 1946—Colonel Franck Lavaud, Major Antoine Levelt, and Paul E. Magloire, then a major. The United States promptly recognized the junta on the grounds that it had made ostensibly honest if futile efforts to involve civilian authorities in governance, succeeded in maintaining law and order, and planned to schedule legislative elections. Five months after Estimé's removal, Paul Magloire was chosen president in the first direct election in Haitian history.[8]

Paul Magloire, born in Cap-Haïtien in 1907, began his career as a distiller's apprentice. In 1930 he took advantage of an opportunity to enroll at the military school in Port-au-Prince. He rose steadily through the ranks, studied law, became an attorney by 1939 and a colonel in the Haitian army seven years later. As commandant of the Casernes Dessalines in 1946, he had refused to move against anti-Lescot dissidents. As one of the few black officers with a prestigious command, Magloire was highly visible. His success in avoiding identification with Lescot had maximized his popularity. A mass demonstration of over sixty thousand persons, mobilized by Daniel Fignolé, protested an early, unsuccessful effort by the mulatto bourgeoisie to keep him out of the junta. Magloire served briefly as minister of the interior in the Estimé government.[9]

Despite his broad appeal, Magloire remained essentially conservative. He neither understood nor sympathized with middle-class rule. For him, the national bourgeoisie was the titular ruling class. Magloire sympathized deeply with its antilabor and traditionalist politics and endeared himself to the United States as a staunch anticommunist.[10] According to one report, Magloire had amassed a small fortune through funds Estimé gave him to buy off the latter's adversaries. Acting as Estimé's lieutenant, Magloire suppressed dissident elements and consequently did himself a favor. MOPists and others would not therefore pose a challenge to him when he, in turn, became president.[11]

Once in the National Palace, Magloire began to mend the traditional fences. He sought out Trujillo through the good offices of Anselmo Paulino and Luc Fouché. The Dominicans in turn facilitated his contacts with the Americans who controlled HASCO, SHADA, Plantation Dauphin and the National Railroad Company. Magloire promised tax holidays to foreign corporations, and with the assistance of a financial adviser appointed from the United Nations, set out to reform the banking system.[12] One of the most pressing financial needs in Haiti at the time was banking assistance for the industrial and agricultural sectors of the economy. To this end, the government established a semipublic agency, the Institut Haïtien de Crédit Agricole et Industriel (IHCAI).

Haiti also joined the International Monetary Fund (IMF) and the International Bank for Reconstruction and Development (IBRD) in 1951. Haiti lacked both a central bank and a savings bank, and the two established commercial banks paid little or no interest on savings deposits. Changes enacted in the early 1950s allowed more credit institutions to operate in the country, and the BNRH, forced to be competitive, soon improved the terms it offered to savings depositors. Haiti also began to attract more foreign capital. In 1951 the value of U.S. investments equaled $50 million.[13]

Magloire's public persona was that of a bon vivant whose colorful state ceremonies enhanced Haiti's reputation as a carefree tourist fantasia. He had not succeeded, however, in eradicating the ancient resentments and inequalities that had ended his predecessors' careers. Disaffection became open by 1954, after the ravages of Hurricane Hazel finally put an end to the *belle époque Magloire* and the president had resorted to jailing dissidents, including MOP leader Daniel Fignolé. Dr. François Duvalier, who had been Director of Public Health in Estimé's cabinet, remained in hiding, from where many believed he carried out acts of subversion.[14]

The erroneous but widespread notion that Magloire's term legally ended on 15 May 1956 caused an outbreak of disturbances, which continued sporadically throughout his remaining year and for the subsequent six months of provisional rule. In early December, U.S. Ambassador Roy Tasco Davis informed him that it would be prudent for him to resign on schedule. Magloire then attempted a subterfuge whereby he publicly agreed but announced a succession vacuum that the army would ask him to fill himself as temporary commander-in-chief.[15] This ruse precipitated more or less spontaneous strikes by both business and labor. Armed with a Thompson submachine gun, Magloire paid individual calls on the business community, key members of which hastily signed an agreement to end the business strike. Magloire went away satisfied, but the following day, the shops remained closed. This act of defiance represented the bourgeoisie's abandonment of Magloire, and he resigned on 12 December.[16]

Haiti had five provisional governments in six months during 1956–

57. Headed by civilians, they were cobbled together by army officers. None of them, however, enjoyed a full enough consensus among the powerful. The commercial elite created additional tension by calling business strikes against the administrations of Joseph Nemours Pierre-Louis (December 1956–February 1957) and Frank Sylvain (February–April 1957). Daniel Fignolé was provisional president for seventeen days, a term that ended when the army moved against the Port-au-Prince slums and killed approximately a thousand of his supporters. A military council followed the Fignolé interregnum and was itself succeeded by the army's choice: François Duvalier.[17]

As the election crisis of 1957 demonstrated, the anger of the urban poor had continued. Additionally, middle-class Haitian blacks refused to surrender the real and figurative gains they had made in the years since the U.S. occupation. Patrick Bellegarde-Smith considers this group's insurgency a key event in Haitian politics. Its ascendancy completed a process begun during the Estimé years. If conditions had permitted, it would have brought Haiti in line with predominantly English-speaking Caribbean states, where middle classes, rather than national bourgeoisies and commercial elites, ruled directly. The latter classes exercise power indirectly, most often through economic control and tacit understandings with foreign powers.[18]

Bellegarde-Smith attributes the elite's loss of authority to its clumsiness in handling middle-class demands and its indifference to U.S. interests. The bourgeoisie's candidate, Louis Déjoie, was a mulatto sugar planter, industrialist, and agricultural engineer whose Francophilia antagonized Washington. Déjoie had criticized the army, which reduced his potential support in that quarter. He was also obtuse enough to have characterized the 1946–56 decade, when opportunities for education and employment for blacks increased substantially, as "ten years of regression." Black nationalists who knew their history could also hold Déjoie's ancestry against him: he descended not only from a French slave holder, but also from President Geffrard, who had overthrown the "black" government of Faustin Soulouque in the mid-nineteenth century.[19]

Approaching the same question from another disciplinary perspective, Simon Fass sees a traditional business sector that by 1957 was too weak to deter a government representing a new class coalition from embarking on commercial ventures in its own right. The extensive network of state enterprises set up by the Duvalier family had its precedent in the 1950s when, partly imitating Trujillo, government officials began to involve the state in corporate enterprise. Washington opposed these forays into government-for-profit ventures, preferring instead that Haiti encourage private rather than state capitalism.[20]

Ideological considerations about the proper relationship between the public and private spheres were not at issue. Rather, objections to state initiatives by the traditional business sector focused on conventional concerns about preserving a balance of power among privileged groups. Governmental entry into capitalist enterprises, a practice that would eventually become a hallmark of the Duvalier dynasty, loaded the balance in favor of the class faction already in control of the state.[21]

Foreign aid came to play a role as another institutionalized resource on which the state could rely, rather than as a source of temporary support for the economy. Indeed, the politics and diplomacy of foreign aid became a significant feature of the relations between Washington and Port-au-Prince after 1945. The United States exercised a protectorate over Haiti from 1915 to 1934, but most of the funds to pay for its ministrations came out of the Haitians' own pockets. The commitment to assist underdeveloped countries in the post–World War II years marked a new departure in U.S. foreign policy, and a consideration of aid is indispensable for a thorough understanding of the Haitian-American dialogue.

U.S. domination of Latin America and the Caribbean in the twentieth century had remained unchallenged. Between 1898 and 1945, only one power, Germany, had had the temerity to do so. Germany was defeated in both world wars, and its plans for commercial expansion and exploitation of Latin American resources aborted. The methods used to effect the removal of German influence during the 1940s included a program of economic assistance, the Institute of Inter-American Affairs (IIAA), founded by Nelson Rockefeller. Rockefeller served as coordinator of inter-American affairs during World War II.[22]

IIAA rewarded states that banished Germans and sequestered their holdings. It provided bilateral assistance in credits for which the recipient country would gradually assume the cost over a specified period. In Haiti, the institute sponsored programs of slum clearance, yaws treatment, and the cleaning and construction of marketplaces. Brazil received the lion's share of these funds because it was perceived as the key to Allied security in the Americas and provided crucial supplies of rubber and other strategic materials. IIAA's total disbursements in Haiti totaled less than $1 million.[23]

Germany's departure and the subsequent reorientation of Soviet-American relations following Harry S. Truman's election strongly reaffirmed the Monroe Doctrine. Here, U.S. military officials took the lead. The Joint Chiefs of Staff regarded the Americas as a critically strategic buffer region in the event of another global conflict. The Pentagon also resolutely opposed any extrahemispheric influence, whether ideological or commercial.[24] In 1946, Secretary of the Navy James Forrestal and Secretary of War Robert P. Patterson endorsed a program of military aid for Latin American states, but the State Department opposed efforts to reinforce regional armies. Its Latin Americanists believed that militarism would abet instability, exhaust the republics' financial resources, and dim the chances for the success of liberal democracies. Secretary of State James Byrnes, in presenting the State Department's objections to military assistance, did not dwell on these questions. He instead argued that the program cost too much and would place resources critically needed in areas where the United States faced challenge, such as Greece and Turkey, in zones where it remained uncontested. Attempts to strengthen Latin American military capabilities then died in Congress in 1947 and 1948.[25]

The White House's Latin American focus proved more amenable to furnishing economic than military assistance. The Truman administration applied its two basic aid models, the Truman Doctrine and the Marshall Plan, to countries in the hemisphere. Administration officials assumed that the principles of postwar rehabilitation that applied to developed European states also suited less developed countries.

Truman's Point Four program, designed to make technical assistance available to such countries, did not consider the qualitative differences between the nations of the South and those of the industrialized North.[26]

On the political front, the United States made use of the largely manufactured crisis in Greece and Turkey to consolidate support for the cold war while simultaneously attempting to improve Latin American relations, which had chilled after 1945. One result was the Rio Pact of 1947, a mutual security alliance designed to repel any extrahemispheric invader.[27] Cold war policies in Latin America most strongly emerged, however, after 1950 when the Korean War, coupled with bitter anticommunism, led to a positive reappraisal of regional military programs. The Mutual Security Act of 1951 merged various military and economic aid programs, including the Technical Cooperation Administration, the heart of Point Four, but excluded the Export-Import Bank. The Eisenhower administration granted a total of $400 million in heavy armaments to Latin American states.[28]

In Haiti, the International Cooperation Agency (ICA) funded irrigation and drainage works. Projects to construct rough roads in the Aux Cayes area worth $1 million and $1.75 million in road and bridge construction around Jérémie were undertaken. In the Department of the North, the *Poté Colé* Project consisted of $1 million of road building and irrigation. USAID in 1959 additionally extended a $7 million cash grant to the Haitian government, even though it "had large 'non-fiscal' (unbudgeted) receipts for which no public accounting was made."[29]

International grantors, lenders, and consultants were also active in Haiti in the early 1960s. UNESCO had initiated multilateral activity in 1949 by establishing an integrated assistance program in the Marbial Valley. UNESCO terminated the Marbial project in 1954 but continued other programs. The IMF maintained a representative in the country and made available to the BNRH a line of credit of up to $6 million. A World Bank subsidiary, the International Development Association, made a fifty-year, low-interest $350,000 loan to Haiti in November

1962. The Organization of American States, the Economic Commission on Latin America, and the Inter-American Bank all had Haitian projects in the works during the winter of 1961–62.[30]

This shower of gold did not change a basic fact of life for Haiti and the region: the poverty and underdevelopment of most states. The Latin American military, working closely with State Department officials, helped suppress popular reaction to this condition, but its ties to the United States only worsened the reputation of the latter in Latin American eyes. Eisenhower and Secretary of State John Foster Dulles belatedly recognized the depth of the problem when citizens of Caracas attacked Vice President Richard Nixon as he rode in a motorcade through their streets in May 1958. The following year, Eisenhower and Dulles, both ill, found themselves confronted with a new insurgency, the Cuban Revolution.[31] Between 1958 and 1961, the administration, with an eye on U.S. presidential election results, established the Inter-American Development Bank (IADB); began a rapprochement with Venezuelan social democrat Romulo Betancourt; and, in August 1960, broke relations with Dominican dictator Rafael Trujillo, a figure who repelled democratic elements in the hemisphere.[32]

The foreign policy failures of the second Eisenhower administration, including its inept handling of Fidel Castro, contributed to a Democratic victory in 1960. The new president, John F. Kennedy, shared Eisenhower's preference for a healthy economy over military aid as a way to thwart communism, now given new immediacy by events in Cuba. Kennedy nevertheless continued to be swayed by cold war considerations in the short run. His administration thus sought Haitian support in its difficulties with Castro. U.S. reliance on Duvalier's anticommunism gave the latter needed leverage. While "Papa Doc's" rejection of external controls over the USAID program eventually led to its being phased out, Haiti in 1961 received $14.1 million in assistance. These funds included $6 million appropriated for "budget support," that is, for the operating expenses of the Haitian government. Money was allocated despite the U.S. ambassador's conviction that Duvalier had little genuine interest in Haitian development.[33]

In the early days of his administration, Kennedy succeeded in shifting the balance so that economic relief enjoyed a greater proportion of the foreign assistance dollar than did military aid. The Foreign Assistance Act of 1961 constituted the Kennedy era's most significant legislative reform in this regard. It replaced the Mutual Security Act and created USAID, an agency organized on geographic rather than functional lines. USAID combined the ICA and the Development Loan Fund. Its chief administrator answered to the Secretary of State and held the rank of undersecretary. His four regional deputies were assistant secretaries of state.

Kennedy drew heavily on the contributions of Harvard and MIT intellectuals who ascribed to a country-specific approach to aid. Rather than organize assistance by project, they endorsed the notion of a total integrated package that would help modernize "entire social structures and ways of thought and life." As in the late 1940s, and, more remotely, the Haitian occupation era, many officials continued to believe that economic assistance alone would lead to political democracy.[34]

Fears of incipient revolution motivated the Kennedy administration's Alliance for Progress development program. The attack on Nixon in Caracas, anti-American demonstrations in Panama, insurgencies in Venezuela and Colombia, and the Cuban Revolution underscored these anxieties. Ultimately, the Alliance for Progress failed because the administration overestimated what it could accomplish. Indigenous conservatives resisted reform and the most impoverished areas did not benefit from a "Marshall Plan" originally designed for Europe's literate, industrialized population and established infrastructure.[35] Stephen G. Rabe has suggested that idealism played little part in the formulation of the alliance. "That [it] was a Cold War policy was never a subject of dispute. . . . Through its recognition policy, internal security initiatives, and military and economic aid programs, the Administration demonstrably bolstered regimes and groups that were undemocratic, conservative, and frequently repressive. The short-term security that anti-Communist elites could provide was purchased at the expense of long-term political and social democracy."[36]

Whatever the faults of the Alliance for Progress, the Cuban Revolution seemed to dictate a policy of strengthening the center, that is, supporting the various social and Christian Democrats in Latin America who had been for decades locked in struggle against the reactionary policies and dictatorships of the right. Latin American governments resented administration efforts to do this in Peru, Ecuador, and Guatemala, and failed to support what they perceived as interventionism. Chastened by these setbacks, pressured by right-wing critics to do something about the communist presence in Cuba, and needing to deeply disguise the secret channels being opened to Castro, Kennedy dropped his moralist stance on Latin American dictatorships.[37]

Edwin M. Martin, assistant secretary of state for inter-American affairs, issued a statement on 5 October 1963 called "Official U.S. Policy for Latin America," which was sent to all diplomatic posts in the region and made public the following day. The statement clarified Washington's attitude toward military regimes. The United States opposed the overthrow of democratic governments everywhere, Martin asserted, but realized that the world is imperfect and, at times, little could be done about undesirable situations. Martin, arguing that democracy had to grow from within a society and could not be imposed from without, denied that he was washing his hands of the issue. The State Department, he affirmed, sought a middle ground between idealism and cynicism. On 9 October, the president publicly expressed his agreement with Martin. He refuted the suggestion that he had reversed policy and declared the new orientation fundamentally consistent with the Alliance for Progress.[38] In this sense, Martin's statement presaged the famous Mann Doctrine of 1964, Lyndon Johnson's subsequent embrace of military rule in Brazil, and the invasion of the Dominican Republic in 1965. As Robert A. Packenham suggests, "The Kennedy administration was already taking a less ambitious position regarding coups in the hemisphere even before Johnson took office."[39]

With regard to Haiti, the revised outlook allowed U.S. officials to go ahead with plans to assist the jet airport construction project, much to the disappointment of Duvalier's adversaries. The $2.8 million loan would make it possible to build Maïs Gâté under the supervision of Pan American Airways, which, according to an unnamed embassy source, would benefit substantially from the project.[40] The outstanding debt repayment issue, which the United States might have used to its advantage in dealing with Haiti, did not figure as a significant instrument of policy. In January 1962 the Duvalier regime was advised to settle up or forfeit additional aid. It moved expeditiously, however, establishing claims machinery in March. By April, Washington had offered Port-au-Prince $7.25 million in technical and economic assistance. It soon followed this sum with a $3.4 million loan for a highway linking Port-au-Prince with Aux Cayes.[41]

Building on the Kennedy legacy, the Johnson administration expressed even fewer criticisms of despotic government. Career State Department officer Thomas Mann, a conventional bureaucrat popular with Johnson and Secretary of State Dean Rusk, represented its perspective on Latin America. LBJ made Mann his voice on hemispheric affairs, and this official simultaneously held the posts of assistant secretary of state for inter-American affairs and special assistant to the president, as well as the title coordinator of the Alliance for Progress. In February 1965 he became undersecretary of state. In the early 1960s Mann began to doubt the capacity of Latin American governments to carry on meaningful reforms.[42]

The 1964 policy associated with his name reappraised militarism on the grounds that it imparted needed stability and efficiency to administration in the American republics. Robert Packenham believes that "the so-called Mann Doctrine represented a significant change in political development doctrines toward Latin America. Whereas Kennedy had initially taken a fairly extreme position in favor of liberal democracy in the region," Packenham writes, and "then moved to a more moderate stance, Johnson and Mann virtually abandoned constitutional democracy as a standard from the start, and more or less maintained that position throughout their terms."[43]

The end of U.S. efforts to levy sanctions on military regimes resulted from the Mann Doctrine. The new policy stressed instead the traditional concern with maintaining a political climate favorable to U.S. business interests and supporting anticommunism. This revision became public in a speech that Mann delivered to a special Washington convocation of ambassadors, chargés d'affaires, and chiefs of Latin America AID missions. The substance of the closed meeting was leaked to the press. A high-ranking audience, its attendance at a policy review conference, and Mann's status within the administration convinced journalists that the speech constituted a major statement. Interestingly, Mann did not mention the Alliance for Progress at any time.[44]

The following day, 21 March, a State Department press release reiterated the U.S. commitment to democracy, while declaring that its position on "unconstitutional governments," would, "as in the past," be guided by the national interest and the "circumstances peculiar to each situation as it arises."[45] The public learned the next day that Washington had approved a $2.5 million IADB loan to Haiti. On 2 April, when the Brazilian army overthrew João Goulart's constitutional government, the United States recognized the provisional junta within twelve hours and accompanied the acknowledgment with Johnson's hearty salutations to the victors.[46]

In Haiti's case, the new soft line on dictators reflected Johnson's belief that the black republic meant little to overall U.S. interests. His ambassador, Benson E. L. Timmons III, termed U.S. policy noninterventionist, " 'correct' and nothing more." The principal U.S. aim in Haiti, he believed, was to maintain a presence in the country. Timmons went a bit further, however. Despite Duvalier's pointed rudeness toward him when he arrived in Haiti, he encouraged the U.S. Navy to grant shore leave in Port-au-Prince to sailors and appeared in public with the dictator.[47]

Dean Rusk in 1966 called for a $1.3 million educational loan to Haiti from the IADB. The United States had previously objected to extending such credits because of its dissatisfaction with the Duvalier regime. Rusk, however, now felt that Washington should find ways to render humanitarian assistance without helping Duvalier. He accordingly encouraged private voluntary work and inter-American agency projects that had little explicit political content. In June 1970, the IADB lent $5.1 million for a water project in Port-au-Prince.[48]

Richard Nixon in 1969 signaled a fresh departure in foreign assistance policy. He endorsed Duvalier's efforts on behalf of anticommunism and restored military assistance to his regime. The 1 July visit to Haiti of Governor Nelson Rockefeller, acting as an official representative of the U.S. government, preceded the gesture. Shortly before Rockefeller arrived, Duvalier massacred an unknown number of "communists" and suppressed dissident media. The apparent friendliness of the governor of New York and enthusiastic public statements from the recently appointed U.S. ambassador, Clinton Knox, suggested that Papa Doc had regained credibility with the White House.[49]

By 1971, when Duvalier died, the United States had made a substantial aid investment in Haiti. Port-au-Prince alone received some $167 million in projects, more than three times the assistance granted to the rest of the country. In addition to PL 480 food supplies, U.S. dollars supported the new light-assembly industry in the capital by providing improved street lighting, road and sewer construction, flood control devices, and enhancements to port facilities. The USAID and other U.S. agencies began to address Haitian development issues in terms of constructing an interdependence between its economy and that of the United States. Their ideas about how the two countries could best cooperate rested on the time-honored conception of Haitians as a source of cheap, docile labor who expected little and got less.[50]

10   The Duvalier Dictatorship: The Consolidation

François Duvalier relentlessly pillaged Haiti by expropriating the proceeds of state industries and inflicted incredible brutality on his compatriots. During the fourteen years of his rule and the fifteen years of his son's, thousands perished in death camps while others died at the hands of the parastatal police, the Ton Ton Makouts. François Duvalier also beat and tortured people himself. He imposed a climate of terror by cynically appropriating black nationalist rhetoric and Vodun beliefs and recruiting many religious leaders, both Catholic and Vodun, into a patronage system. Abject poverty made the political realities even harsher. The contrasts between the fetid urban slum and the balmy hillside suburb deepened despite the *noirist* discourse of Duvalier's supporters. The manner in which the United States came to terms with the dictatorship, moreover, sheds more light on the historical contours of Haitian-American relations.

Duvalier devoted his first presidential year to consolidating power in the face of severe factionalism among contending political forces. He accomplished this by terror and repression. He also neutralized the aspirations of some who had backed him to further their own ambitions. One of these, General Antonio Kébreau, became intimate with Trujillo. He soon lost his position as army chief of staff and was sent away as ambassador to Italy.[1] Trujillo had come to regard Kébreau as his man in Port-au-Prince and began making trouble for Duvalier after Kébreau's removal. The Dominican media broadcast anti-Duvalier tirades and supported Haitian exile activity. Kébreau's exile had been relatively simple to accomplish, but other problems did not so easily dissolve. One of these was the U.S. embassy, which had tacitly favored Déjoie's candidacy during the elections. The new president's relations with the embassy soured almost immediately as a result of the murder of a U.S. national, Shibley Talamas, a few months before his inauguration.[2]

Talamas, a Syrian-American Déjoie supporter, had complained to the U.S. consul after Pétionville police detained him for a curfew violation. The consul, having received assurances from authorities of Talamas's personal safety, encouraged him to return to the police station for further questioning the following day and escorted him to his destination. Talamas was then taken from the police station to Fort Dimanche and beaten to death by Haitian army personnel.[3] U.S. protests led to the suspension of several aid programs, but after assuming the presidency, Duvalier agreed to indemnities for Talamas's family and ordered mild punishments for the suspected killers.[4]

The Kébreau and Talamas incidents were important because the United States and the Dominican Republic formed the two main axes of Haitian diplomacy. The character of Haitian relations with one state is fully revealed only in the context of its relations with the other. The long-standing antagonism between Haiti and the Dominican Republic, exacerbated by Trujillo, concerned the United States because of its obsession with regional stability, and because these regimes had antirevolutionary credentials.

In reality, Duvalier had less to fear from dissidents attempting to invade the country than from the use of Haiti as a stepping-stone to a Dominican overthrow of Trujillo. A filibustering expedition that originated in Haiti might invite severe reprisals from the east. The implications of the emerging Cuban Revolution also sobered Port-au-Prince. In its militant early phase, the Twenty-Sixth of July Movement hoped to eventually sweep away all vestiges of dictatorship from the region. A mutual fear of leftist insurgency ultimately brought Trujillo and Duvalier together in a 1958 mutual security agreement signed at the frontier town of Malpasse.[5]

The terms of the Malpasse agreement compelled Haiti in March 1959 to accept the Dominican army's creation of a "Foreign Legion" composed of mercenaries recruited from as far away as Greece and Yugoslavia. These soldiers, under the command of generously remunerated Dominican officers, included several hundred Spaniards from the fascist "Blue Division" that had helped the Wehrmacht during World War II. In the following months, the Dominican military maintained an intrusive surveillance of Haiti, violating its air space and territorial waters.[6]

Trujillo had ostensibly strengthened his relations with Port-au-Prince but secretly planned, with Ton Ton Makout founder Clément Barbot, to undermine Duvalier. For his part, Duvalier appeared supinely cooperative with Trujillo's anticommunist crusade but knew how to profit from the Cuban insurgency. Early in Duvalier's presidency, the Cuban democrat Carlos Prío Socarrás offered to pay him for the use of Haiti as a Castroite base. Duvalier accepted but took an even larger sum from Cuban President Fulgencio Batista himself. Doc had placed bets on both sides.[7]

Haiti benefited from increasingly chilly Dominican-U.S. relations in 1960. The Cuban Revolution had shaken Washington out of its complacency. Policymakers now weighed the costs and benefits of supporting a dictatorship whose agenda included trying to assassinate President Romulo Betancourt of Venezuela. Subtle attempts to persuade Trujillo to retire from politics had proven unavailing—he firmly declared his intention to remain in power until the year 2000.[8] The plot against Betancourt provided the opportunity Haiti needed to distance itself from its bothersome Dominican alliance. In September 1960 it followed the lead of other Latin American nations and the United States, which had broken relations with Santo Domingo in June, and recalled its ambassador. The assassination of Trujillo in 1961 took a load off Duvalier's mind. In 1962 Haiti supported the lifting of OAS sanctions against the Dominican Republic and resumed formal relations with it.[9]

A long-awaited normalcy seemed in the offing. After a period of instability, Juan Bosch, then a social democrat, became president of the Dominican Republic. Bosch received information that Duvalier, upset by his moderate politics, planned to have him murdered. The former Dominican poet in turn conspired at Duvalier's overthrow with Haitian exiles. When Port-au-Prince policemen searching for anti-Duvalierist fugitives violated the Dominican embassy, another rupture ensued.[10]

John Martin, the U.S. ambassador to the Dominican Republic, assured Bosch that the United States would support his drive for OAS sanctions against Haiti. Haiti, however, checkmated Bosch's move by successfully directing UN Security Council attention to the issue. The Security Council debated the conflict for two days. Port-au-Prince planned to obtain African and Soviet support for its complaints against Dominican air space incursions, troop build-ups on the frontier, and the twenty-four-hour ultimatum it had received. The OAS argued that the matter belonged under its jurisdiction. It requested that Haiti drop UN proceedings and eventually persuaded it to agree to an inter-American settlement.

Bosch's attempts to unseat Duvalier ultimately failed. As Georges A. Fauriol observes, "There is evidence that Washington cautiously encouraged Bosch to move against Duvalier politically. However, Bosch overplayed his hand and also threatened military action. With a showdown on the horizon, Haiti outflanked Bosch, Washington, and the OAS by directly appealing to the United Nations. Duvalier ordered the recall of the American ambassador, and waited for Bosch's bluff. It never came. Instead, five months later Bosch was overthrown by his own military."[11] Bosch's defeat owed much to U.S. fears that Duvalier's resignation would lead to a leftist takeover. An attack on Haiti would further undermine the already weak authority of the OAS. In any case, the Dominican military refused to back up Bosch's belligerency. Port-au-Prince consequently supported the U.S. intervention in the Dominican Republic in 1965. Duvalier liked and respected the ultimate beneficiary of that invasion, Joaquin Balaguer. For the remainder of François Duvalier's life, Dominican-Haitian relations remained low-key.[12]

The U.S. preoccupation with communism and, specifically, with the Cuban Revolution forms a motif that runs through Haitian diplomacy with Santo Domingo as well as with Washington. U.S. officials found Duvalier repugnant very early in his fourteen-year stint as dictator, but cold war anxieties overshadowed their concern for the human misery in Haiti. The Eisenhower administration, the first to deal with Duvalier, preferred his leadership to the uncertainties associated with democratic reform in countries that lacked traditions of orderly political transition.[13]

This point is illustrated by the U.S. response to a crackdown which followed an explosion in a secret bomb cache on 30 April 1958. The bombs were evidently intended for Duvalier the following day. The incident provided a rationale for calling an emergency meeting of the national legislature, which suspended the constitution and voted extraordinary powers to the president. Duvalier thus received carte blanche to move on his enemies, and his responses included gunfire aimed at opponents' houses. Among these was the villa of the U.S. ambassador, Gerald Drew, apparently resented for his partiality to Louis Déjoie.[14]

In this instance the United States chose to accept the explanation that the bombardment had been in error and acknowledged official Haitian apologies. Two weeks later a U.S. military assistance mission arrived in the country. The Haitian government had requested the naval mission in an effort to improve the quality of its forces and to provide a disincentive for Dominican aggression. Washington held a dim view of most Latin American armies and saw the mission's main task as bolstering the Haitian army as a counterweight to Duvalier and his terrorist militia. A strong military, hopefully, would keep Ton Ton Makout excesses in check and provide continued access to power for the elite elements with whom U.S. policymakers could best communicate. Given the uncertainties of Haitian politics, Eisenhower administration officials proved unwilling to help depose Duvalier.[15] The decision to send a naval mission to Haiti also corresponded to the Pentagon's general policy on hemispheric military assistance. Rather than withhold aid from what they considered inept and irresponsible powers, the Joint Chiefs preferred to give Latin Americans enough help to prevent European countries from establishing military missions. It would be even more undesirable if such assistance helped create markets for European hardware right under North Americans' noses.[16]

Vice-President Richard Nixon's Latin American tour in 1958 forced the Eisenhower administration to reevaluate its hard-line policies.

The debate touched on mounting public dissatisfaction with the administration's lackluster response to Soviet trade initiatives in Latin America, Sputnik, growing sophistication in Soviet defenses, and mounting unrest in the underdeveloped world. The physical decline of Secretary of State Dulles accompanied the growing unpopularity of his ideas. Liberal forces in the Western Hemisphere had begun to stir: between 1956 and 1960 ten dictators had fallen. The Vatican had also begun to rethink its traditional commitment to the status quo in the region.[17]

The Democratic party victory in the 1960 U.S. presidential elections occasioned a policy review of Latin American relations. Adolf A. Berle, Jr., headed a study group for the Kennedy administration that examined current events in the region and made recommendations. The choice of Berle was no accident. He and his team did not hide their criticisms of the attachment of the United States to some of the most retrograde political figures. As a former New Dealer, Berle was also associated with welfare state policies which, in the Latin American context, meant liberal grants of assistance. Berle's report drew attention to the threat posed by Cuba and called for strengthening the center in Latin America. The United States should oppose both insurgencies of the left and tyrannies of the right. The report limned out a plan for economic assistance, later called the Alliance for Progress.[18]

In line with the task force's recommendations and his own convictions, President Kennedy did not resume diplomatic relations with Trujillo, which Eisenhower had broken, and he sent a fleet to the Dominican Republic to prevent Trujillistas from regaining power following the dictator's May 1961 assassination. Kennedy admired Venezuela, a country he had visited, as well as Colombia, Mexico, and Costa Rica, all which had constitutional governments.[19] Kennedy's commitment to Latin American democracy was not, however, as staunch as it appeared. While JFK opposed a July 1962 military coup in Peru, the extent of his hostility to military leaders depended on their attitudes toward the linked issues of communism and Cuba. Juntas soon learned that a tough stand on reds would soften U.S. antagonism. In October 1963 Assistant Secretary of State Edwin M. Martin, speaking for the administration, declared that the United States would continue to oppose the overthrow of constitutional governments but would use force only against "intervention from outside the hemisphere by the international Communist conspiracy." Kennedy had come to realize that the military shared his sentiments more fully than many Latin American democrats, especially insofar as stability and unassailable authority counted as paramount virtues.[20]

The changed attitude had significant consequences for U.S. relations with Haiti. While Secretary of State Dean Rusk regarded Duvalier as "a disgrace to this hemisphere," he and others in the administration increasingly regarded him as a useful tool for excluding Cuba from the inter-American community and maintaining a watchful surveillance over the spread of revolution. State Department officials realized that Duvalier would divert any economic aid to projects that enhanced his own power and prestige, but they counted on his departure after his presidential term expired in 1963.[21]

Duvalier quickly realized the advantage that professional anticommunism gave him and went out of his way to bestow services on Washington. He offered it the Môle St. Nicolas as a naval station through the good offices of Representative Victor L. Anfuso, invited to visit Haiti for two days in 1961. The Môle need not be used to threaten Cuba, Anfuso assured the hesitant, but could give the OAS a patrol depot. He recommended a satellite tracking station to replace the one Cuba had expropriated. According to Anfuso, Duvalier wanted Kennedy to know that Haitians "would cooperate with the United States in presenting the Western viewpoint to new African countries." The gift of the Môle had by that time become a standard ploy of Haitian presidents. Duvalier had earlier made a similar proposal to Eisenhower. His son would do the same to Reagan in 1985.[22] Haiti also cooperated fully with the U.S. embargo of Cuba, providing port facilities and even putting its own army and militia on alert in case of a Cuban invasion. This was, of course, largely symbolic. The conquest of Port-au-Prince held little interest for Havana.[23]

More significantly, Haiti lent its support to U.S. efforts to impose sanctions on Cuba and expel it from the OAS. Given the opposition to these measures by the major continental powers—Mexico, Argentina, Chile, and Brazil—Washington needed the assistance of any country with a vote. Haitian Foreign Minister René Chalmers pressed this point home to U.S. delegation chief Dean Rusk at a January 1962 OAS meeting at Punta del Este, Uruguay. In James Ferguson's words, "Chalmers reminded [Rusk] that Haiti was a poor nation, in need of US aid, and suggested that this consideration might well determine Haiti's vote in the Cuban issue. Witnesses report that Rusk, with considerable *sang froid*, agreed that the questions of the vote and aid were indeed linked, adding that future financial support was likely to be assessed on the strength of Haiti's position in the debate. The tables thus turned, Haiti duly voted with the US."[24]

Fear of communism led to the Kennedy administration spending $77 million annually for military aid to Latin America. Such assistance also included schooling in police and counterinsurgency methods by USAID's Office of Public Safety. Some nine thousand soldiers received such training between 1961 and 1964. U.S. agencies educated more Latin American personnel in police science than in health and sanitation programs because administration analysts believed the former gave better cost/benefit results.[25]

Stephen G. Rabe comments: "By fostering these new programs, the Kennedy Administration increased the coercive abilities of Latin American armed forces and violated Kennedy's pledge, in his Alliance for Progress speech, to reduce military expenditures in the region. Officials justified these programs on national security grounds and by claiming that internal security programs strengthened democratic institutions." The notion that Latin American officers would absorb U.S. attitudes on the proper role of the military in a liberal society enjoyed great currency. The Defense Department itself belied this idea, however, in a 1964–65 study that found no link between strong armies and strong democracies.[26]

Haitian-U.S. relations had chilled when the military aid program ended in 1963. Duvalier had taken precautionary measures to prolong his tenure through a fraudulent election in 1961 that Washington did not recognize as legitimate. While cold war considerations muted

U.S. protest over this maneuver—it was limited to the ambassador absenting himself from Duvalier's annual holiday celebration—officials bided their time and began pressing in 1962 for Duvalier's anticipated retirement the following year.[27]

When Papa Doc canceled Haitian army officers' stateside scholarships in June, fearing undue foreign influence over them, the United States suspended military assistance. In July, the U.S. military attaché, Marine Corps Colonel Robert D. Heinl, recommended abolishing the militia to the Haitian army chief of staff. Heinl thought this outfit inefficient and potentially subversive. The uniformed Milice Civile, like the plain-clothes Volontaires de la Sécurité Nationale (VSN) or Ton Ton Makouts, were loyal only to Duvalier. Both organizations had originated as ways of neutralizing the Haitian army and its bourgeois constituencies. The appearance in Port-au-Prince of the U.S. commander of the southern forces underscored Heinl's advice, and days later Washington officials announced the suspension of substantial aid.[28]

Efforts to directly control military affairs in Haiti proved fruitless. In January 1963, a group of Haitian officers began plotting a coup d'état with the knowledge and tacit encouragement of U.S. diplomats. The intrigue came to light before it could be carried out. Port-au-Prince condemned seven officers to death in absentia and dismissed over sixty. The beating death inside the Casernes Dessalines of the popular, pro-U.S. Colonel Charles Turnier shocked embassy personnel. Two months later, the U.S. government honored Duvalier's request that Colonel Heinl's posting not be renewed. The entire military mission was recalled in May.[29]

According to the Haitian constitution, Duvalier was to cede power to a successor on 15 May. He countered the growing popular unrest with repression, personally tortured political adversaries, and freely used his secret police and militia to intimidate, jail, and murder. The Central Intelligence Agency in the 1960s made halfhearted plans to abet Duvalier's overthrow with a combined Cuban-Haitian exile force. Haiti would serve as a launch pad for an invasion of Cuba. President Kennedy authorized the CIA to train one hundred Haitian exiles at two U.S. bases. They would then go to a secret U.S. Navy camp in the Dominican Republic. The CIA involved itself in some half-dozen plots to depose the dictator between 1962 and 1968 but invested few resources in them. Exile guerrillas received paltry equipment and very little training. During the subsequent Johnson presidency, U.S. officials were ready to publicly disavow any association with the insurgents. This tepidity indicated a fundamental ambivalence about ousting Duvalier.[30] Since Trujillo's demise, Duvalier had become all the more useful as a check on Cuba. As a result, most of the poorly prepared *flibustiers* who made amphibious landings in Haiti and attempted to raise insurrections during this era met horrible deaths at the hands of Duvalierist forces.[31]

In late April, as described above, Dominican President Juan Bosch made his own unsuccessful attempt to dislodge Duvalier. As in the early 1900s, U.S. Navy ships appeared off the coast. The combined pressure of Haitian dissidents, the U.S. and Dominican governments, the OAS, and international opinion on Papa Doc proved enormous. He and his family had arranged flights out of the country on the day his term expired, 15 May. That very evening, however, saw him still in place at the National Palace. Doc had simply waited out the crisis.[32]

After the recall of the U.S. military and training missions, Washington rendered no further military assistance, despite Haitian envoys' reminders of the conformist posture that Port-au-Prince had been assuming in the OAS.[33] Termination of this aid, which had never met all of Haiti's perceived needs, sent the dictatorship in search of alternative resources. Haitian regimes had viewed criminal syndicates as possible sources of funding and useful contacts as early as the 1940s. In 1957, before federal authorities showed interest in airport construction at Port-au-Prince, Haiti approached the Mafia. Organized crime activity in Haiti did not become prominent, however, until after the Cuban Revolution eliminated opportunities for mobsters in the entertainment and tourist industries of Havana. A member of the Carlo Gambino organization proposed a successful deal to Duvalier in 1961, which involved the sale of Haitian lottery tickets in the northeastern United States. A few years later another racketeer obtained a casino concession. Criminal investment in Haiti also extended to trying to safeguard the future of this hospitable regime. Denied U.S. arms, Papa Doc turned to Mafia brokers, who provided him with guns and planes, customized to order by a Miami-based firm whose clients included the CIA.[34] Weapons also came from places as diverse as Panama, Nicaragua, and Israel. Duvalier's shady deals with unsavory characters, while not unprecedented in Haitian history, were significant for several reasons. They occurred frequently, they put government functionaries in contact with an international criminal network, they involved persons with links, albeit covert, to U.S. government officials, and they corresponded to certain desiderata of U.S. foreign policy.[35]

After Duvalier's successful resistance to international pressure to resign, he moved quickly to strengthen his position through a publicity blitz. The United States, which had "suspended," rather than broken, relations with Haiti, resumed them on 3 June, whereupon Duvalier sought and obtained not only the entire removal of the military mission but also the recall of U.S. Ambassador Raymond Thurston, who was subjected to indignities as he left the country.[36] Port-au-Prince subsequently evaded U.S. attempts at rapprochement which, Duvalier clearly understood, could readily disguise a coup attempt. His steady objections in late 1963 and 1964 to various U.S. embassy career officers, it was suggested, related to this concern. If a conspiracy existed, Duvalier must have believed, then U.S. efforts to execute it would be hampered by inadequate staffing. If no plot materialized, however, he would have lost nothing.[37]

Thurston's successor, Benson E. L. Timmons III, assumed his post in January 1964. He was made to wait five weeks before presenting his credentials. When the belated ceremony took place, Duvalier publicly criticized Timmons's predecessors before the press. In the first two and a half years of Timmons's tenure, according to the Washington Star, Duvalier received him only six times. The Haitian president could follow this course of action with impunity because he had correctly assessed the rigidities in U.S. foreign policy that made him more acceptable than a democratic alternative.[38] Timmons himself recognized this. "The essential character of Duvalier's regime, including its disregard of human rights," he wrote in a subsequent dispatch, "is of course most repugnant. But it remains in control, and we see no alternative to dealing with it on this basis, in U.S. national security interest." It was therefore necessary to "maintain [a] U.S. presence against [the] day of inevitable change, and deny [the] country to communists."[39]

President John F. Kennedy, in the meantime, had died, an event that Duvalier noted with satisfaction and even claimed to have predicted. The succeeding Johnson administration's attitude toward Port-au-Prince proved conciliatory. In line with the Mann Doctrine, a period of cooperation and comparative generosity toward Haiti began. The United States decided to live with Duvalier because of his valuable anti-Castro vote in the OAS and the desire to create security for U.S. investments in Haiti. The White House and State Department had come to see Duvalier as a necessary prop to broader foreign policy objectives. They feared the consequences of the collapse of the "machine" he had built, for a radical regime could inherit this police state. As one Foggy Bottom official opined: "The greatest danger in Haiti is not the slow growth of Communism among students, intellectuals, etc., but rather the fact that the regime, having crushed all opposition and destroyed almost all Haitian institutions, could be taken over intact in a bloodless coup by pro-Communist members of the regime after Duvalier's passing."[40]

Aside from these considerations, the U.S. embassy, reviewing Duvalier's appalling record, realized that despite all, there had been no nationalizations of foreign property, no forced labor, no collectivization, no "state trading" or "capital levies." Doc's had remained a conservative regime whose oratory, confined to appeals to racial consciousness, eschewed the rhetoric of class. Moreover, Timmons did not view specific development plans put forth by the Haitian government as inimical to the Alliance for Progress.[41] State Department recommendations for Haiti in 1964 included cutting back bilateral assistance and budget-supporting grants and allowing European powers to shoulder more of the aid burden, provided that they did not do enough to give them—or Duvalier, for that matter—undue leverage.[42]

Duvalier faced his gravest military challenge in the summer of 1964 when rebels staged an amphibious landing in the southwest peninsula and worked their way into the hills. According to former U.S. Military Attaché Robert D. Heinl, the CIA had tried but failed to dissuade the insurgents from going ahead with the invasion. Unable to take the southern town of Jérémie, the guerrillas pushed eastward through the mountains. They fought ten engagements, downed a Haitian military plane, and marched two hundred miles through the raging gusts of Hurricane Cleo. While U.S. officials doubted that Cuba supported the invasion—its coast had remained under constant surveillance since the 1962 missile crisis—they wanted to be sure so that Duvalier could not use public opinion to embarrass the U.S. government. Timmons recommended that Washington not appear to be helping Duvalier if the rebels seemed to be winning. If they seemed to be losing, the United States should emphasize the food assistance program, which "could constitute [a] useful card in [the] never-ending poker game to maintain U.S. presence here."[43]

The Haitian government, for its part, asked for U.S. assistance in quelling the insurgency, citing its anticommunist fidelity.[44] Port-au-Prince had cordoned off the southwest peninsula, sent in General Henri Namphy and the Bataillon Tactique, and raised the rural militia. The Haitian air force maintained a constant armed aerial reconnaissance. By September, the insurgents clearly had not been able to hold any towns of significance and all indications suggested that they were withdrawing from previous footholds. The public later learned that there had been only thirteen rebels, all exiles and members of the Jeune Haïti movement. Attrition had reduced their number to three when they finally perished near l'Asile in late October. They were decapitated and their heads brought to Duvalier.[45]

The Jeune Haïti invasion of 1964 marked the last time that filibusters truly threatened the regime, although coup attempts continued. In February 1966 Haitian officials prepared for a Florida-based invasion by Cuban exile Rolando Masferrer. Each recruit would receive arms and a cash payment, and planes from Somoza's Nicaragua would supply air cover. An exile "colonel" from Yugoslavia, currently employed at a Miami car wash, would command the expedition. Haitians believed to be involved in the conspiracy included supporters of Daniel Fignolé. An official complaint to the U.S. ambassador brought assurances that Masferrer and associates would be watched and brought to justice if they violated any federal law. Haiti insisted that Masferrer was already breaking the law and pointedly asked for a summary of actions that federal authorities had taken to date.[46]

Masferrer nevertheless enjoyed the ear of at least one highly placed functionary, a career State Department official and the president's Latin Americanist on the National Security Council. According to Masferrer's account, William G. Bowdler okayed the mission as long as the insurgents, and Masferrer in particular, maintained a very low profile. The Immigration and Naturalization Service nevertheless de-railed Masferrer's invasion of Haiti. He and others went to jail for violating neutrality acts. So many filibusters of this type failed in the 1950s and 1960s that it is difficult not to believe that they were blocked from on high.[47]

Jeune Haïti launched another unsuccessful raid in 1968. The CIA backed these student insurgents, and their organization joined an anti-Castro coalition that exchanged support from Cuban exiles for a promise to assist future anti-Castro insurgencies.[48] Duvalier's willing-ness to cooperate with Cuban exile elements himself compromised such arrangements from the very beginning. He knew that insurrec-tionists planning to overthrow Castro could unseat him as well. Cuba was far superior militarily, and Duvalier could trust neither his own officers nor the United States, despite its rhetoric. Haiti could conceiv-ably function as a base of operations against Castro with or without Duvalier's help—or presence. Duvalier therefore prohibited defect-ing Cubans from entering Haiti directly. He maintained secret con-tact with Havana, and persuaded the Cubans to stop training Louis Déjoie's partisans and cancel the broadcast of a Creole language radio program. This laissez-faire arrangement with Cuba gave him some respite from assaults from that quarter.[49]

Internal enemies were another question. As a result of a 1967 army plot, Duvalier reorganized the military leadership structure as well as that of the Ton Ton Makouts. The usual bloodletting, interestingly, did not accompany his initial response. Doc waited six months to have the nineteen officers suspected of high treason shot. The suspense, the cashiering, and arrests, Timmons speculated, represented the end of the violent phase of his regime. Improved relations with the Dominican Republic and the Vatican, a visit by Haile Selassie, and prospective cabinet changes favorable to U.S. interests all projected a return to normalcy by the now invincible leader.[50]

11   The Duvalier Dictatorship: Decline and Fall

During the presidency of Lyndon Baines Johnson, Haitian-U.S. relations became markedly more pacific than under Kennedy. The so-called Mann Doctrine of 1964 reappraised militarism as a stabilizing institution in Latin America. U.S. officials came to accept the idea that social change should be attendant on expanding capitalism, and financier David Rockefeller grew increasingly influential in policymaking circles.[1] Friends of the Johnson administration found investment in Haiti attractive. One of LBJ's most valued campaign contributors, oilman Clint Murchison of Dallas, owned ranches and other enterprises there, and he cherished good relations with Duvalier. Murchison shared a U.S. lobbyist with the Haitian president, one Irving Davidson, who had held accounts with both Trujillo and the Central Intelligence Agency. Johnson aide and confidant Bobby Baker had also joined Murchison in an influence-peddling scheme involving the Haitian-American Meat Packing Company (HAMPCO). Rumor had it that Lady Bird Johnson was also a HAMPCO investor. Whatever the possible influence exerted by Mann, Timmons, Murchison, Baker, and the first lady, the Johnson administration maintained a conciliatory policy toward Port-au-Prince.[2]

Comfort with Duvalier's economic conservatism explains some of the U.S. acquiescence in his continued tenure. The black nationalist rhetoric of the regime did not disguise its willingness to allow labor exploitation in the foreign light-assembly re-export industries. As Michel-Rolph Trouillot points out, these appeared in the country as early as the 1950s. Real factory operations, unlike the single windfall profits that characterized trafficking in paper concessions in the nineteenth century, allowed a continuous stream of benefits. Light assembly would palpably demonstrate the government's commitment to diversifying the economy, stimulating employment, and befriending expatriate business interests.[3]

Manufacture for export developed as an important sector of the Haitian economy. It failed, however, to improve life chances for a significant part of the labor force because of its close linkages to a fickle U.S. economy. According to Alex Dupuy, manufacturing grew by a prodigious 56.2 percent between 1972 and 1976, but slowed to only 2 percent between 1980 and 1984. Indeed, the fact that Haitians would absorb the shocks of economic retrenchment more passively than U.S. workers made locating these industries in Haiti all the more attractive. The population of the Port-au-Prince metropolitan area, where the factories were, meanwhile expanded by an average of thirty-five thousand a year in the 1970s, with an unemployment rate of 38 percent.[4]

Light assembly in Haiti failed to overcome its enclave character. It used few locally produced raw materials and sold none of its output in the country. It did, however, rehabilitate the commercial middleman function historically served by the old import-export sector. François Duvalier's erstwhile enemy, the traditional bourgeoisie, which had opposed black middle-class ambitions since the days of Estimé, could now tout Haiti as a Caribbean Hong Kong. "The formulas that best explained the survival of the second Duvalier [Jean-Claude]," Trouillot comments, "notably the systematic search for the explicit endorsement of the local bourgeoisie and the U.S. government, had been on the drawing board before the death of Papa Doc."[5]

The election of a conservative U.S. president in 1968 further enhanced the attractiveness of this strategy. Richard M. Nixon admired right-wing governments that kept popular disaffection in check and provided a favorable climate for U.S. corporate investment. Nixon pulled out all the stops in rekindling friendship with Haiti during his first administration. While Jeune Haïti insurgents were being martyred, a Republican White House renounced the Alliance for Progress as a signal failure and restored full aid to Haiti. The 1969 visit to Port-au-Prince of Nelson Rockefeller, traveling as a personal representative of the president of the United States, inaugurated a period of big casino and tourism profits for Duvalier. A massacre of hundreds of "communists" preceded the visit. U.S. authorities repaid Papa Doc's ideological conformity when they licensed export of an F-51 fighter and permitted Haiti to use shop facilities in Miami with funds ostensibly provided by the mob. Washington granted licenses to firms to sell light arms and six 65-foot patrol boats to the Haitian Coast Guard late in 1970.[6]

François Duvalier began grooming his son Jean-Claude for the succession as early as 1964. When in 1971 the president-for-life died, Jean-Claude stepped into his shoes. Due to the heir's personal limitations, he became in many respects a titular ruler, with real power vested in the Duvalier family as an entity and in certain trusted lieutenants. Jean-Claude's ascent nevertheless created an opportunity to forge a new public image without changing the fundamental features of Duvalierism. It also gave Washington a rationale for renewed financial support of the regime. From 1972 to 1981, Haiti realized $584 million in development assistance from the United States and other donors, with U.S. aid equaling 80 percent of the total.[7]

Haiti also received military aid during this period, supposedly structured in such a way as to prevent its use for internal security. Subsidies focused on sea and air rescue and "logistic and communications capabilities." Citing a supposedly improved human rights record, in 1976 the United States resumed the military mission it discontinued in 1963. Washington officials reasoned that canceling the mission would not lead to further improvements in human rights and would simply reduce their already limited influence in the country.[8]

In some respects, *Jean-Claudisme* represented an attempt at modernization. It intended to modify some of the more infernal aspects of the family tyranny without actually ending repression. In the late 1970s the authorities carried out some limited experiments with an uncensored press. The advertisement of Jean-Claude as a young, dynamic Third World leader suffered as a result of the adipose idol's lack of panache. Some second-generation Duvalierists nevertheless dimly perceived the future possibility of a united ruling class that would have evolved beyond the bloody, debilitating factional struggles of the past. The most far-sighted envisioned a day when black middle-class elements loyal to the regime, the traditional mulatto elite, foreign business interests, and the military could all peacefully share the golden eggs laid by the Haitian goose, untroubled by the threat of foreign intervention or internecine strife.[9]

The 1980 wedding of Jean-Claude and Michèle Bennett symbolized in dynastic terms the maturation of this vision. The union represented a reconciliation and consolidated an alliance between Duvalierists and the parvenu commercial elite. Bennett's first marriage had been to the son of Alix Pasquet, an officer killed in the July 1958 coup attempt against François Duvalier. After the union with the Duvaliers, the Bennetts' economic fortunes improved substantially. They became politicians in their own right, effecting in 1982 the firing of finance minister Marc Bazin, who tried to curb their spending, and the removal of the Port-au-Prince police chief, whose growing authority they feared. Not satisfied with an unlimited franchise for legitimate business, the Bennetts also involved themselves in the drug trade, which later netted Michèle's brother Frantz an arrest in Puerto Rico for cocaine distribution.[10]

Beyond the standard larceny, the second Duvalier regime occasionally tried to mask practices that made its crimes unpleasantly obvious, such as the trade in blood. The endemic presence of infectious disease made Haitian blood rich in antibodies, and, before disputed information about AIDS targeted Haitians as being particularly at risk, desirable for transfusion purposes. Accordingly, some six thousand Haitians a month gained modest sums of money by selling blood at three dollars per liter. Minister of the Interior Luckner Cambronne profited from shipping five tons of blood a month to the Armour Pharmaceutical, Cutter, and Dow Chemical companies' laboratories in the United States. Cambronne lost his position as a result of condemnation of this traffic, but he later reappeared informally as a powerful, if low-profile, figure in the government. The commerce in corpses for medical schools continued.[11]

In 1975 international agencies responded with emergency food supplies to relieve a famine in northwest Haiti caused by drought and soil erosion. Some three hundred thousand persons faced starvation. To the dismay of donors, a substantial amount of food failed to reach the hungry, for bags of rice clearly marked for relief purposes wound up on sale at markets. As James Ferguson relates, "a handful of token arrests—principally of scapegoat Lebanese and Syrian merchants—did little to counter suspicions of governmental complicity." [12]

The food problem was not only a matter of corruption. Haiti by the mid-1970s depended heavily on foreign imports, and Haitian governments had been traditionally sensitive to this issue. Dependency underlay the historic attempts to ban foreign participation in the retail sector. These date back to the French colonial regime's realization that controlling food resources in an island economy is a strategic necessity. Jean-Claude, however, made few strides in addressing this critical issue. [13]

Traditional exploitation of Haitian agricultural workers continued during the 1970s. In 1978 the UNESCO Commission on Human Rights targeted forced labor practices in the Dominican Republic. The Commission's Working Group on Slavery reported the annual sale of twelve thousand cane cutters to government-owned, privately leased estates, including one operated by a U.S. corporation, Gulf and Western. These seasonal workers received meager food and wages and lived in a state of virtual debt peonage. Most lacked sanitary facilities in the crowded quarters that some shared with their malnourished children. All attempts they made to organize met repression. The migrants suffered from "a variety of preventable diseases, high maternal and infant mortality, illiteracy, and hopelessness." Allegations that the Duvaliers profited from this slavery constantly recurred. [14]

These depredations took place in the context of Haiti's declining ability to absorb the profligate waste of resources and outright theft that characterized the behavior of government officials and favorites. The cumulative effect of generations of social inequity and injustice—a rising population and a declining land base, soil erosion and progressive deforestation, and industries that reinvested little in the nation—contributed to the malaise of the 1970s.

The bleak prospects for most citizens of Duvalier's Haiti contributed to emigration. Reports of "boat people," Haitians fleeing by sea, appeared in the U.S. press. Many risked drowning to escape. A global fuel shortage, which hit underdeveloped countries the hardest, exacerbated the crisis. Fallout from the decaying U.S. economy, which by mid-decade worsened the distress being experienced in Haiti and other satellite states of the Caribbean, also played a role. Canadian restrictions on West Indian entry increased the chances that people would gamble on illegal entry in the United States. There they sought poorly paid employment in agriculture, the garment industries of New York and Florida, or the unskilled sectors of the marine and construction industries.[15]

The Haitian exodus, which had not yet reached mammoth proportions in the mid-1970s, was accompanied by new pressures from Washington. The "liberal" phase of *Jean-Claudisme* thus began in 1977 under President Jimmy Carter's instigation. Carter based his Latin American and Caribbean policy on the realization that the role of the United States as a powerful, unilateral actor in world affairs had diminished. His renowned "trilateralism" thus embodied a conventional bloc politics aimed at uniting Japan and the Western powers. Carter hoped to deal with Western Hemisphere states as part of a larger North-South dialogue between developed and underdeveloped nations. A degree of political diversity would be tolerated, but the flexible question of human rights would help the administration maintain leverage.[16]

Carter tied aid to demonstrable improvements in democratic rights. Port-au-Prince responded by releasing some political prisoners, permitting representatives from the Inter-American Human Rights Commission to investigate internal conditions in 1978, and holding national legislative elections. The Haitian government also allowed a limited freedom of the press, and mildly critical media, such as the review *Petit Samedi Soir* and the radio station Haiti Radio Inter, flourished briefly. The Inter-American Human Rights Commission wrote a negative report on human rights in Haiti, as did Amnesty International during the same and succeeding year. U.S. assistance nevertheless continued on the grounds that it was vital to keep the pipeline to Haiti open and offer some assistance, however token—and pilfered—to its suffering people.[17]

Aside from U.S. support, Haiti remained isolated in the Caribbean of the 1970s. It had rarely associated itself closely with the ideologies and interests of the larger Third World, preferring instead the dubious security of close clientelistic relations with Washington. Haiti was excluded from the Caribbean Community and Common Market (CARICOM) because of its record of human rights abuses and concerns about its subsistence wage practices.[18] In the lands around Haiti, however, agitation for change had mounted. The leftist Sandinista insurgency in Nicaragua brought down the Somoza dynasty dictatorship in 1979. Other Central American countries—most notably El Salvador, long controlled by a small oligarchy—were in transition. Jamaica's ruling People's National Party, defeated by the 1980 election of a conservative candidate, had, in the 1970s, flirted with a socialist agenda. In the neglected and impoverished eastern Caribbean, a radical movement in 1979 deposed Grenada's increasingly repressive populist leadership. The leftist drift in the Caribbean and Central America suggested to U.S. policymakers the necessity of returning to traditional postures in Latin America. The incoming Reagan administration thus inaugurated the Caribbean Basin Initiative (CBI) in 1981.[19]

In the spirit of Dollar Diplomacy, the CBI was to pump millions into some of the restive republics of the southern rim, partly through boosting offshore assembly industries that employed cheap labor. In exchange, regional governments would maintain an anticommunist stance and ostracize Cuba and Nicaragua. As Lester D. Langley comments: "It took extensive lobbying from the administration and concessions to American textile and shoe manufacturers before Congress finally approved the CBI. In the end, the biggest beneficiaries were American exporters and not the neediest Caribbean recipients." Ultimately, the bulk of CBI funds went to Central American states perceived as being on the front lines of Sandinista penetration. The CBI in Haiti enhanced the already significant development of an export-oriented economy organized around the private sector.[20]

Fanfare over the CBI nearly overshadowed social justice issues, but certain congressmen continued to press independently for human rights in Haiti. Some of these responded to the Caribbean immigrant voters among their constituents, and others to what they considered collateral economic issues. Liberal congressmen frequently linked Haiti to broader dissatisfactions with the conservatives' domestic and foreign policy agendas. Representative Walter Fauntroy typified this perspective in remarks made at 1980 hearings on Caribbean migration. "Relationships which, bluntly put, are based on gross exploitation are not in the interests of the people of the United States of America," he declared. "It is not in our national interest for our government to be on the side of seven thousand families and a few special interests in the United States at the expense of the five million people of Haiti. More directly, many of the jobs which are now available in Haiti and other countries with regressive labor practices, might otherwise have been available to the poor here in the United States of America. It is the structure of exploitation existing in Haiti which has caused us to lose jobs here in the United States and is making Haiti a cheap labor export platform that benefits not the American people and the Haitian people but only a few Haitians and a few Americans."[21]

Despite the objections of Fauntroy and similar critics, it was just this policy that the Reagan administration sought to pursue in Haiti. On the diplomatic front, the White House encouraged Haiti to break out of its regional quarantine by cultivating closer ties with Edward Seaga's government in Kingston, Jamaica. The Free Zone in Kingston, widely promoted as a model for Haiti, is an industrial enclave of light-assembly and manufacturing plants where a largely female labor force works at paltry wages. Joint policies of opposition to communism, cultivation of close ties with the U.S. economy, and export-oriented industrialism linked Kingston and Port-au-Prince in spirit.[22]

Reagan's advent also gave Jean-Claude the green light to get tough with domestic critics. He shut down *Petit Samedi Soir* and deported dissidents. Vandals ransacked the offices of the candid Haiti Radio Inter. Internal criticism of the Haitian government's role in the "boat people" crisis was the immediate cause of the crackdown.[23] U.S. immigration officials' harsh responses to the growing Haitian influx provided the general context. Routine incarcerations even included children who arrived alone and unsponsored. As some of them were as young as six years old, their solitary journeys indicated the depth of their parents' desperation.[24]

New congressional legislation in 1980 distinguished between so-called economic and political refugees. The former were ineligible for asylum. In September 1981, the White House announced a radical plan to prevent small craft carrying Haitians from landing on the Florida coast. This included Coast Guard apprehension of vessels outside U.S. territorial waters and the return of undocumented aliens. U.S. officials held some Haitians indefinitely in detention centers. The Reagan administration widely publicized its attempts to develop permanent camps in some of the continent's least hospitable climates. Sites considered included an air force base near Glasgow, Montana, where "winter temperatures plunge to forty degrees below zero." A court decision of June 1982 fortunately thwarted this scheme.[25]

Haitians also suffered discrimination because the public identified them with the AIDS pandemic. In the early 1980s, the international medical community slowly came to realize the gravity and universal implications of the disease, and its etiology remained poorly understood. Many believed AIDS to be widespread in Haiti, and Haitians especially at risk. Reports of rampant tuberculosis in Haiti (a disease often linked to AIDS), scattered cases of leprosy, and the resurgence of yaws further prejudiced official opinion. The AIDS scare put a damper on Haitian tourism, which had just begun to revive as a result of the widely touted liberalization policies. It particularly damaged the prostitution industry, part of which moved across the border into the Dominican Republic.[26]

The "boat people's" suffering engaged the concern of Afro-American congressmen. The Congressional Black Caucus appointed a task force headed by Walter Fauntroy and Shirley Chisholm to study their plight. Two factors sparked caucus members' interest. First, the policy of discriminating against black refugees while favoring those from Eastern Europe had been brought to their attention by three major civil rights organizations: the NAACP, Urban League, and Operation PUSH. Second, a large and assertive Haitian community had developed in New York City and some newly hyphenated Americans had already begun to play a role in electoral politics.[27]

Racism clearly figured in Washington's decisions, but another reason, more intimately linked to Caribbean policy per se, also accounted for prejudicial policies. An emerging Haitian community in the United States would inevitably challenge the Duvaliers' power. Without repression, the regime could not manage an expendable labor force whose permanence and low cost resembled slavery and thereby increased the profit margins of its multinational employers. The extent to which the Haitian government could pose as a bulwark against communism in the Caribbean also colored U.S. policymakers' assessments. Threats to such a state open the door to insurgency, upset the regional balance of power, and, to those steeped in the bromides of the cold war, lead ultimately to Soviet penetration.[28]

To Port-au-Prince, the boat people constituted an embarrassment and a possible source of danger. While the economy might benefit from their remittances, the regime did not want exiles plotting resistance, enjoying better lives than at home, and making invidious comparisons. Rising expectations could contaminate Haiti. The escapes also demonstrated the permeability of national borders. Authorities did not tolerate media discussion of the subject because it would inevitably lead to talk about the implications of the conditions from which Haitians sought relief. The Coast Guard and other U.S. agencies captured three thousand immigrants and returned them to Haiti where many faced severe retribution.[29]

Haiti in 1980 was a country where 5 percent of the population controlled half the national income. Per capita consumption in the cities tripled that of rural areas, where 80 percent of the population dwelled. A regressive tax structure reinforced these inequities. As in the past, the government severely taxed staples but barely assessed luxury goods and imports. Funds provided by foreign donors did little more than match expenditures for imported goods and the expatriation of capital earned in Haiti.[30]

In 1981 a swine flu epidemic struck over one million black pigs traditionally raised by peasants. The pigs constituted an important part of the peasant economy. In the absence of other means to control the disease, and fearing its spread throughout the Caribbean, U.S. agricultural experts recommended the mass extermination of the swine population. USAID accordingly carried out the slaughter. The original program guidelines provided for new pink pigs sent from the United States to compensate peasants for the destruction of their livestock. The swap did not prove equitable however: the pink pigs differed from the Creole breed. These more costly animals required imported food and medicine whereas the native swine had been hardy experienced foragers. Many peasants could not afford to keep them. The exchanges took place, furthermore, not with individual peasants, but with government officials, who were free to be capricious in distributing the dubious restitutions.[31]

While Haitian poverty deepened during the first and second Duvalier regimes, Washington officials developed strategies for lessening the burdens of assistance expectations. The United States as early as 1964 supported small-scale activity by Canada and European states and encouraged the operations of private voluntary organizations (PVOs). Many of these agencies established what development analysts called community development projects.[32] Community development, a strategy originating in rural U.S. communities during the depressed 1930s and later exported to colonial India and to China, promoted the idea of self-help. Rural villagers would involve themselves in daily planning of such projects as road building, water resource improvement, and adoption of new agricultural technologies.

Community development projects began in Haiti following the U.S. occupation. The first few were connected to literacy programs, including Creole literacy instruction, which President Lescot endorsed as an adjunct to the church-sponsored "anti-superstition" campaign. After 1945 UN specialists and those working with British and U.S. agencies championed the concept. Community development became part of the struggle against communism. As a result of the UN projects in Haiti and the major increase in aid under the Truman administration's Point Four program, Port-au-Prince in 1953 established a bureau to manage assistance programs. This represented the institutionalization of an assistance bureaucracy in Haiti. After the ravages of Hurricane Hazel the following year, a number of PVOs launched their own Haitian missions.[33]

Internationally, community development became unpopular in the early 1960s among many Asians, Africans, and Latin Americans, who believed that it imposed a Western idea of community on less developed countries. Critics felt that it focused more on providing social services than on increasing rural income; that it evaded such highly political questions as land distribution, the relation of the rural to the urban sector, and labor exploitation.[34] Such objections did not seem liabilities to the Duvalier dictatorship. On the contrary, community development appeared a conservative approach to the problem of rural poverty that did not evoke the specter of insurgency or even of mild challenge to the status quo. In the context of mounting pressures to liberalize in 1978, Port-au-Prince encouraged the proliferation of apolitical rural community councils. The Conseil National d'Action Jean-Claudiste (CONAJEC) supervised these councils. CONAJEC also organized grass roots support for *Jean-Claudisme*.[35]

Some commentators have seen CONAJEC as an embryonic effort to found a ruling political party and have it in place should the Carter administration insist on permitting opposition parties to function.[36] In any event, the Haitian government had to concern itself with rural councils. These mass organizations represented a channel to more foreign aid, to greater legitimacy, and a better public image for the government abroad. They also provided a mechanism through which the state could consolidate its control over peasants in rural areas where its presence and authority had historically been weak. Finally, the interweaving of the councils with already existing governmental structures would provide sources of manpower for public works and enlarge the patronage system on which the regime depended.[37]

Port-au-Prince found privatization of assistance in this regard disadvantageous. Privatization multiplied the number of players, and as community development was to be apolitical, made it impossible for the state to operate unobtrusively. The emphasis of some programs on rural self-sufficiency or on transactions that did not include the usual commercial middlemen further complicated matters. The growing exclusion and irrelevance of the town to the council structure were, from Port-au-Prince's perspective, undesirable consequences. PVOs additionally provided some of the services that government normally furnishes in other countries and thus upstaged the state. Some Haitian officials regarded this as a threat.[38] By 1985 as many as four hundred separate agencies operated assistance programs in an increasingly privatized milieu. USAID spent some 57 percent of its funds indirectly by granting them to PVOs, a practice also followed by the Canadian International Development Agency. Most of the U.S. PL 480 program food was channeled through private agencies, and a portion of it found its way to black markets or Miami grocery stores.[39]

The "Reagan revolution" in Washington gave new life to the Duvalierist hope of controlling rural PVO activity. Laws passed in 1981 more closely regulated community councils and returned their power to the towns. In general, the PVOs hardly constituted revolutionary organizations. They avoided disturbing the rural class system. Albeit dependent on local Duvalierist elites and apolitical, the councils nevertheless created an important precedent for peasant organization that would emerge much more sharply after the flight of Jean-Claude in 1986.[40]

The Catholic Church also played a part in developing organizational structures ultimately capable of challenging the regime. Motivated by Protestant missionary successes, by tacit Vatican encouragement, and by the deepening influence of liberation theology, many members of the lower clergy began to reconcile their actions with their moral conscience. The media liberalization policy pursued in the early 1970s permitted church radio stations to discreetly criticize the government, and this continued even after the collapse of "freedom of the press." Christian "base communities," organized around particularly effective priests and other religious, began as ostensibly simple church organizations. They subsequently evolved into the *Ti Egliz*, or popular church, led by militant clergy who, following the Duvalier regime, called for radical reform of Haitian institutions.[41]

Duvalier's efforts to mend relations with the Vatican included re-linquishing his right to name bishops. This arrangement had resulted from François Duvalier's battles with the Church hierarchy, which ultimately led to his excommunication in the 1960s. Return of episcopal rights to the Church coincided with Pope John Paul II's brief visit to Haiti on 9 March 1983. The pope had come as part of an extended tour of the Americas, which included a number of countries experiencing rapid social change. His speeches in Haiti clearly rebuked the government for the poverty and injustices inflicted on the populace.[42]

The papal visit had a catalytic effect on the Haitian clergy. As a self-styled black nationalist, the late François Duvalier had militated for more native priests. His insistence paralleled traditional Haitian fears of the Catholic Church as a stalking horse for the imperialist ambitions of France and other European states. The ironic consequence of his efforts to Haitianize the Church was that the indigenous clergy, which Duvalierism had largely created, proved highly responsive to the pontiff's message. It agitated for greater social justice in Haiti and more freedom of expression for the Church itself. Clerics increasingly defied conservative members of the ecclesiastical hierarchy to become major spokesmen for change. Their number included a young priest, the charismatic Father Jean-Bertrand Aristide, whose inner city parish of St. Jean Bosco became a major center of dissidence. Aristide, of rural origin, showed promise in school. His education took him to Europe and Canada, where he excelled. Aristide's accomplishments proved Duvalier right in demonstrating Haiti's capacity to supply its own priests.[43]

Aristide's education also refined his awareness of what was wrong with the system, and by 1985 he became a powerful voice demanding change. The Duvaliers responded to the growing clamor by enacting reforms meant to be no more than window dressing. They legalized political parties, for example, with the proviso that they all accept the principle of the life presidency and *Jean-Claudisme*. Michèle Bennett Duvalier sought to benefit from the publicity accompanying Mother Theresa's visit to a clinic and dispensary for women and children that the first lady had established. Though put in good order for the renowned nun's visit, the institution normally lacked vital medicines and supplies and depended totally on allocations from *la Présidente*. These abuses simply fueled the widely felt resentment.[44]

Aside from the pressures from without, disintegration from within began to shake the Duvalierist system by the mid-1980s. The deaths or dismissals of veteran stalwarts, governmental vacillation on dissidence, mulattoes' visibility in Jean-Claude's circle, and the unpopularity of the extravagant Michèle Bennett contributed to internal conflict. The VSN as well as the army experienced dissatisfaction. Precautions taken by the regime to isolate and reduce Old Guard Duvalierists thought to be a threat from the right indicate the extent of the disorder. Jean-Claude ultimately proved incapable of mounting an emphatic, successful, and final assault on his numerous adversaries from right to left. Antigovernment sentiment escalated, and more important, found open expression in demonstrations that would have been unthinkable during Papa Doc's era. The visible decay of the regime provided the context in which the mass insurgency and, finally, the insurrection of 1986 took place.[45]

In response to mounting food prices, riots broke out in February 1984 in the provincial city of Gonaïves, regarded as the historic seat of the Haitian revolution. Angry crowds invaded a warehouse stocked with CARE provisions and launched assaults on the local prison and police station. Six people died in these conflicts. The following year Gonaïves erupted again in student protests over government efforts to create and manipulate a youth movement. On 28 November, during a second day of demonstrations, army troops fired on hundreds of protesters and killed at least three. A week later, the U.S. State Department condemned the military action, and more important from the Duvalierist standpoint, suspended foreign aid. Port-au-Prince then offered a compensation of $2,000 each for the murdered students, a gesture that further rankled rather than soothed spirits. Vexed by the Catholic station Radio Soleil's coverage of the Gonaïves incident, the government temporarily shut it down, as well as Radio Ave Maria, and arrested a number of dissidents.[46]

At this point, indignation in the provincial towns began to quicken and the public increasingly defied the state as repression, in turn, mounted. The number of assaults and jailings of opposition figures, school boycotts, and confrontations between slum dwellers and soldiers multiplied in Cap-Haïtien, Gonaïves, and Aux Cayes. Port-au-Prince found its efforts to deal with the situation hampered by a changed attitude in Washington. In the early 1980s the Reagan administration, obsessed by developing insurgencies and general unrest in the Caribbean basin, had not objected to Baby Doc terminating his brief flirtation with civil liberties. By the mid-1980s, however, the White House had become more pragmatic and less ideological about its commitments. Reagan administration officials now partially endorsed the popular liberal wisdom that neglect of the democratic center in developing countries led to tyrannies of the right and left. In the absence of a leftist or populist threat, they were content to allow the business of dictatorship to go on as usual. In Haiti's case, however, and in the Philippines (which also ejected a despot in 1986), it thought the dangers of radical usurpation great enough to warrant better support for the center. Some commentators have congratulated Reagan for perspicacity in the timely shedding of links to Duvalier and Marcos. One wonders, however, how much wisdom is required to jump out of the way of a speeding train.

In late December 1985 the State Department announced a general review of assistance programs and threatened to terminate all of them unless political conditions improved. Duvalier then hastily reorganized his cabinet and fired his principal advisers. He also took the precaution of closing schools, so that youthful incendiarism would not light the match that reduced his government to cinders. A temporary peace reigned during the Christmas season, but open resistance to the regime, strongly encouraged by religious leaders, persisted. On 25 January heavy fighting erupted in Cap-Haïtien between troops and thousands of demonstrators. Violence also occurred in Limbé, Petit-Goâve, Léogâne, and recurred in Aux Cayes. The following week, arson and looting broke out in Jérémie and St. Michel de l'Attalaye. In St. Marc, soldiers disarmed and detained members of the VSN. In many towns, hungry mobs targeted food depots. Poor families depended heavily on the free lunches that pupils received, and some weaker children died as a result of the school closings.[47]

The army withdrew its support from the regime late in January 1986, giving orders to common soldiers to refrain from shooting at protesters save in self-defense. On 30 January, the United States announced the postponement of a $26 million aid package to Haiti. The following day, White House spokesman Larry Speakes erroneously announced to the media that the Duvalier regime had collapsed and that Jean-Claude was in exile. Baby Doc took to the air waves to deny that he had fled and declared a state of siege and the suspension of all civil rights. Duvalier nevertheless had already begun negotiating his exit behind the scenes.[48] With the assistance of the diplomatic corps and the foreign offices of friendly powers, Jean-Claude departed on a U.S. cargo plane for France and a golden exile on 7 February 1986. Rumor had it that he had distributed machine guns to loyal Makouts remaining in Haiti.

12   The Balance Sheet

Haitians have been tropical commodity producers who relied heavily on the metropolis, an inheritance from the colonial past. Dominant social and cultural attitudes, which placed high value on things North American and European, assisted this process of unequal exchange. Containment had always been a cornerstone of the U.S. attitude toward Haiti. During the war between the Haitians and the French, the United States took steps to prevent revolutionary "contagion" from spreading to its own enslaved black population. In subsequent years it imposed a blackout on the rebel republic, isolating it diplomatically even while enjoying a profitable commerce with it. It explained away Haitian sovereignty in exceptionalist arguments (often seconded by Haitians themselves), which maintained that Haiti did not follow the patterns of historical development discernible in the evolution of other nations. This permitted proslavery advocates to deny the legitimacy of the Haitian Revolution and neutralize the real danger to their interests that the spread of democratic ideology among blacks represented. With emancipation, this brand of containment helped to rationalize perpetuating unequal relations between Haiti and more developed countries.

Following the defeat of Spain in 1898, the United States enjoyed maritime supremacy in the Caribbean and continued to exercise control of the independent republics. The Theodore Roosevelt administration's particular type of navalism was a containment policy in that it emphasized policing the Caribbean and preventing internal civil strife within sovereign states from attracting European interest. By contrast, the Dollar Diplomacy of William Howard Taft, Roosevelt's successor, appeared progressive. It stressed regional stability through governmental solvency. However it may have operated in other Latin American countries, Dollar Diplomacy became a license to steal in Haiti. Far from stabilizing conditions, the loan of 1910 helped sweep away the government that had negotiated it. Credits to the state did not provide it with the capital needed to generate infrastructure, attract foreign investment, and alleviate the most disruptive social ills. Rather, it bought time for those who received the money, and for a few short years it contained a host of growing contradictions.

The desire for political stability in the Caribbean region is a thick thread running through the fabric of U.S. diplomatic history. Policymakers unfortunately equated stability with the promotion and retention of regimes that could neutralize endemic popular discontent. Sometimes this involved judicious concessions to power factions and interest groups within a given country, but at other times it simply entailed stern repression. Whatever the right combination for a particular state, when coupled with a favorable attitude toward U.S. trade and investment, this "stability" assured reliable support from Washington.

Why was genuine peace and security so difficult to achieve? Overpopulation, unemployment, monocultural dependency, and social injustice lay at the root. Most countries had unresponsive governing elites that defined their interests in terms of Western allegiances. The West, for its part, saw Caribbean republics only in terms of their productive capacities or strategic potential. This orientation brought the region to attention only when immediate crises threatened the status quo.

Containment arguments took on a particularly racial character in the Haitian case. U.S. and Dominican officials in the 1930s wished to preserve Santo Domingo's "whiteness" against a possible Haitian migrant onslaught. The sparsely populated Dominican Republic had considerable range land suitable for small-scale farming, but concerns about racial purity emanating from Washington as well as Santo Domingo encouraged efforts to exclude Haitians. Anyone aware of island demography knew that Dominican whiteness had never been more than wishful thinking, but the desire to keep Haitians out of the East was couched in explicitly racial terms. The senseless murder of thousands of migrant Haitian workers in 1937 stemmed from the violence of a regime installed with the help of U.S. arms. Port-au-Prince's failure to press for a full investigation of the matter, and its acceptance of the insultingly small indemnity Trujillo offered it, clearly indicated its own indifference to its citizens' plight. Selective genocide proved the ultimate expression of containment.

If the massacre of 1937 represented an enactment of the racist tragedy of Europe, Trujillo could not sustain this parody after the Allied victory in 1945. Nazi Germany's horrors discredited racism as an ideology. The United States, aspiring to cold war global leadership, had to confront its own racist legacy and history of cultural misunderstandings with southern neighbors. The sentiments of some statesmen during the era indicated that they lacked strong commitment to an ideal of racial justice and knowledge of Latin American civilization. State Department Counselor George Kennan, for example, doubted "that there could be any other region of the earth in which nature and human behavior could have combined to produce a more unhappy and hopeless background for the conduct of human life than in Latin America." In Kennan's 1950 policy memorandum, the Spanish *conquistadores* bequeathed little to the Americas except "religious fanaticism." The tragedy of the *conquista* was so profound that it permanently impaired the republics' capacity to enjoy democratic rule. Even worse, "the large scale importation of Negro slave elements into considerable parts of the Spanish and other colonial empires, and the extensive intermarriage of all these elements, produced other unfortunate results which seemed to have weighed scarcely less heavily on the chances for human progress."[1]

Kennan's views closely resembled those of earlier policymakers. Secretary of State Philander Knox had suggested in 1910 that only "champagne and other alcoholic preservatives" could bridge the cultural gap with Latin states. Kennan similarly found little basis for mutual understanding:

> The price of diplomatic popularity, and to some extent of diplomatic success [in Latin America], is constant connivance at the maintenance of a staggering and ubiquitous fiction: the fiction of extraordinary human achievement, personal and collective, subjective and objective, in a society where the realities are almost precisely the opposite, and where the reasons behind these realities are too grim to be widely or steadily enter-

tained. Latin American society lives, by and large, by a species of make-believe: not the systematized, purposeful make-believe of Russian communism, but a highly personalized, anarchical make-believe, in which each individual spins around him, like a cocoon, his own little world of pretense, and demands its recognition by others as the condition of his participation in the social process.[2]

The negativity and despair that Kennan depicted perhaps captures the compliant spirit that accompanied the U.S. response to President François Duvalier's ascendancy and subsequent activities. In 1957 the Haitian army helped secure the presidency for Duvalier. Duvalier later used his position to weaken this benefactor and attack the bourgeoisie, which it represented. This class had long served as the conduit through which metropolitan interests exploited the country. Duvalier did not seek to end this but rather to eliminate intermediaries. He clothed his strategy in the rhetoric of mystical black nationalism. In the name of defending Haitian cultural values and black political hegemony, he deferred generously to foreign investors.[3] Washington officials repudiated the corruption, terror, and arbitrariness that Duvalier's government deliberately practiced but did little more than issue strong protests. U.S. vessels hovered near Haitian shores and Marines staged brief mock landings, but the Kennedy administration proved reluctant to authorize invasion or sever relations.

The desire to keep an antileftist regime in power increased after the Cuban Revolution became manifestly Marxist, and after Havana's interest in the candidacy of a Duvalier rival became known. Dean Rusk asserted that "Batista had prepared the way for Castro in Cuba and . . . the same thing could happen in Haiti."[4] The United States therefore helped Duvalier withstand an amphibious attack mounted from Cuba in 1959. "Papa Doc" played the anticommunist obsession to the hilt. He demanded and received payment for supporting the U.S. position at the OAS meeting in Punta del Este, where Washington sought to have sanctions imposed on Cuba. The Central Intelligence Agency covertly assisted certain exile groups while the U.S. government simultaneously helped Duvalier resist coup attempts directed by Haitians. Haitian "stability" then, was purchased at the very high price these manipulations demanded. During the Johnson administration, combined business pressure and fear of insurgency led to rapprochement between the United States and the Haitian president, who by now had appointed himself "president for life." Duvalier efficiently contained the misery of the masses and stunted their ambitions. The Nixon and Ford administrations in their turn continued cordial relations with his son, Jean-Claude Duvalier, who succeeded him after his death in 1971.

This trend exemplifies the changes that overtook U.S. Latin American policy following the Kennedy administration. During the early 1960s some liberals thought that only sincere and sustained support for genuinely popular regimes in Latin America could forestall inevitable revolution. This perspective succumbed to elite opposition to substantive change, the recognition of structural barriers to development, and the belief that U.S. business would suffer if Latin American conditions improved. Communist revolution in Cuba soon closed the lid on the Alliance for Progress, and policymakers once again returned to cold war preoccupations. Repressive governments and brutal poverty seemed intractable problems given the assumption that the security of dependable "allies" took precedence over social and economic justice.

A conservative trend in U.S. domestic opinion over the past quarter century rapidly followed the demise of liberalism on hemispheric issues. This conservative revival had profound effects for subsequent relations with Haiti. By 1968 the United States had begun losing ground in heavy industry to countries boasting newer physical plant and lower production costs. The savings these countries realized usually involved the exploitation of unorganized labor. Some domestic manufacturers sought to compensate for their comparative disadvantages by relocating industries to regions within the United States where they could employ cheaper labor. Others moved abroad to developing countries. In both cases, domestic conservatism paved the way by weakening trade unionism and making the practice of expatriating jobs more acceptable to the general public. Within the United States itself, the transition to a postindustrial "service economy" created menial jobs without the protections afforded by strong labor organizations, a pattern repeated overseas.[5]

Possibilities for offshore assembly industries in Haiti attracted numerous U.S. companies. The relationship to Haitian politics is discussed in the preceding chapter. Offshore industries supposedly helped the Haitian economy by creating jobs at home, blunting the force of emigration, and consequently protecting the natural resource that Haiti's low-wage labor force represented. They failed in this mission, partly because they did not create enough jobs, but also because meeting the needs of U.S. firms always remained the highest priority, and this did not necessarily equate with stable, continuous, and permanent employment.[6]

Veteran U.S. managers in Asia and Latin America found that they could benefit from hiring an ephemeral, heavily female work force. Transience guaranteed that workers would neither gain mastery of all work processes nor accumulate the required seniority to begin organizing as a constituency and making demands. Women of childbearing age who dropped in and out of the labor market characteristically evinced this impermanence. The temporary nature of any individual worker's employment also meant that most jobs would remain poorly paid and low-skilled, affording little opportunity for upward mobility. Haiti set the minimum wage at three dollars a day in 1984, but, in practice, worker payoffs to foremen and hiring agents caused some laborers to work at below-subsistence rates.[7]

The foreign low wage sector not only cut production costs for stateside manufacturers, it also buttressed the ideology and political agendas of U.S. conservatives as interpreted and popularized by President Ronald Reagan and others. The actuality of Haitian and other foreign workers toiling in offshore sweatshops disciplined labor at home and curtailed its demands for constant economic growth. It lent the illusion that poorer countries were making substantial progress in development, even though the assembly industries provided, at best, stopgap remedies. It reinforced the message that healthy economies must respond to the supply-and-demand imperatives of the traditional market. More broadly, this neoclassic economic wisdom helped undermine the institutionalized liberal welfare state and justify the profitable—for corporations—export of jobs.[8]

The offshore phenomenon carried other ideological baggage. In the process of redefining the job market, manufacturers identified Haitian factory employees and others as expendable labor. Characterizing such personnel as docile played into convenient racist and sexist stereotypes. U.S. employers were already accustomed to an informal system in which racial minorities received lower wages than others. The leap from this to rationalizing the requirement that the poor abroad work for less was not difficult to make. Factories could furthermore reinforce patriarchal attitudes already existing in the host country to justify low pay and poor working conditions for women. In most countries, a tradition of female subservience enhanced the fluidity of the labor pool. Women in Haiti, socialized to hard labor without complaint, had worked in factory-like settings since at least 1919 sorting coffee beans. Women's labor ranked as casual and of little significance. Even when they independently supported their families, society could regard women's jobs as intrinsically less important than men's.[9]

The racism and containment themes that pervade Haitian-U.S. relations are also apparent in the clamor surrounding the AIDS pandemic. Here, the association of AIDS with Haitians and calls for Haitian exclusion ironically evoked the past. In 1983 a theory that the viruses causing AIDS originated in Central Africa gained currency. Scientists surmised that Haiti subsequently assisted their spread through the United States via homosexual tourists who became infected in Port-au-Prince. Haitian expatriates who had lived and worked in Central Africa in the 1960s and 1970s supposedly provided the link between Africa and the New World. This widely publicized explanation devastated the Haitian tourist industry and further contributed to the negative popular perception of Haitian immigrants, for researchers pinpointed Haitians specifically as carriers of the disease.[10]

The Centers for Disease Control (CDC) in Atlanta repudiated this theory in 1985, and removed Haitians from a list it had created of groups at special risk. The CDC now understood that less developed countries incurred general risk because of their inability to safeguard blood banks and furnish medical personnel with a continuous supply of disposable syringes. It also realized by then that AIDS did not affect homosexuals only. The damage done to Haiti's reputation recapitulated the old repulsion and horror that the West had felt for the black republic, and it was expressed in similar metaphors of isolation and quarantine.[11]

Jean-Claude Duvalier and his advisers had a plan to remedy Haiti's bad press while simultaneously benefiting themselves. They sought to maintain the system while adding some grace notes of political liberalization consonant with gradual and conservative democratization. Duvalierists had in mind a Caribbean Taiwan or Hong Kong, but they failed to understand that these Asian economies had never served exclusively as revenue-generating scams. On the contrary, they represented a commitment to producing foreign exchange earnings to reinvest locally or expatriate as working, rather than retired, capital. Capitalism to the Duvaliers still represented little more than an opportunity for insiders to net bonanzas. Jean-Claude ultimately had to confront a world different from his father's. The reconciliation with the bourgeoisie that Jean-Claude effected had been one of François Duvalier's long-range objectives. Now realized, it inadvertently removed the camouflage with which black nationalist rhetoric had clothed ongoing foreign and elite exploitation. The continuous degradation of rural Haiti and growing urban migration worsened dependence on food imports and contributed to rising prices for basic commodities. The increasing diaspora, on whose remittances the economy came progressively to rely, became a nest of dissidence. The United States by 1986 realized the consequences of past policy failures in Cuba and Nicaragua, and faced democratic challenges in other developing countries. It could no longer afford unquestioning support of the most blatantly repressive dictatorships. As in the Philippines, where U.S. pressure helped to topple Ferdinand Marcos and put a centrist in his place, Washington prevailed upon Jean-Claude Duvalier to leave the country.[12]

Jean-Claude's flight amid frenzied celebration and expressions of

rage did not solve for Washington the problem of Haiti's continuing vulnerability to leftist problem-solving. The quiet realization that
many Haitians had little to lose in the event of a socialist revolution
undoubtedly highlighted fears of communist penetration. Underlying
the cold war issue, moreover, lurked an even older anxiety about foreign influence in the black republic. The State Department's concern
about Libyan "covert funding" to Haitian radicals in 1986 revealed
Haiti as an Achilles heel on Washington's ideal of hemispheric stability.[13]

A provisional government, the Conseil National de Gouvernement
(CNG), immediately succeeded Jean-Claude Duvalier, crafted, like
other interregnum regimes, with the help of foreign powers represented in Haiti. The U.S. embassy played a major role in persuad-
ing U.S. Army–trained general Henri Namphy to be chief of state.
Washington resumed the suspended foreign assistance programs and
almost doubled grants to Haiti over the previous 1985 fiscal year.[14]
These included nearly $500,000 worth of riot equipment, ostensibly
for use against diehard Duvalierist conspirators. The CNG had six
members: initially, Colonel Williams Régala, minister of defense and
interior; Colonel Prosper Avril, Namphy's adviser on military affairs;
and Colonel Max Valles, minister of information had all held top appointments during the Duvalier regime. Civilian Alix Cinéas, minister
without portfolio, had served Duvalier as minister of public works.
Gérard Gourgue and Rosny Desroches, civilians with no ties to the
previous government, were the remaining members. Gourgue, an
attorney, had headed the Haitian League for Human Rights and now
functioned as minister of justice.[15]

In the course of the following week, people in the street exacted
a popular justice of their own. In a process referred to as *dechoukaj*,
in Creole, "uprooting," the public tried to purge political life of all
remnants of the dictatorship. This included lynching the most brutal
Makouts, harassment of others, refusals by civil service employees to
cooperate with Duvalierist superiors, and denunciations of collaborators. Mobs desecrated François Duvalier's grave and pillaged the prop-

erties of wealthy Duvalierists. Crowds demonstrated vociferously for economic and social reform.[16]

The CNG set itself the task of restoring order. It policed the mass protests and maintained curfews. To many, its actions seemed aimed at preserving the status quo or, as some termed it, Duvalierism without Duvalier. The CNG, consequently, enjoyed little popularity, especially when it became evident that its officials took a dim view of retribution against the Makouts and shared none of the spontaneous exhilaration. The CNG outlawed the Volontaires de la Sécurité Nationale (VSN) on 10 February, but the army still protected besieged Makouts, who enjoyed continued access to power. Justice Minister Gérard Gourgue resigned his position on 20 March to protest the ongoing Duvalierist presence and influence in government. (Some evidence suggests that the CNG even helped some of the more nefarious to escape.) Certain minor functionaries, daunted by the persistent fraud and corruption in government and disappointed at the lack of support their reformist efforts generated from top officials, also left the civil service. The shooting of demonstrators who were commemorating the martyrs of the infamous Fort Dimanche prison further embittered the populace.[17]

Haiti after Duvalier had changed as a result of politicization unprecedented in recent times. Organizations sprang up seemingly over night, and many of them derived from supposedly apolitical agrarian or church-based collectives and associations. For the first time in decades, workers arrogated to themselves the right to strike. People freely discussed the kind of changes they wanted to see made in Haiti, and they wanted them made posthaste. Some reforms proved relatively easy to effect. The CNG quickly returned the Haitian flag to its original red and blue, removed Duvalierist names from towns, and reduced the high food prices that had helped fell Duvalierism in the first place. It endorsed Mision Alfa, a massive church-sponsored program, designed to tackle Haiti's 85 percent illiteracy rate. It was more difficult to satisfy the demand that the government recoup the wealth stolen from the national treasury and hold Duvalierists legally accountable for their crimes. Most importantly, Haitians wanted a popularly elected, civilian government. Matters came to a head late in March as strikes and violence beleaguered Port-au-Prince. Namphy reorganized the CNG into a triumvirate consisting of Régala, the ex-diplomat Jacques François, and himself. The army remained in control, but its individual officers and enlisted men proved susceptible to the unrest sweeping the country.[18]

CNG officials and the Reagan administration shared a similar worldview. Men like Finance Minister Lesley Delatour advocated fiscal conservatism and austerity for Haiti, an agenda that hardly meshed with the aspirations of a community emerging from generations of deprivation. They called for less state intervention in the economy, belt-tightening, and subsidies to foreign investment. Delatour and others realized that the fall of Jean-Claude and *dechoukaj* had led to U.S. capital flight as some four dozen overseas firms packed up and left the country. Many such companies cited political instability as the reason for relocating their businesses, but in truth, many departed when the magnet that had originally drawn them to Haiti ceased to attract. The erstwhile docile labor force had begun asserting itself despite management resort to yankee "union busting" consultants. On 10 June a general strike shut down Port-au-Prince.[19]

The demise of Duvalierism had also strengthened rural organizations that had already acquired some experience. These groups faced two entrenched powers: large landholders who had exploited impoverished peasants for generations, and *chefs de section* who exerted tyrannical authority over their districts. Bitter, bloody clashes occurred between peasants and landlords during the summer of 1987 in Jean-Rabel, a northwestern town. Large proprietors attempting to break the organization Tèt Ansamn hired thugs to shoot and hack members and sympathizers to death.[20]

Namphy recognized that he could not withstand popular pressures indefinitely. He accordingly scheduled presidential elections for November 1987, and the government proceeded halfheartedly with prosecutions of persons accused of crimes against the people. It simply released certain alleged assassins and torturers, including the former mayor of Port-au-Prince. The CNG's patent lack of enthusiasm for democracy owed much to the paucity of democrats within. The Duvaliers had allowed few dissenters to acquire experience as public administrators. Over a thirty-year period a bureaucratic style incompatible with genuine reform had consolidated. Even those who retained some sympathy for the provisional government worried about the disappearances and harassment of literacy workers and other community activists. Just as François Duvalier had used the Haitian army to acquire power and then reduced it, some military officers may have contemplated a similar use of the remaining Duvalierists. Makout terror could help subdue the population and curtail radicalism until the army, still representing its long-time clients, the bourgeoisie and foreign interests, could take full control.

Plans for constitutional democracy continued. Guidelines for functioning political parties excluded small cliques and limited the funds parties could receive from any individual donor. The CNG scheduled elections on 19 October 1986 for members of a constituent assembly empowered to draft a new constitution. The resultant document addressed the chronic problem of autocratic rule by strengthening the legislative branch of government, creating the post of premier, and limiting presidential terms. It excluded former Duvalierists from office for ten years. The bill, approved by the electorate on 29 March 1987, guaranteed freedom of the press and religion and protected political parties and trade unions. Haitian Creole became the official language. The document set up the machinery for supervising the forthcoming elections through the offices of a provisional electoral council, the Conseil Electoral Provisoire (CEP).[21]

Politicians, including many newly arrived from exile without grassroots constituencies, began organizing their campaigns. Conventional politics in the style of Western democracies was a novel experience for many Haitians, but it did not overshadow popular insistence that the country's long-neglected needs be addressed at once. Strikes and demonstrations continued. The government moved to the right, accelerating the arrests and detention of outspoken critics. Early in 1987 the CNG dismissed the ministers of justice, education, foreign relations, and health, all anti-Duvalierist civilians. Catholic bishops, still catalyzed by their recent roles, reproved the CNG for its indifference to public welfare and seeming collusion with the old regime.[22]

The CEP meanwhile began preparing for the forthcoming elections despite top-level opposition. It found its voter registration work stymied by bureaucratic obstruction and harassment, and on 22 June the government dissolved it, ostensibly for technical reasons. The CNG banned one of two major trade union federations, the Centrale Autonome des Travailleurs Haïtiens (CATH), on the same day. Soldiers destroyed its office shortly after the organization called for another general strike.[23]

These heavy-handed actions met a tidal wave of popular opposition. The general strike turned into a month-long moratorium on work and the conduct of business. The army met strikes, demonstrations, and riots with deadly firepower as the CNG lost its remaining legitimacy in the eyes of the people. It found itself forced to rescind its prohibitions of CATH and CEP. Even though it proved capable of suppressing protests, the army appeared less able to prevent the growing crime that plagued Port-au-Prince. Rumor had it that Makouts were committing the numerous armed robberies in order to further destabilize the environment and prepare themselves financially for a coup d'état. They added political assassination to their crime inventory, murdering two presidential candidates.[24]

In Washington, the Congressional Task Force on Haiti let its disapproval of the CNG's attitude toward the CEP be known. Representative Walter E. Fauntroy, in a letter published in Haïti-Observateur, claimed that the provisional government had gravely erred in its "attempt to violate the Constitution by usurping the role of the CEP." Fauntroy reiterated congressional support of the CNG and suggested that it "make a sharp break with the Duvalierist past and those in its ranks who cling to its mentality and practices." It was to do so, he added, "without significantly modifying the electoral calendar." A U.S. Senate resolution passed 23 July backed up Fauntroy's message.[25]

When the CEP, according to constitutional fiat, disallowed presidential candidates with links to Duvalierism, Duvalierists, now openly terrorists, responded by fire-bombing CEP offices and strafing the homes of remaining candidates. The army took no action as Makouts with automatic weapons openly patrolled slum areas. In many instances, their military garb proved officers' collusion. Courageous slum residents organized watch committees to protect their communities from Makout pillage and bloodshed. The CNG, unwilling to stop the terrorism, nevertheless found the resources to ban these neighborhood groups on 25 November.[26]

Eight major candidates had made it unscathed to 29 November, election day. They ranged from René Théodore, a communist, on the left, to Louis Déjoie, an old-fashioned mulatto elitist, on the right. They included Marc Bazin, a former World Bank economist in great favor with the Reagan administration, and Leslie Manigat, an academic of international repute and protegé of Venezuelan statesman Romulo Betancourt. The CEP had managed, assisted by foreign donations, to register over 70 percent of the electorate, and some still held high hopes for the election's outcome.[27]

Terrorism continued during the days leading up to the twenty-ninth. On the night of the twenty-eighth, mortar fire hit Port-au-Prince and destroyed three radio transmitters, a ballot depository, polling places, and other sites. The following morning a death squad armed with machine guns and machetes shot and hacked voters to death at a downtown school in the capital. These and other incidents clearly illustrated that Duvalierists planned to stop the elections. Two hundred people died in the election eve and day violence. Using the terror as an excuse, the CNG suspended polling at 9:00 a.m. and once again abolished the CEP, even though most disturbances had occurred only in the capital. The provisional government established a curfew and forbade late night assemblies in the days that followed. It suspended independent radio transmissions, closed the airport and limited telephone service.[28]

The United States had strongly endorsed the elections. Ever since the Wilson era, Washington had wanted to see constitutional government established in Port-au-Prince. It provided 80 percent of the $10 million to organize the balloting. Bogged down in Central America, the White House in particular paid little attention to Haiti. Yet U.S. officials on the ground and others sent to observe the political process had first-hand information about the election day violence. They had been shot at themselves and experienced the *couri,* or panicky escape through the streets. Many blamed the U.S. embassy for its lack of preparation and inadequate knowledge of CNG motives. There was no longer any denying that Namphy's government collaborated with Duvalierists. State Department officials called for swift apprehension of the election day assassins and suspended direct aid as a punitive measure.[29]

Despite these ministrations, anti-Americanism increased. This sentiment had several sources. Many Haitians held the United States directly responsible for sustaining the thirty-year dictatorship and holding Haiti hostage to the cold war. When a crowd in downtown Port-au-Prince threw the statue of Christopher Columbus into the Caribbean Sea, they meant the gesture to symbolize rejected foreign influence and imperialist usurpation.[30] Recent, specific grievances dating from the Duvalier period involved the U.S. role in abusing Haitian boat people, stigmatizing Haitians as AIDS carriers, destroying and then failing to adequately replace the badly needed Creole pigs. Once the Duvaliers had gone, segments of the public saw Washington's hand again upholding the repressive military-dominated CNG. U.S. officials disliked the left-of-center trade union federation, CATH. They preferred instead the more conservative Fédération d'Ouvriers Syndiqués (FOS), which received funds from the AFL-CIO's American Institute for Labor Development, an international service agency with a history of Central Intelligence Agency support.[31]

Some interpreted as meddling the admonitions of U.S. Protestant missionaries against radical reform, which the latter presented as communistic. Duvalierists used anti-Americanism to grind their own axes. The United States had toppled their system and now had the impudence to intrude upon Haitian decision making. Given all these provocations, it is not surprising that many people resented rather than applauded U.S. assistance, and viewed candidates with known pro-U.S. sympathies as suspect. There was talk of a conspiratorial "American plan" designed to subordinate Haiti and thwart its budding democracy.[32] When the CNG aborted the elections, the belief was widespread that the United States had known all along that it would happen.

Many who held to this conviction could cite not only the points enumerated above, but also the White House's apparent skirting of the direct payments ban after November 1987. As Josh DeWind notes, "The Reagan administration continued to seek 'leverage' with the military by providing funds that violated the intent of the Congress even though they may not technically have been 'economic development assistance.'" These monies included wheat sales to the Haitian government on favorable terms with the knowledge that it would resell at a profit, and the release of seventy-five thousand gourdes escrowed by USAID.[33]

Washington, nevertheless, refused to abandon its insistence that elections be held. The CNG organized a new electoral council made up of its creatures who elaborated procedures for a 17 January 1988 election. Their plan ensured that no Haitian could vote in safety. There would be no registration and no secret polling. Only four of the former candidates, Leslie Manigat among them, agreed to run in this second election. A massive public boycott of the polls accompanied the refusal of popular candidates to put their names in the ring, despite a CNG ban on boycotts.[34]

The resultant election proved a travesty. As James Ferguson described it: "According to foreign witnesses, at most ten per cent of the electorate voted. Many of those who did vote did so often. Outside polling stations voters, and particularly children, could be seen scrubbing the indelible ink from their fingers, and returning to cast another vote. Their enthusiasm was understandable; at some stations, a five-gourde note was included with every ballot paper. Most of these, reported journalists and observers, were Leslie Manigat's, while at some stations only Manigat's papers were available. At one station a

US journalist jokingly offered to vote for Manigat as he seemed to be the army's man; to her amazement, her ballot was accepted and put into the urn." [35]

Not surprisingly, Manigat won the election. He had cut a deal with the CNG, which remained the kingmaker. Manigat's cynicism disappointed those who would have seen in him the intellectual statesman of integrity that his training warranted. These credentials had given him legitimacy in the generals' eyes. The United States also endorsed his electoral "victory" despite the patent fraud with which he obtained it. Williams Régala stayed on in government, ominously, as minister of defense and armed forces. [36]

Manigat proved no more able to govern than the military, which remained close at hand. His association with it and his selection of cabinet members with Duvalierist connections compromised his standing with the public and injured his reputation abroad. If he had an agenda, events soon ensured that he would be unable to execute it. The generals made it clear that they alone ruled Haiti by acts of disrespect and violations of protocol. Toward the end of Manigat's term, he received token Venezuelan military assistance, but this proved ineffective. Whatever his own need for them, bringing foreign troops to Haitian soil would hardly win the hearts and minds of the public. [37]

Manigat believed that he, like François Duvalier in the past, could string the Haitian army along until he saw an opening to thrust it aside. In addition to their role as the powers behind the throne, ranking army officers involved themselves in Byzantine intrigues against one another. Manigat tried to exploit their differences but ultimately, like the proverbial grass in the African adage, was trampled when the elephants began to fight. On 17 June he had General Namphy arrested and replaced by Colonel Jean-Claude Paul, a rival militarist linked to international drug smuggling and wanted by the United States on drug charges. Paul, however, would not play along. Namphy, quickly released from prison by troops, deposed Manigat on 20 June. His presidency had lasted only four months. This palace revolution caused hardly a ripple in a Haiti already embittered by the debasement of its aspirations. [38]

The junta now dominated Haiti plain and simple, with Namphy as president. Namphy regarded representative democracy as an alien implant in the Haitian body politic and promptly abolished the legislature, establishing in its place a military council. Responding to these events, the Permanent Council of the OAS resolved on 19 June 1988 to have the Inter-American Commission on Human Rights study and report on human rights in Haiti. Indifferent to hemispheric disapproval, those wishing to reverse the tide of history continued to target persons and groups deemed subversive. On 11 September 1988 they burst into the church St. Jean Bosco to assassinate Father Jean-Bertrand Aristide while he said mass. Twelve people died and eighty were wounded by an armed group which set fire to the church. Aristide escaped.[39]

Why did the Haitian army prove so recalcitrant, faced with the weight of public indignation and adverse world opinion? Namphy and others regarded themselves as guardians of a praetorian tradition, long predating Duvalierism, to which they hoped Haiti would eventually return. In the meantime, they were not uncomfortable with Papa Doc's authoritarian methods: they made useful instruments. Politically, top officers could see in Panama's General Manuel Noriega an example of a militarist who ruled successfully behind a puppet president and enjoyed Washington's formal support, plus proceeds from the informal drug economy.[40]

There were other reasons. The Duvaliers had controlled many private sources of profit. The army, as the most powerful and articulated institution in the country, inherited these. International drug trafficking drew some criminally disposed persons into the shadowy underworld of the Medellín, Colombia, cocaine cartel. Revelations about a secret Haitian bank account maintained by U.S. Army Colonel Oliver North, embroiled in scandal himself, raised questions about Washington's role. U.S. insouciance on such matters was limited, however, as a result of domestic pressure to stem the epidemic of drug abuse and eliminate narcotics as a factor in foreign policy.[41]

Suspicions about widespread smuggling of basic commodities, including food, which badly hurt local producers, also fell on the military. Confrontations erupted in the Artibonite when cultivators tried

to stop trucks loaded with contraband rice from reaching local markets. In January 1988 the barge *Khian Sea,* cruising the hemisphere for
a place to dump four thousand tons of waste from Pennsylvania and
New Jersey, ended its journey near Gonaïves. After securing permis-
sion of the port's military authorities, it dumped its cargo outside the
city where its toxic payload sickened hundreds. The lucrative and still
semiclandestine forced-labor schemes that delivered Haitian agricultural workers to Dominican sugar estates had netted large sums for
Duvalierists and continued to do so for their successors. Those who
could stay on top would enrich themselves handsomely. These and
other rackets contributed to the internecine power struggles that resulted in Colonel Jean-Claude Paul's murder and the removal of Namphy himself in a supposed "sergeant's coup" on 17 September 1988.[42]

General Prosper Avril, once Namphy's adviser, succeeded him.
Avril rose on the shoulders of noncommissioned officers and enlisted
men who had tired of autocratic rule and official irresponsibility. The
maneuver was an ingenious one which cloaked his ascent in a mantle
of legitimacy and democratic appeal. After a few token reforms and
routine purges of objectionable militarists, Avril dispensed with the *ti
soldats* (privates and sergeants) and settled down to business as usual.
The elections were again postponed into the future. Avril managed
to withstand attempts to unseat him and secured the approval of the
U.S. Congress and State Department. Washington restored some of
the assistance cut off after the election violence of 1987.[43]

The Bush administration appeared at first to continue Reagan era
diplomacy, accepting the notion that democracy could occur in Haiti
under a military dictatorship. It tried hard to divorce human rights
abuses from junta policy (despite blatant evidence to the contrary),
view free elections as a panacea, and see the CNG as cheerfully preparing for them. Josh DeWind has sagely recognized that "in relying
upon the military the United States compromised the support it could
otherwise have given to the creation of alternative popular democratic
movements and civilian democratic institutions." The small grants it
made to civilian organizations tended to favor foreign development
projects rather than indigenous ones. It estranged itself from the very

forces that would necessarily constitute the backbone of a truly free, independent Haiti.[44] Congress, whose liberalism on Haitian questions reflected partisan divisions in government, did not squarely confront this issue either. It did, however, guardedly advocate a phased program of aid restoration, linked to visible progress toward democracy, to be implemented through the foreign aid authorization law of 29 June 1989.[45]

Prosper Avril did not bring democracy to Haiti. He tried to manage unrest through the carrot-and-stick technique: featherbedding and payoffs combined with repression. Few attempts were made to hide brutalities—the authorities displayed battered dissidents on television as a warning to others. Human rights violations continued, as did popular resistance. By November 1989 when the new U.S. ambassador, Alvin Adams, assumed his post, Avril had lasted over a year. He had shown he could survive, but this was no longer enough. Adams represented the Bush administration's new approach to Haiti. Lacing his speeches with Creole, he made a point of emphasizing democratic transition wherever possible. His first address of this kind so nettled Avril that he initially refused to accept Adams's credentials.[46]

The parsimony with which the U.S. and other habitual patrons doled out aid tied Avril's hands. Early in 1990, Avril went to Taiwan, ostensibly to negotiate economic assistance and break out of the bind that customary donor countries' restrictions had placed on the government. He returned to Haiti on 15 January, apparently having been wined and dined, but not promised anything specific. Avril attributed this to a telegram a democratic coalition sent to the president of Taiwan, which dissociated the Haitian people from Avril's policies. It is also probable that the U.S. State Department dampened his prospects with the Taiwanese. Avril made an angry speech upon his return, thought to have instigated the gunning down of a well-known radio commentator. The murder of a Presidential Guard officer on 19 January led Avril to declare a state of siege.[47]

The state of siege was illegal, according to the constitution of 1987. Troops nevertheless arrested and beat prominent civilian politicians, including two who had campaigned for president in 1987. A soldier extinguished a cigarette in the eye of former candidate Hubert de Ron-ceray. Police beat Serge Gilles in the presence of his wife and small children. Others subjected to detention, assault, and, in the case of communists, expulsion, ran the gamut of the Haitian political spectrum from center to left. Soldiers and police also arrested dissidents in Cap-Haïtien and Aux Cayes.[48]

Avril lifted the state of siege on 29 January, but because the reprisals were so sweeping, brutal, and indiscriminate, they met universal condemnation. The Catholic bishops issued a strong rebuke, and the United States had no choice but to further distance itself from Avril by coaxing him to resign. France suspended all economic assistance. Statements emanated from Canada, the European Economic Community, and the OAS. At home, Avril had stepped on the toes of the wealthy bourgeoisie as well as ordinary citizens and enjoyed no further credibility in Haiti. He now maintained himself in power by mere force of arms. Spurred on by Avril's isolation and dwindling influence, civilians meanwhile worked on guidelines for a successor regime.[49]

Even while Avril bowed to pressure to pardon those arrested during the state of siege, he continued a sub rosa program of harassment. Public opposition proved obdurate, however, and the month of February and early March passed in turmoil. The victory of a non-Marxist government in Nicaragua the same month and the end of the counter-revolutionary insurgency there focused more of the Bush administration's attention on Haiti. With its help, and that of other foreign powers, a coalition of Haiti's major political parties obtained Avril's resignation. He retired to exile on 12 March 1990.[50]

A new provisional government took office the following day. The next president of Haiti, the jurist Ertha Trouillot, was the first female head of state in Haitian history. The entirely civilian character of the administration and the demobilization of the twelve-hundred-member Presidential Guard augured well for change if lawless, reactionary elements could be contained. This proved the major challenge of the Trouillot administration. Secondary problems stemmed from countering resistance from lackadaisical bureaucracies with little experience of integrity and efficiency.[51]

The army was out of power and out of control. Its now open alliance with Duvalierism hovered like a sword of Damocles over the Haitian political process. Certain notorious Duvalierists, most importantly Williams Régala and Roger Lafontant, returned to Haiti, knowing that they could elude arrest and detention. Perhaps as a gesture of appeasement, Trouillot had offered the finance ministry to a former Jean-Claudist. The appointment incited considerable indignation outside Duvalierist circles. In the course of 1990, army and police elements colluded with attacks on civic organizations, activists, and citizens exercising their constitutional rights.[52] Among the most shocking of these was the 21 June assault on the Council of State, a group of nineteen prominent citizens who acted in an advisory capacity to the administration.

A hit squad arrived at the Santos Hotel in Port-au-Prince where the council was meeting with a popular organization. It retreated after spraying the *salle* with automatic fire and killing two persons, one a council member. The public widely condemned Trouillot for failing to decisively condemn the murders and launch a genuine investigation. She dismissed the finance minister, but inability to gain mastery over the army suggested that the administration might prove too weak to carry Haiti over the transition to elected government.[53]

In spite of these problems, the United States had still not completely divorced itself from its unrequited romance with the Haitian army, on which it planned to bestow more riot-suppressing equipment. The avowed purpose was to allow the army to sustain the government and restrain public excesses while the elections, first set for November then postponed to December, took place. This idea derived from a U.S. Defense Department that had not kept abreast of events, or remained cynical, naive or worse. Opposition from the Senate Foreign Relations Committee postponed execution of the grant.[54]

This time, the elections featured the candidacy of Father Aristide, who—despite expulsion from his Salesian order, reprimands from the ecclesiastical hierarchy, deportation orders, and attempts on his life—had become one of the most popular and influential figures in Haiti. His fiery sermons gave voice to the rage of the dispossessed and pinpointed with acuity the crimes committed by Duvalierists and the depravity of their elite and foreign collaborators. Aristide did not spare the United States, which he heavily criticized for its long-time support of Duvalier and subsequent repressive military regimes. The logic of Christian ethics formed the moral basis of his discourse.

On 16 December 1990 Haitians finally went to the polls in a historic democratic election. No violent incidents marred the voting. The UN peacekeeping troops that some had thought necessary were not called for. To the shock of some and delight of others, Haitians elected Jean-Bertrand Aristide president. The United States recognized his presidency immediately. It could not do otherwise. The U.S. embassy in Port-au-Prince had not liked the president-elect, however. One official described him to journalist Amy Wilentz as "a Marxist maniac."[55] But one phase of the political process had ended, and another was yet to begin. Aristide's enemies included conservatives of all kinds— members of the business community who deplored his radicalism, the Catholic hierarchy who opposed his candidacy, as well as Duvalierist traditionalists. Many feared his influence with the hundreds of thousands of poor people in Port-au-Prince. Under Aristide's direction, they believed, the urban poor could wreak untold havoc on the propertied classes.

According to the constitution of 1987, the president shared power with a premier. Accommodation with centrist interests might well blunt the radical thrust of the new president's energies and limit what he could accomplish in the social welfare realm. Resistance to redistribution policies would be felt from within and without the country. Aristide himself rejected collectivism and spoke against expropriating small farmers and businessmen. He did oppose, however, the monopolies, scams, and offshore operations that exploited the country without giving anything in return. The new government would also have to contend with the continuing Makout presence and its capacity for chaos and destabilization. Its relationship with the military remained unresolved. Washington, moreover, planned to resume assistance to the armed forces now that a democratic government was in place.[56]

This persistent fondness for the military rested in part on the notion that the army and Duvalierists remained two separate entities. They had, after all, been antagonistic during the presidency of François Duvalier. The U.S. military mission of 1957–63 had refused to train the VSN or militia, and its antagonism to Duvalier's personal troops, among other factors, led to its eventual expulsion.[57] But the Haitian army was not the same institution that Marine officers had put together during the occupation. It had begun changing as soon as the Marines withdrew, and it continued to change thereafter. Robert Debs Heinl, head of the U.S. military mission, wrote in 1959 that "Haiti's armed forces are not only the fulcrum of the country's internal stability but also an important agency for progress."[58] That view was overtaken by events.

U.S. officials sometimes made the mistake of believing that education in the United States meant acceptance of its political culture. Intelligent, sophisticated aspirants to power readily imbibed North Americans' cultural idioms without absorbing their values. During the U.S. military occupations in the early twentieth century, baseball caught on as a popular sport in Cuba and the Dominican Republic. Dominican dictator Rafael Trujillo hardly exemplified the virtues of the game, but he liked it so much that, in a gesture reversed by later impresarios, he tried to recruit talented U.S. players from the Negro Leagues to his national team.[59]

The ethic common to baseball and military organization, cooperative work toward a shared goal, often proved attractive in societies short of skilled personnel. Armies could be marshaled to do work performed by civilians in more developed countries. Colonel Heinl, for example, noted that Haitian army functions included "communications, rural medical service, immigration, prisons, lighthouse service, the national airline, coast guard, and commercial ship-repair."[60] Given the sheer magnitude and critical importance of these functions, it would be folly to think that those executing them would remain unsullied by politics. One might also wonder why military government, unthinkable if imposed on the United States, seemed appropriate for Caribbean republics.

Underlying fears of disorder partly explain the ready resort to military expedients. The new Haitian politics has been messy: it spills out into the public arena, sweeping up crowds in rage and enthusiasms. U.S. policymakers' distrust of the people as a mob or multitude dates back to the writings of the federalist era. An almost reflexive impulse to repress revolts of people of color, buried deeply in U.S. history and society, also contributes to the prominence of repressive measures in addressing Haitian problems.

In the early morning hours of 30 September 1991 a military junta began the overthrow of Aristide's seven-month-old regime. Unknown persons brutally murdered Christian Democratic leader Sylvio Claude in the streets of Aux Cayes. Attacks by soldiers on the urban slums that housed Aristide's supporters, on orphaned children that he had encouraged, and on popular mass organizations that arose during the post-Duvalier interregnum, soon followed. In the Lamentin shantytown, victims included toddlers. "A pair of preschoolers, one boy and one girl, died in their house," the *Washington Post* reported, "which the troops then torched. All that remains of their short lives are a tiny pair of charred shoes and two small lunch pails decorated with cartoon characters." The terrorism seemed directed at forestalling any popular mobilization in support of Aristide and effectively deterred an immediate mass response. Threats against broadcast media ensued. After a period of detention, army officers permitted Aristide to go into exile and ceded formal power to a provisional government. The military had resumed its traditional role as executor of the status quo.[61]

Coup leaders claimed that they had taken action because "undemocratic tendencies" had emerged within the Aristide government. Commentators associated with conservative Haitian interests accused Haiti's first popularly elected president of violating provisions of the 1987 constitution and of condoning the burning alive of opponents. They quickly adopted a newly strident tone in discussing the alleged shortcomings of the fallen administration. A joint report released on 1 November by three human rights organizations, the U.S.-based National Coalition for Haitian Refugees, Americas Watch, and the Barbados-headquartered Caribbean Rights, however, noted the Aristide government's achievements in the human-rights domain. The president had begun dismantling the generations-old system of *chefs de section*, suppressed army abuses of the civilian population, and had initiated reforms of the criminal justice system. The debate over Aristide exposed the rift in the Haitian community between the haves, who resented the inroads that reform would necessarily make on their privileges, and the have-nots, who remained committed to change. Many affluent Haitians made their support of the coup visible, as wealthy individuals personally bestowed small gifts of cash and food on soldiers patrolling the streets.[62] In the United States, however, resident Haitians participated in pro-government demonstrations, which were prohibited in Haiti. Refugees in New York and Miami organized marches and picket lines following the coup d'état. In some instances, they targeted businesses of affluent Haitian members of the community believed to support anti-democratic forces.[63]

On 7 October 1991 the Haitian Senate, blockaded in their chambers by guntoting soldiers, approved the coup d'état. They had been given a choice of electing a provisional civilian government or continuing General Raoul Cédras' direct military rule. They opted for the former, making their decision without a quorum and over the protests of the Organization of American States and U.S. ambassador Alvin P. Adams. Neither the OAS nor the U.S. State Department accepted the legislators' decision as legitimate. The action nevertheless complicated OAS efforts to effect a reconciliation between the Aristide government, the military, and conservatives. Mediators hoped to persuade Aristide to moderate what some considered a harsh politics of class by replacing Prime Minister René Préval. They also advocated sending to Haiti an OAS watchdog force to assist in reporting and keeping order. The army wanted complete guarantees that Cédras and other putschists would not be punished should Aristide return to power, a demand that the legitimate government refused to accept.[64]

OAS member states sought to soften military and conservative opposition to the elected government by initiating a rigorous trade embargo against Haiti that prohibited all but humanitarian assistance. Venezuela terminated shipments of oil, and the United States froze

Haitian assets. The embargo, though aimed at the consuming classes, would nonetheless further depress Haiti's weak economy and, it was hoped, create sufficient social unrest to force the usurpers to bargain. The massive brutality unleashed against the populace, however, stifled early efforts to mount a popular defense against military terror. The cessation of imports also meant that the offshore assembly-manufacturing enterprises would grind to a halt, throwing laborers out of work. Many Haitians, hopes of democracy bitterly dashed, chose instead to escape.[65]

During October and November, over three thousand Haitian refugees braved the choppy Caribbean Sea seeking political and economic asylum. Washington's response to their plight had not changed significantly since the days of the Reagan administration. The U.S. government continued to define Haitians as economic rather than political refugees and thus deny them the right of asylum. The U.S. Coast Guard began intercepting refugee vessels and escorting them back to Haiti, claiming concern that they might drown at sea. Official handling of Haitian refugees continued to contrast starkly with the treatment of Cubans leaving an economically depressed homeland. Cubans who illegally entered the United States typically experienced short periods of detention, followed by parole to Cuban-American organizations. The Immigration and Naturalization Service detained Haitians for longer periods of time and failed to cooperate with Haitian organizations. The Coast Guard proved ever ready to return escapees to the tender mercies of Haitian authorities.[66]

A 19 November restraining order, the result of pressure mounted by Haitian refugee organizations and their Congressional sympathizers, temporarily suspended this policy. A few weeks earlier, a bill was introduced in Congress that would suspend deportations. Protests by the NAACP, the Southern Christian Leadership Conference, and the National Coalition for Haitian Refugees against the continuing and seemingly racially motivated detention policies led authorities to fruitlessly seek alternative host countries for some refugees. Others remained in judicial limbo in detention camps or on the high seas, escorted by the Coast Guard and in search of a safe harbor. The Republican senator from Florida, Connie Mack, joined the chorus of complaints about Haitian immigrant treatment, which would not, he claimed, have been inflicted on Vietnamese, Russians, Jews, or Nicaraguans fleeing communism.[67]

Notes

Introduction

1. W. B. Seabrook, *The Magic Island* (New York, 1929), 3, 4.
2. Rayford Logan, *The Diplomatic Relations of the United States with Haiti, 1776–1891* (Chapel Hill, N.C., 1941), 7–26.
3. Sidney Kaplan, *The Black Presence in the Era of the American Revolution, 1770–1800* (New York, 1973), 59.
4. Gordon K. Lewis, *Main Currents in Caribbean Thought* (Baltimore, 1983), 206.
5. Franklin W. Knight, "The American Revolution and the Caribbean," in *Slavery and Freedom in the Age of the American Revolution*, edited by Ira Berlin and Ronald Hoffman (Baltimore, 1983), 243–46.
6. James Oakes, "From Republicanism to Liberalism: Ideological Change and the Crisis of the Old South," *American Quarterly* 37 (Fall 1985):551–71; Sidney Mintz, *Caribbean Transformations* (Baltimore, 1974), 9.
7. David M. Streifford, "The American Colonization Society: An Application of Republican Ideology to Early Antebellum Reform" *Journal of Southern History* 45 (May 1979):209–12.
8. Prince Saunders, *Haytian Papers: A Collection of Very Interesting Proclamations and Other Official Documents* . . . (Boston, 1818), 82–83, 91; Oakes, "From Republicanism to Liberalism," 553; Lynn Avery Hunt, *Politics, Culture, and Class in the French Revolution* (Berkeley, 1984), 20.
9. Beaubrun Ardouin, *Etudes sur l'histoire d'Haïti* (Port-au-Prince, 1924–30), 2:68.
10. Vergniaud Leconte, *Henri Christophe dans l'histoire d'Haïti* (Paris, 1931), 110–28, 134–35.
11. Hunt, *Politics, Culture,* 56, 72.
12. Ardouin, *Etudes,* 1:207; Hunt, *Politics, Culture,* 20, 88; Mona Ozouf, *La fête révolutionnaire* (Paris, 1976), 7–17.
13. Leconte, *Henri Christophe,* 179.
14. Oakes, "From Republicanism to Liberalism," 553–59; C. L. R. James, *The Black Jacobins* (New York, 1938), 27–33.
15. Joyce Appleby, "Republicanism and Ideology," *American Quarterly* 37 (Fall 1985):470.

16. Philip C. Jessup, *Elihu Root* (New York, 1938), 1:555.

1. The Foundations

1. C. L. R. James, *The Black Jacobins* (New York, 1938), 225–40; David Geggus, "Slave Resistance Studies and the Saint Domingue Slave Revolt: Some Preliminary Considerations," Florida International University, Latin American and Caribbean Center, Occasional paper no. 4 (Winter 1983), 13, 15.
2. Roger Norman Buckley, *Slaves in Red Coats: The British West India Regiments, 1795–1815,* (New Haven, Conn., 1979), 9, 49; Beaubrun Ardouin, *Etudes sur l'histoire d'Haïti* (Port-au-Prince, 1924–30), 1:144, 155, 209; David Geggus, *Slavery, War, and Revolution: The British Occupation of Saint-Domingue, 1793–1798* (New York, 1982).
3. Geggus, "Slave Resistance Studies," 22.
4. James, *Black Jacobins*, 143; Buckley, *Slaves in Red Coats*, 86–87.
5. On maroons, see Richard Price, comp., *Maroon Societies: Slave Rebel Communities in the Americas* (Garden City, N.Y., 1973); Jean Fouchard, *The Haitian Maroons* (New York, 1981); Geggus, "Slave Resistance Studies."
6. Richard Price and Sally Price, *Afro-American Arts of the Suriname Rain Forest* (Berkeley, Calif., 1980), 9.
7. Henock Trouillot, "La guerre de l'indépéndance en Haïti," *Revista Historica de las Americas* 72 (1971): part 1, p. 272; vol. 73–74 (1971), part 2, pp. 118, 121.
8. Ibid., part 2, pp. 120–23.
9. Remy Bastien, "Procesos de aculturación en las Antillas," *Revista de Indias* 24, nos. 95–96 (1964):184, 192.
10. Lynn Avery Hunt, *Politics, Culture, and Class in the French Revolution* (Berkeley, 1984), 38–40.
11. Jonathan Brown, *The History and Present Condition of St. Domingo* (Philadelphia, 1837, rep. London, 1971), 204; Alfred Métraux, *Voodoo in Haiti* (New York, 1959), 360.
12. Prince Saunders, *Haytian Papers: A Collection of Very Interesting Proclamations and Other Official Documents . . .* (Boston, 1818), 142; Buckley, *Slaves in Red Coats*; Montilus Guerin, "Africa in Diaspora: The Myth of Dahomey in Haiti," *Journal of Caribbean Studies* 2 (Spring 1981):73–84.
13. Pickering to Mayer, 22 Nov. 1797, United States Department of State, Dis-

patches from U.S. Consuls in Cap-Haïtien (DUSCCH), 1797–1806, micro-copy 9, National Archives Microfilm Publications; Walter LaFeber, *The American Age: United States Foreign Policy at Home and Abroad Since 1750* (New York, 1989), 48, 50–51.

14. Lester D. Langley, *America and the Americas* (Athens, Ga., 1989), 24–25; Alfred N. Hunt, *Haiti's Influence on Antebellum America* (Baton Rouge, 1988), 34–35.
15. Pickering to Mayer, 30 Nov. 1792, DUSCCH.
16. W. E. B. Du Bois, *The Suppression of the African Slave-Trade to the United States of America, 1638–1870* (New York, 1896), 71.
17. Pickering to Mayer, 22 Sept. 1797, DUSCCH; Vergniaud Leconte, *Henri Christophe dans l'histoire d'Haïti* (Paris, 1931), 135; James, *Black Jacobins*, 225–40.
18. Tobias Lear to James Madison, 7 July 1801; 20 July 1801; 7 Aug. 1801, DUSCCH.
19. Pickering to the President of the United States, 5 June 1799; Pickering to Consul-General Edward Stevens, 20 Apr. 1799, DUSCCH; Toussaint Louverture to John Adams, 16 brumaire, An I.
20. Tobias Lear to James Madison, 7 July 1801; 20 July 1801; 4 Aug. 1801, and 7 Aug. 1801, DUSCCH.
21. Lear to Madison, 7 July 1801, DUSCCH.
22. Gordon K. Lewis, *Main Currents in Caribbean Thought* (New York, 1983), 69; LaFeber, *American Age*, 53.
23. David Brion Davis, *The Problem of Slavery in the Age of Revolution, 1770–1823* (Ithaca, N.Y., 1969), 150–51; LaFeber, *American Age*, 52–54.
24. Davis, *Problem of Slavery*, 152.
25. Patrick Bellegarde-Smith, *Haiti: The Breached Citadel* (Boulder, Colo., 1990), 43; Hunt, *Haiti's Influence*, 35–36; LaFeber, *American Age*, 53.
26. Thomas Lawrason to Lear, 10 Jan. 1802; Lear to Madison, 17 Jan. 1802, DUSCCH; Franklin W. Knight, *The Caribbean*, 2d ed. (New York, 1990), 208–9.
27. B. Dandridge to Madison, 3 Mar. 1802, DUSCCH.
28. Lee to Timothy Pickering, 20 Feb. 1799, DUSCCH; Leconte, *Henri Christophe*, 153.
29. James, *Black Jacobins*, 334, 363.
30. Ibid., 337–66.
31. Rayford Logan, *The Diplomatic Relations of the United States with Haiti, 1776–1891* (Chapel Hill, N.C., 1941), 142–45.

32. Brenda Gayle Plummer, *Haiti and the Great Powers* (Baton Rouge, La., 1988), xii–xiv, 40, 66.

33. *Commercial Relations of the United States, Year Ending Sept. 1861* (Washington, D.C., 1862), 382–83; Bellegarde-Smith, *Haiti*, 51–52; William Javier Nelson, "The Haitian Political Situation and Its Effect on the Dominican Republic, 1849–1877," *The Americas* 45 (October 1988):228.

34. Samuel Hazard, *Santo Domingo Past and Present* (New York, 1873), 158–62; Logan, *Diplomatic Relations*, 237–50; Murdo J. MacLeod, "The Soulouque Regime in Haiti, 1847–1859: A Reevaluation," *Caribbean Studies* 10 (October 1970): 39–40; Nelson, "Haitian Political Situation," 28.

35. Hazard, *Santo Domingo*, 170–71.

36. Hubert Cole, *Christophe, King of Haiti* (New York, 1967); Earl Leslie Griggs and Clifford H. Prator, eds., *Henry Christophe and Thomas Clarkson: A Correspondence* (Berkeley, Calif., 1952).

37. *Analectic Magazine* 9 (May 1817):403, 406.

38. William Hutchinson Rowe, "The Maine West India Trade," *American Neptune* 8 (July 1948):165–78; Logan, *Diplomatic Relations*, 195–96; Basil Hall, *Travels in North America, in the Years 1827 and 1828* (Philadelphia, 1829), 2:394–95.

39. A. Armstrong to the Secretary of State, 16 Dec. 1820; William Taylor to the Secretary of State, 9 Jan. 1814, 30 Aug. 1814, DUSCCH. Logan, *Diplomatic Relations*, 195–96; F. M. Dimond to the Secretary of State, 3 May 1837, Dispatches from U.S. Consuls in Port-au-Prince (DUSCPP), microcopy T346, National Archives Microfilm Publications.

40. Bellegarde-Smith, *Haiti*, 45.

41. Drew R. McCoy, "Republicanism and American Foreign Policy: James Madison and the Political Economy of Commercial Discrimination," *William and Mary Quarterly* 31 (October 1974):633–46.

42. Paul Moral, *Le paysan haïtien* (Paris, 1961), 22; Michel-Rolph Trouillot, *Haiti: State Against Nation* (New York, 1990), 76–77.

43. James Oakes, "From Republicanism to Liberalism: Ideological Change and the Crisis of the Old South," *American Quarterly* 37 (Fall 1985):553, 555, 557–58.

44. Ibid., 563, 568–69; Joyce Appleby, "Republicanism and Ideology," *American Quarterly* 37 (Fall 1985):470.

45. David Nicholls, *From Dessalines to Duvalier, Race, Colour, and National Independence in Haiti* (Cambridge, Eng., 1979).

46. Leslie F. Manigat, "The Relationship Between Marronage and Slave Revolts in St. Domingue-Haiti," in *Comparative Perspectives on Slavery in New World Plantation Societies*, edited by Vera Rubin and Arthur Tuden (New York, 1977), 422.

47. Eric Williams, *From Columbus to Castro: The History of the Caribbean, 1492–1969* (London, 1969), 307–8; Griggs and Prator, *Henry Christophe*, 120–21.

48. Merton L. Dillon, *Benjamin Lundy and the Struggle for Negro Freedom* (Urbana, Ill., 1966), 83–84; Griggs and Prator, *Henry Christophe*, 162, 142, 124.

49. J. Catts Pressoir, *Le Protestantisme en Haïti* (Port-au-Prince, 1945), 78, 79.

50. David M. Streifford, "The American Colonization Society: An Application of Republican Ideology to Early Antebellum Reform," *Journal of Southern History* 45 (May 1979):201–20.

51. Saunders, *Haytian Papers*; B. Romain, *Quelques moeurs des paysans haïtiens* (Port-au-Prince, 1969), 32, 33.

52. Berquin-Duvallon, *Vue de la colonie espagnole du Mississippi; ou des provinces de Louisiane et Floride occidentale en l'année 1802* (Paris, 1803), 23–28, 231, 239, 275; Claiborne to James Mather, 9 Aug. 1809, in Dunbar Rowland, ed., *Official Letter Books of W. C. C. Claiborne, 1801–1816*, 6 vols. (Jackson, Miss., 1917), 4:402; *idem* to *idem*, 8 July 1809, 4:388; Mayor's Office, Passenger Lists, 7 Aug. 1809 and 18 July 1809, 4:381–82 and 4:409; Claiborne to Andrew Jackson, 28 Oct. 1814, 6:294, all Rowland, *Official Letter Books*; Harold Shoen, "The Free Negro in the Republic of Texas," part 1, *Southwestern Historical Quarterly* 39 (April 1936):302, 305; Laura Foner, "The Free People of Color in Louisiana and St. Domingue: A Comparative Portrait of Two Three-Caste Societies," *Journal of Social History* 3 (Summer 1970):421 n. 80; *African Repository* 5 (February 1830):381–82.

53. Cyril Griffith, "Martin R. Delany, Emigration Advocate," paper read at the Association for Afro-American Life and History annual meeting, Chicago, 29 Oct. 1976.

54. Griggs and Prator, *Henry Christophe*, 141.

55. *Niles Weekly Register*, 11 Sept. 1824, 30–31, and 18 Dec. 1824, 255; Dillon, *Benjamin Lundy*, 92.

56. Loring Dewey, ed., *Correspondence Relative to the Emigration to Hayti of the Free People of Colour in the United States . . .* (New York, 1824), 8–9, 22–26.

57. Alexander Barclay, *A Practical View of the Present State of Slavery in the West Indies*, 2d ed. (London: 1827), 350; Dillon, *Benjamin Lundy*, 95; *Niles Weekly Register*, 18 Dec. 1824, 245; and 25 June 1825, 263–64.

58. Floyd J. Miller, *The Search for a Black Nationality* (Urbana, Ill., 1975), 79, 81, 82 n.46.
59. Dillon, *Benjamin Lundy*, 100, 142; *African Repository* 5 (April 1829):61–62.
60. James Leyburn, *The Haitian People* (New Haven, Conn., 1941):71–79; Benjamin S. Hunt, *Remarks on Hayti as a Place of Settlement for Afric-Americans, and on the Mulatto as a Race for the Tropics,* cited in Leyburn, *Haitian People,* 315–16; Hazard, *Santo Domingo,* 182, 378, 453; Amos L. Mason, ed., *Memoir and Correspondence of Charles Steedman, Rear Admiral, United States Navy, with His Autobiography and Private Journals, 1811–1890* (Cambridge, Mass., 1912), quoted in Logan, *Diplomatic Relations,* 233–34. See also the letters of Serena Baldwin to E. J. Cox in Abigail Field Mott, comp., *Biographical Sketches and Interesting Anecdotes of Persons of Color* (New York, 1838):331–34.
61. *Niles Weekly Register,* 11 June 1825, 228; Julie Winch, *Philadelphia's Black Elite* (Philadelphia, 1988), 57.
62. Elsie Clews Parsons, "Spirituals from the 'American' Colony of Samana Bay," *Journal of American Folklore* 41 (October–December 1928):55–58; Brookings Institution, *Refugee Settlement in the Dominican Republic* (Washington, D.C., 1942), 105–6; Hans Hoetink, "'Americans' in Samana," *Caribbean Studies* 2 (1962–63):3–22.
63. Leonard I. Sweet, *Black Images of America* (New York, 1976), 136.
64. Samuel Flagg Bemis, *The Latin American Policy of the United States* (New York, 1971), 53–58; Alonso Aguilar, *Pan-Americanism from Monroe to the Present* (New York, 1968), 23–25.
65. Ibid., 25–26.
66. Logan, *Diplomatic Relations,* 204–9.
67. Plummer, *Haiti and the Great Powers,* 21–22.

2. Race and Nation

1. Alfred Hunt, *Haiti's Influence on Antebellum America* (Baton Rouge, La., 1988), 142; Cedric Robinson, *Black Marxism: The Making of the Black Radical Tradition* (London, 1983), 10–13, 122–24.
2. Bertram Wyatt-Brown, *Southern Honor* (New York, 1982), 406.
3. Prince Saunders, *Haytian Papers: A Collection of Very Interesting Proclamations and Other Official Documents . . .* (Boston, 1818); James Theodore Holly,

"Thoughts on Hayti," parts 1–6, *Anglo-African Magazine* 1 (June 1859):185–87; (July 1859):219–21; (August 1859):241–43; (September 1859):298–300; (October 1859):327–29; (November 1859):363–67; Sterling Stuckey, *Slave Culture: Nationalist Theory and the Foundations of Black America* (New York, 1987), 184.

4. *Le Phare*, 2 Sept. 1830; Higinbotham to the Secretary of State, 10 Aug. 1839, Dispatches from U.S. Consuls in Aux Cayes (DUSCAC), microcopy T330, National Archives Microfilm Publications; Eugene D. Genovese, *From Rebellion to Revolution: Afro-American Slave Revolts in the Making of the New World* (Baton Rouge, La., 1979), 49.

5. *L'Union*, 15 Feb. 1838; William Miles to the Secretary of State, 10 Dec. 1835, 25 May 1838; Higinbotham to the Secretary of State, 15 Dec. 1838; 7 Jan. 1839; 4 Feb. 1839; 9 Mar. 1839; Apr., n.d., 1839, DUSCAC; Rayford W. Logan, *The Diplomatic Relations of the United States with Haiti, 1776–1891* (Chapel Hill, N.C., 1941), 188, 190.

6. *Le Phare*, 2 Sept. 1830; Higinbotham to the Secretary of State, 10 Aug. 1839; Gooch to Webster, 12 Aug. 1842; 1 Oct. 1842; 21 Jan. 1842; Thomas Wattson and Sons to the Secretary of State, 24 May 1844, DUSCAC; Logan, *Diplomatic Relations*, 84–85, 231.

7. G. Eustiss Hubbard to the Secretary of State, 15 Apr. 1857, Dispatches from U.S. Consuls in Cap-Haïtien (DUSCCH).

8. Arthur Folsom to the Secretary of State, 23 Oct. 1862; G. Eustiss Hubbard to the Secretary of State, 27 Jan. 1857; 23 July 1859, DUSCCH.

9. United States, Bureau of Foreign and Domestic Commerce, *Commercial Relations of the United States, 1864*, part 2, p. 715; André Georges Adam, *Sylvain Salnave, une crise haïtienne, 1867–1869* (Port-au-Prince, 1982), 86–87, 174–77.

10. G. Eustiss Hubbard to the Secretary of State, 15 Apr. 1857, 22 Jan. 186[?], DUSCCH.

11. A. Armstrong to the Secretary of State, 5 Apr. 1823, DUSCCH; "Shod by Order," *Time*, 2 Feb. 1948, 26; K. Onwuka Dike, *Trade and Politics in the Niger Delta* (Oxford, 1956), 47, 48, 112, 115–16.

12. Jonathan Elliot to the Commander in Chief of the Haitian forces, 7 June 1850; Bulwer to Viscount Palmerston, 2 Mar. 1850, Dispatches from U.S. Consuls in Port-au-Prince (DUSCPP); Hubbard to the Secretary of State, 8 Feb. 1856, 14 Apr. 1856, DUSCCH; Murdo J. MacLeod, "The Soulouque Regime in Haiti, 1847–1859: A Reevaluation," *Caribbean Studies* 10 (October 1970):37, 39–40, 46.

13. Samuel Hazard, *Santo Domingo Past and Present; with a Glance at Hayti* (New York, 1873), 252–61, 263.
14. Joseph Lewis's two 15 July 1861 communications to the Secretary of State mention the indemnity variously as $200,000 and $250,000 in Spanish currency. Lewis to the Secretary of State, 15 July 1861, DUSCPP; Arthur Folsom to the Secretary of State, 21 July 1863, DUSCCH.
15. Seth Webb to the Secretary of State, 7 Apr. 1862, DUSCPP; Arthur Folsom to the Secretary of State, 15 Aug. 1864, DUSCCH.
16. Hazard, *Santo Domingo*, 265.
17. Charles H. Wesley, "Lincoln's Plan for Colonizing the Emancipated Negro," *Journal of Negro History* 4 (January 1919):7–21; George M. Fredrickson, *The Black Image in the White Mind: The Debate on Afro-American Character and Destiny, 1817–1914* (New York, 1971):149–52.
18. Logan, *Diplomatic Relations*, 303.
19. *Congressional Globe*, 37th Cong., 2d sess., part 2, 24 Apr. 1862, p. 1807; 23 Apr. 1862, pp. 1773–76.
20. Ibid., 24 Apr. 1862, p. 1806.
21. Ibid., 4 June 1862, pp. 2501–3, 2505.
22. Ibid., p. 2503.
23. Ibid., p. 2505.
24. Ibid., p. 2500.
25. Ronald T. Takaki, *Iron Cages: Race and Culture in 19th Century America* (Seattle, 1979), 115; Fredrickson, *The Black Image*, 149–52.
26. Fredrickson, *The Black Image*, 149–52; Eric Foner, *Free Soil, Free Labor, Free Men* (New York, 1970), 278–79.
27. Foner, *Free Soil, Free Labor*, 42, 47.
28. Andrew N. Cleven, "Some Plans for Colonizing Liberated Negro Slaves in Hispanic America," *Journal of Negro History* 11 (January 1926):35–49; Warren A. Beck, "Lincoln and Negro Colonization in Central America," *Abraham Lincoln Quarterly* 6 (September 1950):162–83; Robert L. Gold, "Negro Colonization Schemes in Ecuador," *Phylon* 30 (Fall 1969):306–16; Thomas C. Miller to the Secretary of State, 11 Nov. 1861; 20 Jan. 1861, Dispatches from U.S. Consuls in St. Marc (DUSCSM), 1861–1891, microcopy T486, National Archives Microfilm Publications; Willis D. Boyd, "James Redpath and American Colonization in Haiti, 1860–1862," *The Americas* 12 (October 1955); Floyd J. Miller, *The Search for a Black Nationality* (Urbana, Ill., 1975), 236–47; J. B. Romain, *Quelques moeurs des paysans haïtiens* (Port-au-Prince, 1969), 32, 33.

29. Philip D. Curtin, *Two Jamaicas: The Role of Ideas in a Tropical Colony* (New York, 1970), 130; Rodolphe Lucien Desdunes, *Our People and Our History* (Baton Rouge, La., 1973), 112–14.

30. James DeLong to the Secretary of State, 29 May 1866; Delong to Henry Conard, 8 July 1863; 27 July 1863; 23 Sept. 1863; DeLong to Benjamin Whidden, 18 Jan. 1864; Richmond Loring to Whidden, 8 Mar. 1864, DUSCAC; P. J. Staudenraus, *The African Colonization Movement, 1816–1865* (New York, 1961), 247.

31. *Congressional Globe*, 4 June 1862, 2501; Paul J. Scheips, "Lincoln and the Chiriqui Colonization Project," *Journal of Negro History* 37 (October 1952): 433–34, 439, 452.

32. Desdunes, *Our People and Our History*, 109–12; Stuckey, *Slave Culture*, 185.

33. James Theodore Holly, "Thoughts on Haiti," part 8, *The Anglo-African Magazine* 1 (August 1859):241–43; Miller, *Search for a Black Nationality*, 108–9, 232–49, and passim.

34. Loring Dewey, ed., *Correspondence Relative to the Emigration to Hayti of the Free People of Colour in the United States . . .* (New York, 1824), 8, 23n.

35. Whidden to the Secretary of State, 6 June 1863, DUSCSM; *L'Opinion Nationale*, 12 Nov. 1864, 26 Nov. 1864. Robert May, *The Southern Dream of a Caribbean Empire* (Baton Rouge, La., 1973).

3. Trade and Empire

1. Samuel Flagg Bemis, *The Latin American Policy of the United States* (New York, 1971), 128–29; Rayford W. Logan, *The Diplomatic Relations of the United States with Haiti* (Chapel Hill, N.C., 1941), 332.

2. George M. Fredrickson, *The Black Image in the White Mind: The Debate on Afro-American Character and Destiny, 1817–1914* (New York, 1971), 305–7.

3. William F. Powell to William Sherman, 7 May 1898, Dispatches from U.S. Consuls in Port-au-Prince (DUSCPP); A. A. Adee to Powell, 5 Oct. 1903, Foreign Relations, 1903, 378; Vansittart to the Foreign Secretary, 17 Mar. 1904, Great Britain Foreign Office (FO), British Foreign and State Papers, General Correspondence, Hayti, FO 35/181; Ludwell Lee Montague, *Haiti and the United States, 1714–1938* (Durham, N.C., 1940), 163–72.

4. Hollister to the Secretary of State, 7 Sept. 1868, United States Department of State, Dispatches from U.S. Consuls in St. Marc (DUSCSM); Logan, *Diplomatic Relations*, 321–22.

5. Logan, *Diplomatic Relations*, 322–23.
6. Seward to Hollister, 1 Sept. 1868, Diplomatic Instructions of the Department of State, 1801–1906, (Instructions), microcopy 77, National Archives Microfilm Publications.
7. Fish to Bassett, 4 Feb. 1870, 8 Feb. 1871, Instructions.
8. Idem to idem, 13 Oct. 1868, ibid.
9. Eric Williams, *From Columbus to Castro: The History of the Caribbean, 1492–1969* (London, 1970), 281; Sidney Mintz, *Caribbean Transformations* (Baltimore, 1974), 236.
10. *Le Peuple*, 22 Feb. 1879, Kurt Fisher Collection, Schomburg Research Center, New York Public Library; André-E. Sayous, *Étude économique et juridique sur les bourses allemandes de valeurs et de commerce* (Paris and Berlin, 1898), 278.
11. Frédéric Marcelin, *Thémistocle Labasterre* (Paris, 1901), 3–5, 161.
12. Paul Déléage, *Haïti en 1886* (Paris, 1887), 64–67.
13. Benoit Joachim, *Les racines du sous-developpment en Haïti* (Port-au-Prince, 1979), 192.
14. Ibid., 200. Roland H. Ebel, "Governing the City-State: Notes on the Politics of the Small Latin Countries," *Journal of Inter-American Studies and World Affairs* 14 (August 1972):325–46.
15. Sanford to the Secretary of State, 30 Apr. 1862; Gould to the Secretary of State, 14 May 1870, Dispatches from U.S. Consuls in Aux Cayes (DUSCAC); Editorials, *L'Opinion Nationale*, 13 Aug. 1892, 22 Oct. 1892; Stephen Leech to Lord Grey, 13 Jan. 1914, FO 368/1309; Michel S. Laguerre, *Urban Life in the Caribbean* (Cambridge, Mass., 1982), 1–3, 149, 151, 156.
16. G. Eustiss Hubbard to the Secretary of State, 27 Jan. 1857; Stanislas Goutier to Assistant Secretary of State Wharton, 31 Dec. 1892, Dispatches from U.S. Consuls in Cap-Haïtien (DUSCCH); John M. Langston to the Secretary of State, Report for 1879–1880, 3 Dec. 1880, DUSCPP; Margaret Priestly, *West African Trade and Coast Society, a Family Study* (London, 1969), 149.
17. Arthur Folsom to the Secretary of State, 23 Oct. 1862; Goutier to the Secretary of State, 19 Jan. 1871, DUSCCH.
18. *Le Peuple*, 22 Feb. 1879; Sayous, *Étude économique et juridique*, 278, 279–81.
19. W. E. Aughinbaugh, *Selling Latin America* (Boston, 1915), 213–20.
20. Ross J. S. Hoffman, *Great Britain and the German Trade Rivalry* (New York, 1964), 191–92.

21. Pichon to the Ministry of Foreign Affairs, 29 Jan. 1895, Archives of the Ministry of Foreign Relations, Quaid'Orsay, France, correspondence politique et commerciale, nouvelle série, Haïti (QDO), vol. 20; Paul Pensac Gourvitch, *How Germany Does Business* (New York, 1917), 16; Arthur Folsom to the Secretary of State, 23 Oct. 1862; Goutier to the Secretary of State, 10 Jan. 1871, DUSCCH.

22. Tobias Lear to James Madison, 7 July 1801; Hubbard to the Secretary of State, 4 Aug. 1852, DUSCCH; Sanford to the Secretary of State, 31 Mar. 1862, DUSCAC.

23. A. Armstrong to the Secretary of State, 5 Apr. 1823, DUSCCH; Langston's annual report, 1879–1880, 11 Nov. 1880, DUSCPP; Gourvitch, *How Germany Does Business*, 18.

24. Henry Peck to the Secretary of State, 28 Oct. 1865 and 18 Nov. 1865, DUSCSM; André Georges Adam, *Une crise haïtienne, 1867–1869: Sylvain Salnave* (Port-au-Prince, 1982), 115.

25. James T. Holly to the Rt. Rev. B. B. Smith, 19 June 1869; Holly to the Board of Missions, 26th annual report, 20 July 1900, Haiti Papers, Domestic and Foreign Missionary Society Papers, Archives of the Episcopal Church in America, Austin, Texas. James T. Holly, "Christian Missions in Haiti," *Missionary Review of the World* 26 (September 1903):651; J. C. Antoine, *Price-Mars et Haïti* (Washington, D.C., 1981), 20.

26. Adam, *Une crise haïtienne*, 72, 77; Folsom to the Secretary of State, 15 June 1866, DUSCCH.

27. Adam, *Une crise haïtienne*, 114–15; David Nicholls, *From Dessalines to Duvalier, Race, Colour, and National Independence in Haiti* (Cambridge, Eng., 1979), 79, 108–9.

28. Adam, *Une crise haïtienne*, 174–77; Stanislaus Stanislas's report, 3 June 1871, *Commercial Relations of the United States*, 1871, 793, 794.

29. Gideon Hollister to the Secretary of State, 17 May 1868; 11 Aug. 1868; 22 Sept. 1868; Hollister to Spenser St. John, 24 June 1868, DUSCSM; Abraham Crosswell to the Secretary of State, 15 Jan. 1870, 22 Jan. 1870; F. St. Clair's memorandum, 16 Feb. 1871, DUSCCH.

30. Adam, *Une crise haïtienne*, 43.

31. Joseph Lewis to the Secretary of State, 15 July 1861, DUSCPP; Arthur Folsom to the Secretary of State, 21 July and 15 Aug. 1864, DUSCCH.

32. Langston to the Secretary of State, 20 Dec. and 31 Dec. 1897, DUSCSM.

33. Ebeneezer Bassett to the Secretary of State, 9 Sept. 1876, DUSCSM.

34. Langston to the Secretary of State, 17 Jan. 1880; *Le Moniteur*, 10 Jan. 1880.

35. Walter LaFeber, *Inevitable Revolutions* (New York, 1983), 33–34.
36. Logan, *Diplomatic Relations*, 412–14.
37. *Le Matin*, 11 Aug. 1898.

4. Trade and Culture

1. Brenda Gayle Plummer, *Haiti and the Great Powers, 1902–1915* (Baton Rouge, La., 1988), 41–66.
2. A. Armstrong to the Secretary of State, 5 Apr. 1823, Dispatches from U.S. Consuls in Cap-Haïtien (DUSCCH).
3. Philip D. Curtin, *Cross-Cultural Trade in World History* (Cambridge, Eng., 1984), 38; Langston's annual report, 1879–80, 11 Nov. 1880, Dispatches from U.S. Consuls in Port-au-Prince (DUSCPP), 1835–1906, microcopy T346, National Archives Microfilm Publications.
4. Eugène Aubin [Léon E. A. C. Descos], *En Haiti* (Paris, 1910), xxi; Eugène Lomier, *A travers les mers* (Saint-Valéry-sur-Somme, France, 1930), 58, 78, 83, 84, and passim; Robert K. Lacerte, "Xenophobia and Economic Decline: The Haitian Case, 1820–1843," *The Americas* 38 (1981):511.
5. James Weldon Johnson, *Along This Way* (New York, 1933), 262; David Nicholls, "No Hawkers and Pedlars: Arabs of the Antilles," in David Nicholls, *Haiti in Caribbean Context: Ethnicity, Economy, and Revolt* (Oxford, 1985), 135–64; Plummer, *Haiti and the Great Powers*, 41–66.
6. David Nicholls, *From Dessalines to Duvalier: Race, Colour, and National Independence in Haiti* (Cambridge, Eng., 1979), 7–8; Micheline Labelle, *Idéologie de couleur et classes sociales en Haïti* (Montréal, 1978).
7. Frédéric Marcelin, *Bric-à-brac* (Paris, 1910), 53–56; Russell to the Secretary of State, 13 Feb. 1928, DF 838.00/2442; David Nicholls, "Idéologies et mouvements politiques en Haïti 1915–1946," *Annales, Economies, Sociétés, Civilisations* 30 (4:1975), 656–57.
8. Lacerte, "Xenophobia," 509. Early twentieth-century examples of such laws appear in *Le Moniteur*, 25 Aug. 1900; Hannibal Price, *Dictionnaire de législation administrative haïtienne* (Port-au-Prince, 1923), 505–6.
9. Celso Furtado, *Economic Development in Latin America* (Cambridge, Eng., 1976), 43; Paul Moral, *Le paysan haïtien* (Paris, 1961), 270–71; Alexandre Battiste to John Hay, 10 Nov. 1903, Consular Dispatches (CD).
10. David Nicholls, *Economic Dependence and Political Autonomy, the Haitian Ex-*

perience (Montreal, 1974), 18–25. On diminishing Haitian entrepreneurial capability, see Dana G. Munro, *Intervention and Dollar Diplomacy in the Caribbean, 1900–1921* (Princeton, 1964), 246–47; Leslie F. Manigat, "La Substitution de la préponderance américaine à la préponderance française en Haïti au début du xxe siècle: la conjoncture de 1910–1911," *Revue d'histoire moderne et contemporaine* 14 (Oct.–Dec. 1967), 326–27, 329; Frédéric Marcelin, *Au gré du souvenir* (Paris, 1913), 20, 21, 107–8.

11. Léonce Bernard, *Antoine Sansaricq, l'homme, sa vie, ses idées* (Port-au-Prince, n.d.), 8; Joseph Jérémie, *Mémoires,* (Port-au-Prince, 1950), 1:95–96; J. Geffrard, "Ce que j'ai entendu et vecu," n.d., MS in the Louis McCarty Little Papers, United States Marine Corps Museum, Washington, D.C.; *Livre bleu d'Haïti/Blue Book of Haiti* (New York, 1920), 75, 201.

12. Oliver Wardrop to the Foreign Secretary, 8 Apr. 1903, FO 35/179; Bellegarde to A. N. Léger, 12 June 1932, Eugène Maximilien Collection, Schomburg Research Center, NYPL; Powell to Hay, 17 May 1902, enclosure no. 1, CD; James P. MacDonald to R. W. Austin, 8 July 1912, DF, 838.6156M14/1; Furniss to Root, 13 October 1908, NF 2126/308; Dantès Bellegarde, *Ecrivains haïtiens* (Port-au-Prince, 1947), 146–48; Waller to Lejeune, 20 Aug. 1917, John A. Lejeune Papers, Library of Congress.

13. Stanislaus Goutier to George L. Rives, 12 Mar. 1890, M9; John Russell, "A Marine Looks Back on Haiti," 64–65, MS in John H. Russell papers, U.S. Marine Corps Museum, Washington, D.C.; Sténio Vincent, *En posant les jalons* (Port-au-Prince, 1939), 1:341–51.

14. Paul Deléage, *Haïti en 1886* (Paris, 1887), 56–57; Powell to Hay, 15 Aug. 1902, CD; Brigade Commander to the Military Governor of Santo Domingo, 17 May 1917, DF 838.00/1458; Léon Audain, *Le mal d'Haïti, ses causes et son traitement* (Port-au-Prince, 1908), 106 n. 1; Stephen Leech to Lord Grey, 13 Jan. 1914, Great Britain Foreign Office (FO) 368/1309; Maurice de Young, "Class Parameters in Haitian Society," *Journal of Inter-American Studies* 1 (October 1959):453; B. Danache, *Le Président Dartiguenave et les Américains* (Port-au-Prince 1950), 154; John M. Street, *Historical and Economic Geography of the Southwest Peninsula of Haiti* (Berkeley, Calif., 1960), 427–28, 429, 464. Michel S. Laguerre, *Urban Life in the Caribbean* (Cambridge, Mass., 1982), 1, 2–3, 145–47.

15. Plummer, *Haiti and the Great Powers*, xii–xiv.

16. Elizabeth Fox-Genovese and Eugene Genovese, *The Fruits of Merchant Capital* (New York, 1983), 5–8.

17. Jules Auguste, *Quelques verités à propos des recents événements de la République d'Haïti* (Paris, 1891), 34, 37; Eugène [Léon E. A. C. Descos], *En Haïti* (Paris, 1910), xxv.

18. Vice-President of the United Steamship Co. to the Bureau of Manufactures, 21 Apr. 1911, DF, 838.802/10; *Proceedings of the Pan-American Commerce Conference*, 13–17 Feb. 1911, (Washington, D.C., 1911), 78; Lamar Cecil, *Albert Ballin: Business and Politics in Imperial Germany* (Princeton, 1967), 58; Benoit Joachim, *Les racines du sous-développement en Haïti* (Port-au-Prince, 1979), 188–92; Brenda Gayle Plummer, "The Syrians in Haiti," *International History Review* (October 1981):517–39.

19. Nicholls, *From Dessalines to Duvalier*; Speech by President Hyppolite, 5 May 1890, in Stanislas Goutier to William Wharton, 17 May 1890; Frédéric Marcelin, *Le Général Nord-Alexis* (Paris, 1909), 1:30; Furniss to the Secretary of State, 25 May 1912, DF, 838.00/688; Vincent, *En posant les jalons*, 1:154–56.

20. Kenneth King, *Pan-Africanism and Education* (Oxford, 1971).

21. Gordon K. Lewis, *Main Currents of Caribbean Thought* (Baltimore, 1983), 261–64; Nicholls, *From Dessalines to Duvalier*, 66–107; Plummer, *Haiti and the Great Powers*, 26–32.

22. Roland H. Ebel, "Governing the City-State: Notes on the Politics of the Small Latin Countries," *Journal of Inter-American Studies and World Affairs* 14 (August 1972):325–46; Laguerre, *Urban Life in the Caribbean*, 148, 156.

23. Demesvar Delorme, *Reflexions Diverses sur Haïti* (Paris, 1873), 6–12, 31, 48, 49.

24. Ibid., 82–84, 103–4, 107.

25. Edmond Paul, *Les causes de nos malheurs* (Kingston, Jamaica, 1882).

26. Anténor Firmin, *Lettres de Saint Thomas* (Paris, 1910), 39–86.

27. Audain, *Le mal d'Haïti*.

28. Anténor Firmin, *De l'égalité des races humaines* (Paris, 1885); Hannibal Price, *La rehabilitation de la race noire* (Port-au-Prince, 1900).

29. Alcius Charmant, *Haïti, vivra-t-elle?* (Le Havre, 1905).

30. Audain, *Le mal d'Haïti*, 45–48, 62–63, 78, 119–20.

31. Charmant, *Haïti, vivra-t-elle?* 4; Audain, *Le mal d'Haïti*, 29–43.

32. Marcelin, *Au gré du souvenir*, 197–98.

33. Anténor Firmin, *M. Roosevelt, Président des Etats-Unis et la République d'Haïti* (New York, 1905), 493, 477.

34. Firmin, *Lettres de Saint Thomas*, v, viii, 109–30, 131, 164–68, 172.

35. *New York Times*, 22 June 1908, 3:1; Pierre Carteron to the Minister of

Foreign Affairs, 25 Aug. 1908, Archives of the Ministry of Foreign Relations, Quai d'Orsay, France, correspondance politique et commerciale,
nouvelle série, Haïti (QDO), vol. 14; Furcy-Chatelain, *Résumé des considerations sur la politique extérieure d'Haïti à propos du 15 janvier, 1908* (Fort-
de-France, Martinique, 1908), 9–10; Rodolph Charmant, *La vie incroyable
d'Alcius* (Port-au-Prince, 1946), 250; B. Danache, *Chose vues: Récits et souve-
nirs* (Port-au-Prince, 1939), 145–46; Thomas Tondée Orum, "The Politics
of Color: The Racial Dimension of Cuban Politics During the Early Republican Years, 1900–1912" (Ph.D. diss., New York University, 1975), 207.
36. New York *Herald*, 12 June 1908, 9:7; see also *Daily Gleaner*, 21 May 1903.
37. James Bryce to Lord Grey, 28 Mar. 1908; Grey to Sénèque Viard, 6 May
    1908, FO 371/468.
38. Orum, "Politics of Color," 207. See also Armando Fernández Soriano, "El
    exilio cubano del expresidente de Haití Rosalvo Bobo," *Cimarron* 2 (Winter
    1990):20–27.
39. Danache, *Choses vues*, 25, 145–47; Charmant, *La vie incroyable*, 219, 249–
    50; Arthur Holly to James Weldon Johnson, 10 Dec. 1920, James Weldon
    Johnson Papers, Sterling Library, Yale University.
40. Murray to the Secretary of State for Foreign Affairs, 27 Oct. 1910, FO 371/
    915.
41. Rayford Logan has treated this subject extensively in *The Diplomatic Rela-
    tions of the United States with Haiti, 1776–1891* (Chapel Hill, N.C., 1941). See
    also, J. N. Leger, *La politique extérieure d'Haïti* (Paris, 1886), 31–32; Deléage,
    Haïti en 1886, 143; Alexandre Poujol, "De la nationalité dans la République
    d'Haïti," *Revue Générale de Droit International Public* (1902):16; Joachim, *Les
    racines du sous-developpement*, 176.
42. Herbert Feis, *Europe, the World's Banker* (New Haven, Conn., 1930), 468–
    69; Jores to the Minister of Foreign Affairs, 12 Nov. 1909; Jores to Murat
    Claude, 9 Nov. 1909, QDO, vol. 22; *New York Times*, 11 Mar. 1910, 4; 7 June
    1912, 8; 13 Apr. 1905, 11; 13 Nov. 1905, 1. See also the obituary of Ernest
    Thalmann, *New York Times*, 27 Feb. 1912, 9.
43. Plummer, *Haiti and the Great Powers*, 71–73.
44. E.g., Sydney Brooks, "The Passing of the Black Republics," *Harper's Weekly*
    52 (16 May 1908):20.

5. The End of an Era

1. Louis Henkin, *Foreign Affairs and the Constitution* (New York, 1972), 268, 330.
2. Dexter Perkins, *The Monroe Doctrine* (Boston, 1955), 240.
3. Ibid., 239–40, 230.
4. Ronald T. Takaki, *Iron Cages: Race and Culture in 19th Century America* (Seattle, 1979), 267–69.
5. Lester Langley, *America and the Americas* (Athens, Ga., 1989), 110.
6. Benoit Joachim, *Les racines du sous-developpement en Haïti* (Port-au-Prince, 1979), 181–87; H. P. Davis' memorandum, n.d., State Department Decimal File (DF), 838.616/175; Louis Gation, *Aspects de l'économie et des finances d'Haïti* (Port-au-Prince, 1944), 191.
7. Samuel McRoberts to Frank A. Vanderlip, 8 Mar. 1910; "Suggestions as to Organization and Scope of Foreign Service," memorandum, n.d., Organizations File, Frank A. Vanderlip Papers, Columbia University; *New York Times*, 19 Oct. 1904, 1.
8. Pierre Carteron to the Minister of Foreign Affairs, 22 Dec. 1908, Archives of the Ministry of Foreign Relations, Quai d'Orsay, France, correspondence politique et commerciale, nouvelle série, Haïti (QDO), vol. 14; Samuel McRoberts to Vanderlip, 9 Apr. 1910, Vanderlip Papers.
9. Furniss to the Secretary of State, 30 July 1910, DF, 874/78; 27 Aug. 1910, 838.51/93; 2 Sept. 1910, 838.51/97; 8 Oct. 1910, 838.51/123; Hoyt to J. R. C, Solicitor's Office, n.d., 838.51/119; memorandum of the Division of Latin American Affairs, n.d., 838.51; State Department to the American legation, 24 Sept. 1910, 838.51; Huntington Wilson's memorandum, 6 Jan. 1911, DF 838.51; Raymond Poidevin and Jacques Bariety, *Les relations franco-allemandes, 1815–1975* (Paris, 1977), 584.
10. Murray to the Secretary of State for Foreign Affairs, 1 Oct. 1910, Great Britain Foreign Office (FO) 371/914; idem to idem, 15 Sept. 1910, 27 Oct. 1910, FO 371/915; Innes to Edward Grey, 28 Nov. 1910, FO 371/915.
11. Paul Cambon to Arthur Nicolson, 8 Dec. 1910, FO 371/915; McRoberts and Milton Ailes to the Secretary of State, 10 Jan. 1911; McRoberts to Ailes et al., 11 Jan. 1911, FO 371/1131; Chatelain, Joseph, *La Banque Nationale, son histoire, ses problèmes* (Port-au-Prince, 1954), 81–82.
12. Lemuel Livingston to the Assistant Secretary of State, 10 Mar. 1910, Records of the Department of State Relating to Political Relations Between the United States and Haiti, 1910–29, (M611) microcopy 611, National

Archives Microfilm Publications, 711.38/9; idem to idem, 15 May 1912, 711.38/14, M 611. Furniss to the Secretary of State, 19 Nov. 1910, DF, 838.77/21; MacDonald to Rep. R. W. Austin, 21 Jan. 1911, Department of State Relating to Political Relations Haiti and Other States, 1910–29, (M612) microcopy 612, National Archives Microfilm Publications, 738.3915/59.

13. Walter LaFeber, *Inevitable Revolutions*, 2d ed. (New York, 1983), 49–54.
14. Arthur S. Link, *Wilson: The Struggle for Neutrality* (Princeton, N.J., 1960), 497–98; Arthur S. Link, *Wilson: The New Freedom* (Princeton, N.J., 1956), 304–14; Richard D. Challener, *Admirals, Generals, and American Foreign Policy, 1888–1914* (Princeton, N.J., 1973), 399–400.
15. Arthur S. Link, ed., *The Papers of Woodrow Wilson* (Princeton, N.J., 1979), 28:50, 451.
16. Link, *Wilson: New Freedom*, 350.
17. Hans Schmidt, *The United States Occupation of Haiti, 1915–1934* (New Brunswick, 1971), 50; Lamar Cecil, *Albert Ballin: Business and Politics in Imperial Germany* (Princeton, N.J., 1967), 152–53; Holger H. Herwig, *The Politics of Frustration: The United States in German Naval Planning, 1889–1941* (Boston, 1976), 67–92, 72–76.
18. Brenda Gayle Plummer, *Haiti and the Great Powers* (Baton Rouge, La., 1988), 194–95.
19. Murray to the Secretary of State for Foreign Affairs, 1 Jan. 1910, FO 371/914; Roger Gaillard, *Charlemagne Péralte* (Port-au-Prince, 1982):64n.
20. Edward W. Said, *Orientalism* (New York, 1978), passim.
21. Michael Dash, *Haiti and the United States: National Stereotypes and the Literary Imagination* (New York, 1988), 101–4.
22. Gérard Pierre-Charles, *L'économie haïtienne et sa voie de développement* (Paris, 1967), 45; Patrick Bellegarde-Smith, *Haiti: The Breached Citadel* (Boulder, Colo., 1990), 71–72.
23. Robert B. Davis to the Secretary of State, telegrams, 9 a.m. and noon, 27 July 1915, *Foreign Relations of the United States, 1915*, 474; Roger Gaillard, *Les cent-jours de Rosalvo Bobo* (Port-au-Prince, 1973), 83–87; testimony of William B. Caperton, U.S. Senate, Inquiry into the Occupation and Administration of Haiti and Santo Domingo, *Hearings Before a Select Committee on Haiti and Santo Domingo*, vol. 1, 67th Cong., 2d sess. (Washington, D.C., 1922).
24. Gaillard, *Les cent-jours*, 87–89; Davis to the Secretary of State, telegram, 6 p.m., 27 July 1915, *Foreign Relations, 1915*, 474–75.

25. Wilson to the Secretary of the Navy, 31 July 1915, Josephus Daniels Papers, Library of Congress; Division of Latin American Affairs memorandum, 29 July 1915, DF, 838.00/1352; Wilson to Bryan, 4 Aug. 1915, DF, 838.00/1418.

26. Counselor of the Department of State to the Secretary of State, 16 June 1914, United States, Department of State, *Personal and Confidential Letters from Secretary of State Lansing to President Wilson, 1915–1918*, microcopy M743, National Archives Microfilm Publications (hereafter referred to as *Lansing Papers*), 460–64.

27. Lansing to Wilson, 24 Nov. 1915, *Lansing Papers*.

28. Lansing to Wilson, 21 June 1915, *Lansing Papers*.

29. Philip N. Pierce and Frank O. Hough, *The Compact History of the United States Marine Corps* (New York, 1964), 153, 157, 172.

30. Caperton to the Secretary of the Navy, 2 Aug. 1915, DF, 838.00/1236; idem to idem, 17 Aug. 1915, 838.00/1255 and 838.00/1256; Livingston to the Secretary of State, 2 Aug. 1915, DF, 838.00/1240; Special Inspector John P. Holleson to the General Receiver of Santo Domingo, in Chargé ad interim Stewart Johnson to the Secretary of State, 25 Sept. 1915, DF, 838.00/1349. Benson to Caperton, 15 Aug. 1915, William B. Caperton Papers, Library of Congress.

31. David Healy, *Gunboat Diplomacy in the Wilson Era, the U.S. Navy in Haiti, 1915–1916* (Madison, Wis., 1976), 160, 167.

32. Outerhout to Waller, 12 Nov. 1915; and Upshur to Captain Durrell and Captain Cole, 12 Nov. 1915, Naval Records Collection, National Archives.

33. Caperton to the Secretary of the Navy, 19 Nov. 1915, DF, 838.00.

34. Daniels to Caperton, 20 Nov. 1915; Caperton to Daniels, same date, and 22 Nov. 1915, DF, 838.00.

35. B. Danache, *Le Président Dartiguenave et les Américains* (Port-au-Prince, 1950), 13; Moorfield Story to Charles Evans Hughes, 6 June 1921, DF 838.00/1780.

36. Faustin Wirkus and Taney Dudley, *The White King of La Gonâve* (New York, 1931), 29, 30, 50.

37. Caperton to the Secretary of the Navy, 17 Mar. 1916, DF, 838.00.

38. Schmidt, *United States Occupation*, 80–81, 86–89; Frank Friedel, *Franklin D. Roosevelt, the Apprenticeship* (Boston, 1952), 279.

39. Alexander Williams, Chef de Gendarmerie, to the American Minister, 9 Nov. 1918, DF, 838.154/4; Senate, *Hearings Before a Select Committee*, 448, 449.

40. Stabler and Mayer to the Division of Latin American Affairs, n.d., DF, 838.00/1620.

41. For example, A. Bruce Bielaski to Boaz Long, 16 Oct. 1915, DF, 711.38/73; Long to Wright, 23 Nov. 1915, DF, 838.51/576.

42. W. E. Aughinbaugh, *Selling Latin America* (Boston, 1915).

43. Frank A. Vanderlip to James Stillman, 2 Feb. 1915; 14 May 1915, 14 June 1915. Vanderlip to Stephen H. Voorhees, 19 June 1915, Vanderlip Papers.

44. Huntington Wilson, "The Relation of Government to Foreign Investment," *Annals of the American Academy of Social and Political Science* 68 (1916):298–311.

45. Ibid., 301.

46. Ibid., 302.

47. Col. Waller to Gen. Lejeune, 3 Apr. 1916, Josephus Daniels Papers; *Hearings Before a Select Committee*; Frederick M. Wise, *A Marine Tells It to You* (New York, 1929), 134; J. W. DuB. Gould, *General Report on Haiti*, 20 Apr. 1916, with Mallet Prevost to J. Butler Wright, 2 June 1916, DF, 838.00/1400; Caperton to the Secretary of the Navy, Report of 31 Oct.–6 Nov. 1915, DF, 838.00/1369; Lélio Laville, *La traite des Nègres au XXe siècle ou les dessous de l'emigration haïtienne à Cuba* (Port-au-Prince, 1933), 4, 5.

48. Woodrow Wilson to Lansing, 16 Dec. 1815, DF, 838.51/1449.

49. Schmidt, *United States Occupation*, 95, 96; Russell to the Secretary of State, 21 Jan. 1929, DF, 838.52/Germans/2; testimony of Carl Kelsey, *Hearings Before a Select Committee*, 2:1256.

50. *New York Evening World*, 27 Feb. 1920; Huttlinger to Tumulty, 7 Feb. 1920, DF, 838.00/1620; Russell, Daily Diary Report, 31 Jan. 1920, and 6 Feb. 1920, DF, 838.00/1571; Farnham's testimony and the Kelsey report in Senate, *Hearings Before a Select Committee*; Tower's Memorandum on the New Business License Law, 22 July 1925, DF, 838.11/221.

51. Ruan to the Secretary of State, 11 Dec. 1916; Ruan to Grief, 11 Dec. 1916, DF, 838.61351H33/2; Stewart's memorandum, 21 Nov. 1917, DF, 838.61351H33/7; Carr to the Auditor, et al., 18 Jan. 1918, DF 125.27382/11; Hengstler to Stabler, 2 Feb. 1918; Bureau of Citizenship to Hengstler, 23 Jan. 1919, DF, 125.27382/10a.

52. *New York Times*, 29 June 1916, 19:4; Pilkington's testimony, *Hearings Before a Select Committee*; Russell, Daily Diary Report, 1 June 1920, DF, 838.00/1645.

6. Under the Gun

1. Hans Schmidt, *The United States Occupation of Haiti, 1915–1934* (New Brunswick, N.J., 1971), 72–75.
2. Ibid., 97.
3. Admiral H. S. Knapp to the Secretary of the Navy, 2 Oct. 1920, State Department Decimal File (DF), 838.00/1704; Schmidt, *United States Occupation*, 101–7; Burke E. Davis, *Marine! The Life of Lt. Gen. Lewis B. (Chesty) Puller, USMC, (Ret.)* (Boston, 1962), 41, 45; Georges Sylvain to James Weldon Johnson, 26 Nov. 1920, James Weldon Johnson Papers, Sterling Library, Yale University; J. Price-Mars to Walter White, 28 Mar. 1934, NAACP Papers, Library of Congress.
4. Gen. Catlin to the Maj. Gen. Commandant, 16 Mar. 1919, DF, 838.00/1572; Charles Moravia to the Secretary of State, 5 Apr. 1919, DF, 838.00/1578; C. Benoit to the Haitian Foreign Office, 9 Oct. 1919, in Russell to the American Minister, 20 Oct. 1919, DF, 838.00/1611; Russell to the Secretary of the Navy, 16 Jan. 1920, DF, 838.00/1612; Russell to Adm. T. Snowden, 10 Mar. 1920, DF, 838.00/1626.
5. Frederick M. Wise and Meigs O. Frost, *A Marine Tells It to You* (New York, 1919), 314, 315; Yvan M. Désinor, *Tragédies américaines* (Port-au-Prince, 1962), 132–33.
6. Suzy Castor, *La ocupación norteamericana de Haití y sus consecuencias (1915–1934)* (Mexico City, 1971), 120–23.
7. Davis, *Marine!* 27; Alex S. Williams to Maj. Butler, 14 June 1916, Smedley Darlington Butler Papers, USMC Historical Museum, Washington, D.C.
8. Harry A. Franck, *Roaming Through the West Indies* (New York, 1920), 149.
9. Alex S. Williams to Maj. Butler, 14 June 1916; Butler to Gen. Lejeune, 23 June 1917, Butler Papers; *History of the Police Department of Port-au-Prince*, 15 May 1934, Haiti Collection, USMC Historical Museum, Washington, D.C.
10. Constantin Vieux to Littleton W. T. Waller, 10 June 1916, Kurt Fisher Collection, Schomburg Research Center, New York Public Library; Damon Woods, "Political Report for July and Aug. 1923," 1 Sept. 1923, DF, 838.00/1965; Winthrop R. Scott to the State Department, 4 Dec. 1924, DF, 838.00/2060.
11. Russell, Daily Diary Report, 1 Apr. 1920, DF 838.00/1634. See Roger Gaillard, *Hinche Mise en Croix* (Port-au-Prince, n.d.).

12. Schmidt, *United States Occupation*, 121–23.
13. Russell, Daily Diary Report, 20 June 1920, DF, 838.00/1647; Russell to Snowden, 10 Mar. 1920, DF, 838.00/1626; testimony of Richard E. Forrest in Senate, *Inquiry*.
14. Bryan to Wilson, 7 Aug. 1915, *Lansing Papers*.
15. Robert Neal Seidel, "Progressive Pan Americanism: Development and United States Policy Toward South America, 1906–1931" (Ph.D. diss., Cornell University, 1973), 11–13.
16. Ulysses B. Weatherly, "Haiti: An Experiment in Pragmatism," *American Journal of Sociology* 32 (November 1926):363.
17. Waller to Lejeune, 11 June 1916; 13 Oct. 1915, John A. Lejeune Papers, Library of Congress.
18. Boaz Long's memorandum, 23 Nov. 1915, DF, 838.42/4; Jordan Stabler's memorandum, 11 Oct. 1918; Carter G. Woodson, *The Negro in Our History* (Washington, D.C., 1922).
19. Domenick Scarpa's report to J. Butler Wright, July 1916, 2–4, DF, 838.00/1404.
20. Ibid., 4–5, 6.
21. Ibid., 7; Louis Gation, *Aspects de 'economie et des finances d'Haïti* (Port-au-Prince, 1944), 7L.
22. Scarpa report, 7, 8.
23. Dunn to the Secretary of State, 1 Sept. 1923, DF, 838.00/1964; W. W. Cumberland in the *Herald Tribune*, 22 Dec. 1929; Millspaugh, 144; undated clipping in NAACP Papers, Library of Congress.
24. Russell to the Secretary of State, 21 Jan. 1929, DF, 838.52/Germans/2.
25. Blanchard to the Secretary of State, 15 Mar. 1921, DF, 838.516/166; Russell, Daily Diary Report, 24 Jan. 1921, DF, 838.00/1748; Hughes to the Secretary of the Treasury, 11 May 1921, DF, 838.516/167. Mayer to the Secretary of State, 11 Aug. 1917, DF, 838.00/1476; Scott to Munro, 12 July 1929, DF, 838.77/374; Grummon to the Secretary of State, 9 Oct. 1929, with enclosure. Mayer's memorandum, 28 Oct. 1918, DF, 838.61333/2. Dunn to the Secretary of State, 1 Sept. 1923, DF, 838.00/1964; *Herald Tribune*, 22 Dec. 1929, undated clipping, NAACP Papers, Millspaugh, 144.
26. Robert Dudley Longyear, "Haitian Coffee: Its Cultivation and Preparation for Shipment," 9 Sept. 1922, DF, 838.61333/40.
27. Munro to White, 9 Apr. 1923, DF, 838.61/26; author's interview with Dana G. Munro, 27 Apr. 1979.

28. Ferdinand Mayer, "United West Indies Company's Plans Regarding Haiti," 12 July 1918, DF, 838.52/12; Franck, *Roaming Through the West Indies*, 153.

29. *Blue Book of Haiti/Livre bleu d'Haïti* (New York, 1920), 205; Senate, *Hearings*, 1354, 1373.

30. Russell to the Secretary of State, 21 Jan. 1929, DF, 838.52/Germans; idem to idem, 28 Oct. 1927, DF, 838.504/5.

31. Winthrop Scott to the Secretary of State, 25 Mar. 1924, DF, 838.6159/ 21; Mayer to the Division of Latin American Affairs, 9 Jan. 1919, DF, 838.61351/7; Josephus Daniels to the Secretary of State, 17 Jan. 1919, DF, 838.61351/8; Clarence K. Streit, "Haiti: Intervention in Operation," *Foreign Affairs* 6 (July 1928):615–32; John McIlhenny's testimony, Senate, *Hearings*; H. P. Davis to Charles E. Hughes, "The Economic Problems of the American Intervention," 16 July 1923, DF, 838.00/1952; Frank B. Kellogg to Sen. Shipstead, 24 Aug. 1927, DF, 838.00/2313; *The Artibonite Irrigation Project*, DF, 838.6113/52.

32. Scott to the Secretary of State, 4 Dec. 1924, DF, 838.00/2060; Gross to the Secretary of State, 8 Aug. 1928, DF, 838.512/30.

33. Candelon Rigaud, *Promenades dans les campagnes d'Haïti, 1787–1928* (Paris, 1928), 127, 105–6, 124, 73, 75.

34. Coolidge to Kellogg, 3 May 1927, Calvin Coolidge Papers; Russell to the Secretary of State, 5 May 1928, DF, 838.52/55.

35. Paul Moral, *Le paysan haïtien* (Paris, 1961), 64–65.

36. *New York Times*, 8 Apr. 1929, 3:1, 7; Russell to the Secretary of State, 18 Jan. 1928, DF, 838.00/2437.

37. Munro to the Solicitor, 3 June 1929, DF, 838.52/91; Arthur F. Millspaugh, *Haiti Under American Control* (Boston, 1931), 152, 153; Munro interview; Perceval Thoby, *Déposessions* (Port-au-Prince, 1930), 11, 18, 19.

38. Thoby, *Déposessions*, 21–23.

39. W. W. Cumberland Memoir, Oral History Collection, Columbia University.

40. State Department to Russell, 16 Nov. 1926, DF, 838.61326/6; Cumberland to Russell, 18 Nov. 1926, DF, 838.61326/9; Merritt to Carr, 27 Jan. 1927, DF, 838.61326/10; memorandum from the Financial Adviser-General Receiver to Staff, 31 Dec. 1927, DF, 838.51a/8.

41. Charles Evans Hughes to the Secretary of the Treasury, 11 May 1921, 838.516/167; Shepherd to Simon, 2 Feb. 1933 and enclosure, Great Britain Foreign Office (FO) 371/16579.

42. Hughes to the Secretary of the Treasury, 11 May 1921; Dana G. Munro, *Intervention and Dollar Diplomacy in the Caribbean* (Princeton, N.J., 1964), 382. Special Report (NAACP) Notes, Haiti, Johnson Papers.

43. State Department to Haimhauser, 21 July 1924; State Department to the French Ambassador, DF, 838.51. French Legation file, Gendarmerie d'Haïti, United States Marine Corps Records, Record Group (RG), 127, National Archives, Washington, D.C.

44. Seidel, "Progressive Pan Americanism," 47–48.

45. Included in the extensive files of the Gendarmerie is a dossier on aliens thought especially dangerous. Gendarmerie Records, RG 127, National Archives.

46. "The Effects of War on Our Latin-American Relations," typescript, 21 Nov. 1914, 3, Francis Mairs Huntington-Wilson Papers, Ursinus College, Collegeville, Pa.

47. Elliott to the Secretary of State, 22 July 1920, DF, 838.153C73/20 and 16 Sept. 1920, DF, 838.153C73/22. McIntyre to Schoenrich, 19 Jan. 1921; Elliott to the Secretary of State, 16 Sept. 1920, McIntyre to the General Receiver, 16 Nov. 1920, in Bureau of Insular Affairs memorandum, Records of the Bureau of Insular Affairs, RG 350, National Archives. *New York Tribune*, 16 Jan. 1921; *Blue Book of Haiti*, 228.

48. *Blue Book of Haiti*, passim.

49. Ibid.

50. Seidel, "Progressive Pan Americanism," 515.

51. Bryce Wood, *The Making of the Good Neighbor Policy* (New York, 1961), 123–35; Samuel Flagg Bemis, *The Latin American Policy of the United States* (New York, 1971), 221–23.

52. Bellegarde to Walter White, 28 June 1931; White to Ernest Gruening, 28 Oct. 1931, NAACP Papers.

53. Dana Munro, "Recent Events in Haiti," in Munro to Sen. Tasker Oddie, 9 Dec. 1929, DF, 9838.00/2639A.

54. Ludwell Lee Montague, *Haiti and the United States, 1714–1938* (Durham, N.C., 1940), 269, 269 n. 20.

55. Dana Munro, "Recent Events in Haiti;" Russell to the Secretary of State, 12 Dec. 1929, DF, 838.911/10.

56. Raymond Wolters, *The New Negro on Campus: Black College Rebellions of the 1920s* (Princeton, N.J., 1975); Kenneth James King, *Pan-Africanism and Education* (Oxford, 1971); Brenda Gayle Plummer, "The Afro-American Re-

sponse to the Occupation of Haiti, 1915–1934," *Phylon* 43 (June 1982):125–43.

57. *Amsterdam News*, 11 Dec. 1929, 20; *The Crisis* 37 (August 1930):275; (April 1930):127; Schmidt, *United States Occupation*, 185; Plummer, "Afro-American Response," 141.
58. The Journal of Cameron Forbes, Library of Congress.
59. Ibid.; Forbes to William Allen White, 4 June 1930; Forbes to Elie Vezina, 19 May 1930; Forbes to White, 15 Apr. 1930, Journal.
60. Wood, *Making of the Good Neighbor Policy*, 392 n. 32.
61. Munro, *Intervention and Dollar Diplomacy*, 337–39; Smith to Little, 26 Sept. 1932, Louis McCarty Little Papers, USMC Historical Museum, Washington, D.C.

7. *Le Vogue Nègre*

1. Booker T. Washington, "Haiti and the United States," *Outlook* 111 (17 Nov. 1915):681; Washington to John S. Durham, 10 Apr. 1905; Richard W. Thompson to Emmett Jay Scott, 2 Dec. 1905, in Louis Harlan and Raymond W. Smock, eds., *The Booker T. Washington Papers*, vol. 8 (Urbana, Ill., 1979); Brenda Gayle Plummer, "The Afro-American Response to the Occupation of Haiti," *Phylon* 43 (June 1982):125–28.
2. Plummer, "The Afro-American Response," 125.
3. W. F. Elkins, "Marcus Garvey, *The Negro World* and the British West Indies, 1919–1920," *Science and Society* 36 (Spring 1972):63–79.
4. W. F. Elkins, " 'Unrest Among the Negroes': A British Document of 1919," *Science and Society* 36 (Winter 1966):66–79. The document in question was not of British origin but had been given to the British government by U.S. officials. I am grateful to Professor Robert Hill for this information. Elkins, "Marcus Garvey," 63–79.
5. For the Negro Factories Corporation, see Amy Jacques Garvey, *Garvey and Garveyism* (London, 1963), and Theodore J. Vincent, *Black Power and the Garvey Movement* (San Francisco, 1972). Commander Russell, Daily Diary Report, 12 July 1920, State Department Decimal File (DF) 838.00/1651.
6. Russell to the Secretary of State, 11 Oct. 838.00/2043; idem to idem, 31 Oct. 1924, 838.00/2049, DF.
7. Idem to idem, 11 Nov. 1924, DF, 838.00/2060 and enclosure.
8. Scott to the Secretary of State, 20 Dec. 1923, DF, 838.00/2060.

9. Ibid.

10. *Les Annales capoises,* 30 Oct. 1924.

11. Ibid.

12. On the origins of the Jamaican community in Haiti, see J. Catts Pressoir, *Le protestantisme en Haïti* (Port-au-Prince, 1945) 218–20. Garvey, *Garvey and Garveyism,* 147–58.

13. Tony Martin, *Race First: The Ideological and Organizational Struggles of Marcus Garvey and the Universal Negro Improvement Association* (Westport, Conn., 1976), 49.

14. Winthrop Scott to the Secretary of State, 11 Nov. 1924, DF, 838.00/2060 and enclosure.

15. Scott to the Secretary of State, 20 Dec. 1923, DF, 838.00/2060.

16. J. A. Rogers, "Jazz at Home," *Survey Graphic* 6 (March 1925):667, Melville J. Herskovits, "The Dilemma of Social Pattern," in ibid., 676–78.

17. Nathan Huggins, *"Harlem Renaissance* (New York, 1971), passim; Léon Laleau's *Le Choc* (Port-au-Prince, 1975), passim; Jean Price-Mars, *La vocation de l'élite* (Port-au-Prince, 1919); J. Michael Dash, *Literature and Ideology in Haiti, 1915–1961* (Totowa, N.J.: 1981), 43–64.

18. Dash, *Literature and Ideology,* 71.

19. The British Minister's report, "Communism in Haiti," 15 Mar. 1947, DF, 838.00B/4-247.

20. Richard A. Loederer, *Voodoo Fire in Haiti* (New York, 1935); William B. Seabrook, *The Magic Island* (New York, 1929); John W. Vandercook, *Black Majesty* (New York, 1928); Faustin Wirkus, *The White King of La Gonâve* (New York, 1931).

21. John H. Craige, *Cannibal Cousins* (New York, 1934); Jervis Anderson, *This Was Harlem* (New York, 1982); Norman Armour to the Secretary of State, 10 Dec. 1934, DF, 838.9111/45.

22. Eder to Chapin, 26 June 1935, DF, 838.4061/Motion Pictures/18. See also Dantès Bellegarde to Lucien Lafontant, 12 Feb. 1931, Eugène Maximilien Collection, Schomburg Center, New York Public Library.

23. Melville Herskovits, *The New World Negro* (Bloomington, Ind., 1966); Zora Neale Hurston, *Tell My Horse* (Berkeley, 1981); George Eaton Simpson, *Melville Herskovits* (New York, 1973).

24. For U.S. perceptions of mulattoes, see George Frederickson, *The Black Image in the White Mind* (New York, 1971); Carl Degler, *Neither Black Nor White: Slavery and Race Relations in Brazil and the United States* (New York, 1971).

25. Léon-François Hoffman, *Essays on Haitian Literature* (Washington, D.C., 1984), 82; J. Michael Dash, *Haiti and the United States* (New York, 1988), 74–75.
26. Mayer to the Secretary of State, 14 Feb. 1939; Patrick Bellegarde-Smith, *Haiti: The Breached Citadel* (Boulder, Colo., 1990), 87.
27. Ghislain Gouraige, *La diaspora d'Haïti et l'Afrique* (Montréal, 1974), 105–8; Mayer to the Secretary of State, 14 Feb. 1939, 838.111/245; John C. White to the Secretary of State, 24 Sept. 1942, 838.404/85; Thomas H. Young, "Some Aspects of the Haitian Class Problem," 13 Apr. 1943, and *Le Matin*, 31 Mar. 1943, enclosed, 838.404/132, DF. Dash, *Haiti and the United States*, 141; "Justice for Judas," *Time* 61 (6 Apr. 1953):45; "Shod By Order," *Time* 51 (2 Feb. 1948):26.
28. Dash, *Haiti and the United States*, 66–72, 74–75, 91. On Lescot and black Americans, see Associated Negro Press releases: 3 Mar. 1941, 23 Apr. 1941; Lieutenant Colonel Thomas H. Young, "Events Tending to Aggravate the Race Question," 20 May 1943, DF, 838.001/78; J. C. White to the Secretary of State, DF 838.001/Lescot, Elie/98.
29. William DeCourcy to the Secretary of State, 16 June 1949, DF, 838.00W 6-1649; Katherine E. Bryan to Ellen B. Gammack, 18 July 1949, Domestic and Foreign Missionary Society Papers, Archives of the Episcopal Church, Austin, Texas; Association for the Study of Negro Life and History brochure in Emmer Martin Lancaster Papers, Division of Negro Affairs, U.S. Department of Commerce, Record Group (RG) 40, National Archives.
30. Selden Rodman, "U.S. Tourists in Haiti," *Americas* 6 (October 1954):32; Herbert Gold, "Americans in the Port of Princes," *Yale Review* (Autumn 1954):88; Herbert Gold, *My Last Two Thousand Years* (New York, 1972), 115–16.
31. Pierre Van den Berghe and Charles Keyes, "Introduction: Tourism and Re-created Ethnicity," *Annals of Tourism Research* 11 (1984):343–52.
32. Elizabeth Abbott, *Haiti: The Duvaliers and Their Legacy* (New York, 1988), 59; Rodman, "U.S. Tourists in Haiti," 32–33; Gold, "Americans in the Port of Princes," passim; Herbert Gold, "Winter in Haiti," *Writer's Digest*, n.d., Schomburg Clipping File (SCF).
33. De la Rue's memorandum, 2 Jan. 1940, DF, 838.51/3877; Finley to Briggs, 9 Jan. 1940, 838.51/3878.
34. De la Rue's memorandum, 2 Jan. 1940, DF, 838.51/3877; Ferdinand L. Mayer to the Secretary of State, 14 Feb. 1939, 838.111/245; idem to idem, 28 Mar. 1939, 838.111/250.

35. For early tourism to Haiti, see Stanislaus Goutier to the Secretary of State, 17 Feb. 1894, U.S. Department of State, Dispatches from United States Consuls in Cap-Haïtien (DUSCCH) NA; De la Rue's memorandum, 2 Jan. 1940, DF, 838.51/3877; De la Rue to Edward J. Sparks, 25 Oct. 1940, 838.502/40; De la Rue to Mayer, 15 Apr. 1940, 838.502/31, DF.

36. De la Rue's memorandum, 2 Jan. 1940; Louis Turner and John Ash, *Golden Hordes: International Tourism and the Pleasure Periphery* (London, 1975), 146.

37. De la Rue's memorandum, 2 Jan. 1940; Finley to Briggs, 9 Jan. 1940, 838.51/3878.

38. U.S. Embassy to the Secretary of State, 9 Dec. 1949, DF, 838.00W/12-949. Montgomery, Alabama *Advertiser*, 3 Jan. 1954; John H. Burns to the Secretary of State, 11 Aug. 1949, 838.00W/8-1149; Paul Blanshard, *Democracy and Empire in the Caribbean* (New York, 1947), 68, 69; *Time*, 17 Oct. 1949; *Reporter*, 28 Mar. 1950, Schomburg Clipping File (SCF); Heinl and Heinl, *Written in Blood*, 590.

39. See, for example, Julian C. Levi to Charles O. Thomas, 26 July 1942, 838.413/2; e.g., U.S. legation correspondence for September–October 1942, DF 838.4061/13.

40. Poppy Cannon, "Haitian Fashions," *Ebony* 6 (April 1950), 44–47; *L'Aurore*, 5 Dec. 1953, 1.

41. Lois Banner, *American Beauty* (New York, 1983), 277; J. C. Furnas, "The Truth About Suntan," *Saturday Evening Post*, 31 July 1948.

42. Daniel J. Leab, *From Sambo to Superspade: The Black Experience in Motion Pictures* (Boston, 1976), 209, 211; Allen L. Woll, *The Latin Image in American Film*, rev. ed. (Los Angeles, 1980), 53–75.

43. Leab, *From Sambo to Superspade*, 204; Donald Bogle, *Brown Sugar* (New York, 1980), 98–102, 130–36.

44. Rodman, "U.S. Tourists in Haiti," 33; Tittman to the Secretary of State, 6 Feb. 1948, and attachment, DF, 838.00/2-648; Edmund Wilson, "Christophe and Estimé," *Reporter* 2 (9 May 1950), 24–25.

45. Athan Theoharis, "The Politics of Scholarship: Liberals, Anti-Communism, and McCarthyism," in Robert Griffith and Athan Theoharis, eds., *The Specter: Original Essays on the Cold War and the Origins of McCarthyism* (New York, 1974), 267.

46. Alonzo Hamby, *Beyond the New Deal: Harry S. Truman and American Liberalism* (New York, 1973), 282.

8. Island Neighbors

1. Hans Schmidt, *The United States Occupation of Haiti, 1915–1934* (New Brunswick, N.J., 1971), 224, 229; J. C. White to Willard Barber, 22 May 1943, 838.00/3645, State Department Decimal File (DF).

2. Schmidt, *United States Occupation of Haiti*, 225–29.

3. Chapin's monograph on Haiti, part 4, chap. 2, p. 3, collection of the United States Embassy, Port-au-Prince.

4. Ibid., part 1, chap. 3, pp. 6–7; part 3, chap. 2, pp. 2, 3.

5. Ibid., pp. 2, 4, 5, 7.

6. Schmidt, *United States Occupation*, 232.

7. Willard F. Barber to Chapin and Briggs, 27 Dec. 1938, 838.51/3761; Mayer to the Secretary of State, 23 Dec. 1938, 838.51/3762, DF.

8. Dana Munro to Lawrence Duggan, 17 Aug., 1939, 838.20/27, DF.

9. Selden Chapin's memorandum, Division of Latin American Affairs, 29 Mar. 1937, DF 838.00/3368; Ferdinand L. Mayer to the Secretary of State, 23 Dec. 1937, 838.00/3388; idem to idem, 5 Dec. 1938, 838.105/520; idem to idem, 7 Jan. 1938, 838.00/3397; idem to idem, 9 Jan. 1938, 838.00/3398; Demosthènes P. Calixte, *Haiti, the Calvary of a Soldier* (New York, 1939), 60.

10. Mayer to the Secretary of State, 8 Dec. 1938, 838.00/3368; Finley to the Secretary of State, 10 May 1939, 838.105/526; memorandum of the Division of Latin American Affairs, 17 Dec. 1938, 838.105/523; Mayer to the Secretary of State, 17 Jan. 1938, 838.51/3548; John C. White to the Secretary of State, 26 Dec. 1941, 838.105/597, DF.

11. Selden Chapin to Duggan, 5 Jan. 1937, 838.51/3281; Julian Pinkerton to the Secretary of State, 22 Aug. 1936, 838.00/3350; Finley to the Secretary of State, 9 July 1937, 838.51/3377; Vincent to Welles, 21 May 1937, 838.51/3338, DF.

12. Ernest Clorissaint to Ernest Gruening, 27 Oct. 1934, in Walter White to James Weldon Johnson, 30 Nov. 1934; idem to idem, 8 May 1934, James Weldon Johnson Papers, Yale University; Committee for the Release of Jacques Roumain to Arthur Schomburg, n.d.; and press release, 1935, in Arthur Schomburg Papers, Schomburg Research Center, New York Public Library; Smith to Little, 26 Sept. 1932, Louis McCarty Little Papers, USMC Historical Museum, Washington, D.C.; Walter White to Sténio Vincent, 9 Oct. 1933; "Memo re Haiti," 17 Mar. 1934; Walter White to Charles B. Vincent, 22 Mar. 1934, NAACP Papers, Library of Congress; Dana G.

Munro, *The United States and the Caribbean Republics, 1921–1933* (Princeton, N.J., 1974), 340.

13. Ferdinand L. Mayer to the Secretary of State, 14 Feb. 1938, 838.,00/3405; R. Henry Norweb to the Secretary of State, 3 Nov. 1939, 838.00/3497, DF.
14. Mayer to the Secretary of State, 14 Feb. 1938; idem to idem, 3 Nov. 1938, 838.00/3432; Norweb to the Secretary of State, 3 Nov. 1939; Chapin to Briggs, Duggan and Welles, 8 Nov. 1938, 838.00/3432; Welles to the Chargé d'affaires ad interim, 19 Oct. 1940. Kern Delince, *Armée et politique en Haïti* (Paris, 1979), 113.
15. Robert D. Crassweller, *Trujillo: The Life and Times of a Caribbean Dictator* (New York, 1966), 160–62.
16. John C. White to the Secretary of State, 29 Mar. 1941, 838.00/3581; idem to idem, 8 Apr. 1941, 838.00/3592, DF.
17. White to the Secretary of State, Bacon's memorandum, both 27 Sept. 1941; Welles to Daniels, 21 Oct. 1941, DF, 838.00/3614.
18. Sparks to the Secretary of State, 15 Jan. 1942, DF, 838.00/3624; Delince, *Armée et politique*, 207.
19. White to the Secretary of State, 24 Feb. 1942, DF, 838.00/3628.
20. White to the Secretary of State, 22 July 1941, 838.105/585; Hauch to Barber and Briggs, 24 Jan. 1946, DF, 838.00/1-1346; Welles, Acting Secretary of State, to the American Legation, 6 Apr. 1942, 838.001/Lescot, Elie/54A; J. C. White to the Secretary of State, 23 Apr. 1944, 838.001/Lescot, Elie/63; Cumberland Memoir, Columbia University Oral History Collection.
21. Lescot to Welles, 5 July 1940; Finley to Duggan and Welles, 9 July 1940, 838.22/1; Bonsal to Welles, 10 Feb. 1942; Bacon to Walmsley and Bonsal, 30 Jan. 1942, 838.2222/6; Barber to Walmsley, Bonsal, Duggan, Wilson, and Welles, 21 Jan. 1942, 838.2222/7; Ellis O. Briggs to the Secretary of State, 9 Dec. 1944, 838.401/12-2044, DF.
22. Williams to C. H. C. Pearsall, 12 Aug. 1942, 838.51/4508; report enclosed with W. F. Barber to Collado, 16 Sept. 1942, 838.51/4518, DF.
23. White to the Secretary of State, 20 Jan. 1943, 838.001/Lescot, Elie/85; memorandum of a meeting with Minister Liautaud, et al., 4 Jan. 1943, 838.105/607; Lt. E. K. G. Borjesson's report, 2 Oct. 1943, 838.105/625; Barber to Duggan, 11 Oct. 1943, 838.105/624, DF.
24. Minutes of the second meeting of Société Haïtienne-Américaine Developpement Agricole (SHADA) board of directors, 20 Oct. 1941, 838.51/Cooperative Program/26; minutes of SHADA board of directors meeting,

10 Nov. 1942, 838.51/Cooperative Program/51; White to the Secretary of State, 11 Aug. 1942, 838.51/Cooperative Program/34; U.S. Naval Attaché (USNA) Lt. Kearley's military intelligence report, *Haiti-Economic Factors, Miscellaneous*, 8 July 1942, 838.51/Cooperative Program/14 1/2; Don Humphrey, "SHADA," report of the Office of Price Administration, 8 Nov. 1943, 838.5017/17, DF.

25. W. M. Jeffers to Cordell Hull, 30 Mar. 1943, 838.51/4589; Minutes of the third meeting of SHADA board of directors, 6 Aug. 1941, 838.51/Cooperative Program/27; USNA Lt. Col. Thomas H. Young's military intelligence report, 15 May 1943, 838.51/Cooperative Program/71; Barber to Cabot, Duggan, Wilson, Phelps, and Collado, 14 Apr. 1944, 838.50/63B; White To Barber, 30 Nov. 1943, 838.51/Cooperative Program/115; M. D. Knapp to J. W. Bickel, 8 Oct. 1943, 838.5018/18; Humphrey, "SHADA."

26. Humphrey, "SHADA;" White to Barber, 12 Aug. 1943, 838.51/Cooperative Program/82; Young's military intelligence report, 1 June 1943, 838.51/Cooperative Program/74; Nelson Rockefeller's memorandum to Robert Lynch, 17 Sept. 1944, 838.5018/7-1444; W. C. Brister to Rockefeller, 12 June 1944, 838.5018/6-1444; Charles Taft to Lawrence Duggan, 24 June 1944, 838.5018/6-2444, DF.

27. Standard Fruit Company memorandum, 6 June 1941, 838.5045/70; "Memorandum on the Industrial Development of Haiti," in White to the Secretary of State, 29 Nov. 1943, 838.50/57; Barber to Cabot, Duggan, and Phelps, 31 Mar. 1944, 838.50/61; Joint Haitian-American Commission, *Industrial Report*, 1 Apr. 1944, 838.50/63, DF.

28. De la Rue, *Summary of Project of Financing by Standard Fruit and Steamship Company for the Extension of Banana Plantations in the Republic of Haiti*, 15 June 1939, 838.51/3813, DF; Louis R. E. Gation, *Aspects de l'economie et des finances d'Haïti* (Port-au-Prince, 1944), 8–50.

29. Williams to C. H. C. Pearsall, 12 Aug. 1942, 838.51/4508; report enclosed with W. F. Barber to Collado, 16 Sept. 1942, 838.51/4518, DF.

30. Vinton Chapin to the Secretary of State, 31 Mar. 1944, 838.51/Cooperative Program/145; Pierre Chauvet to Duggan, 15 May 1944, 838.51/Cooperative Program/147, DF.

31. Remy Bastien and Harold Courlander, *Religion and Politics in Haiti: Two Essays* (Washington, D.C., 1966), 65; White to the Secretary of State, 2 Feb. 1942, 838.404/48; idem to idem, 19 Feb. 1942, 838.404/55; idem to idem, 26 Feb. 1942, 838.404/58; memorandum of a conversation between Willard Barber and Rev. M. P. Cross, 6 Oct. 1943, 838,404/137, DF; *Annual Report*

of the Missionary Bishops, 1941, Domestic and Foreign Missionary Society of the Protestant Episcopal Church, 52; David Nicholls, "Religion and Politics in Haiti," *Canadian Journal of Political Science* 3 (1970):405.

32. White to the Secretary of State, 11 Mar. 1942, 838.404/65; Bacon's memorandum, 11 Mar. 1942, 838,404/64; Sumner Welles to Harold Tittmann, 7 Mar. 1942, 838.404/62; Halleck L. Rose to the Secretary of State, 11 Mar. 1942, 838.404/66; Harrison to the Secretary of State, 10 Apr. 1942, 838.404/ 75; Lescot to Welles, 25 May 1943, 838.404/128, DF; Associated Negro Press release, 7 Oct. 1942.

33. Orme Wilson to the Secretary of State, 9 Jan. 1946, 838.00/1-946; idem to idem, 10 June 1946, 838.00/6-1046; Crassweller, *Trujillo,* 153; George F. Scherer to the Secretary of State, 5 June 1946, 838.00/6-546, DF; Nicholls, "Ideologies," 672.

34. *Annual Report of the Missionary Bishops, 1946,* Domestic and Foreign Missionary Society of the Protestant Episcopal Church, 45; Orme Wilson to the Secretary of State, 7 Jan. 1946, 838.00/1-746; idem to idem, 10 Jan. 1946, 838.00/1-1046; idem to idem, 11 Jan. 1946, DF, 838.00/1-1146; Delince, *Armée et politique,* 114.

35. Allan Dawson to the Secretary of State, 17 Jan. 1946, 838.01/1-1746; Wilson to the Secretary of State, 12 Jan. 1946, 838.00/1-1246; Briggs's note attached to Hauch to Barber, Briggs, and Braden, 7 Feb. 1946, DF, 838.00/2-546; Hauch to Barber and Briggs, 14 Feb. 1946, 838.00/2-946; W. P. Cochran to Butler, Briggs, and Braden, 21 Feb. 1946, 838.01/2-2146; Cochran's memorandum, 26 Mar. 1946, 838.01/3-2646; Barber's memorandum of a conversation with J. C. Antoine, 29 Jan. 1946, 838.00/1-2946; Hauch to Briggs and Braden, 16 Jan. 1946, 838.01/1-1546, DF. *Annual Report of the Missionary Bishops,* 45.

36. Orme Wilson to the Secretary of State, 29 Jan. 1946, 838.00/1-2-946; Hauch's memorandum of a conversation with Braden, et al., 29 Apr. 1946, 838.00-4-2946, DF. State Department, "Political and Economic Relations of the United States and Haiti," *Foreign Relations of the United States, 1951,* 2:1461. U.S. ambassador to Haiti Raymond L. Thurston in 1963 echoed the view of Haitian Communism as essentially a French import. Thurston's testimony, U.S. Senate, Subcommittee on Inter-American Affairs, *Castro-Communist Subversion in the Western Hemisphere,* 88th Cong., 2d sess. (Washington, D.C., 1963).

37. Enclosures in Wilson to the Secretary of State, 13 Jan. 1946, 838.00/1-1346, DF; idem to idem, 19 Mar. 1946; Hauch to Barber et al., 25 Mar. 1946,

838.00/3-1946; Jack West's memorandum for the ambassador, 12 Nov. 1946, 838.00/11-1346, DF; *Haïti-Progrès*, 15–21 June 1988, 8.

38. West's memorandum; *Haïti-Progrès*, 15–21 June 1988, 8.

39. Wilson to the Secretary of State, 22 Jan. 1946, 838.00/1-2246, DF.

40. "Communiqué du Secretariat Général du Mouvement Ouvrier Paysan," 26 Mar. 1949; MOP, *Actes et Principles*, 24 Mar. 1949, 838.00/4-849; Miss Hale to Hauch et al., 8 June 1949, 838.00/6-849; DeCourcy to the Secretary of State, 15 Nov. 1949, 838.00/11-1849; Harold Tittmann to the Secretary of State, 11 June 1948, 838.00B/6-1148; Tittmann's memorandum, 22 June 1948, 838.00B/6-2946, DF.

41. Alex Dupuy, *Haiti in the World Economy: Class, Race, and Underdevelopment Since 1870* (Boulder, Colo.: 1989), 147.

42. Orme Wilson to the Secretary of State, 17 Aug. 1946, 838.00/8-1746; Tittmann to the Secretary of State, 10 Mar. 1947, 838.00/3-1047; Lyon's memorandum, 27 Jan. 1948, 838.00/1-2748; DeCourcy to the Secretary of State, 13 Jan. 1949, 838.00/1-1249, DF. Edmund Wilson, "Christophe and Estimé," *The Reporter* 2 (9 May 1950):25–26.

43. U.S. Embassy to the Secretary of State, 29 Sept. 1949, 838.00W/9-2949; idem to idem, 16 Dec. 1949, 838.00W/12-1649.

44. William Javier Nelson, "The Haitian Political Situation and Its Effect on the Dominican Republic, 1849–1877," *The Americas* 45 (October 1988):227–36; Thomas Fiehrer, "Political Violence in the Periphery: The Haitian Massacre of 1937," *Race and Class* 32 (October–December 1990), 8–9.

45. Jesus Galíndez Suarez, *The Era of Trujillo* (Tucson, Ariz., 1973), 209; Crassweller, *Trujillo*, 150–51, 224–25; Horatio Mooers to the Secretary of State, 17 Sept. 1946, 838.00/9-946, DF.

46. Galíndez Suarez, *Era of Trujillo*, 9; Sumner Welles to the Secretary of State, 26 Apr. 1923, 738.3915/238; idem to idem, 1 Apr. 1924, 738.3915/265, DF; Fiehrer, "Political Violence," 10–11.

47. Howard J. Wiarda, *Dictatorship and Development* (Gainesville, Fla., 1986), 2.

48. Crassweller, *Trujillo*, 152, 153; Mayer to the Secretary of State, 10 Feb. 1939, 838.00/3447; Duggan's memorandum, 31 Oct. 1939, 838.00/3489, DF.

49. Munro to the Secretary of State, 1 Aug. 1931, 738.3915/430; idem to idem, 12 Feb. 1932, 738.3915/455, DF; Crassweller, *Trujillo*, 153.

50. Munro to Welles, 6 Nov. 1937, 738.39/36; De la Rue to Heath, 6 Nov. 1937, 739.38/88; F. B. Attwood's memorandum, 15 Feb. 1938, 838.00/3406, De la Rue to Welles, 18 Dec. 1937, 838.51/3514, DF.

51. Juan Manuel Garcia, *La matanza de los haitianos* (Santo Domingo, 1983); Galíndez Suarez, *Era of Trujillo*, 207–8; G. Pope Atkins and Larman C.

Wilson, *The United States and the Trujillo Regime* (New Brunswick, N.J., 1972), 52–57.

52. Crassweller, *Trujillo*, 156–57.
53. Ibid, 157, 158, 213; De la Rue to Welles, 18 Dec. 1937, 838.51/3514, DF.
54. Mayer to the Secretary of State, 26 Nov. 1937, 738.39/132, DF.
55. Selden Chapin to Lawrence Duggan, with Cordell Hull to Rep. James A. Shanley, 30 Dec. 1937, 738.39/230; Franklin Folsom to Hull, 6 Jan. 1938, 738.39/251; Finley to the Secretary of State, 20 Oct. 1937, 738.39/11, DF.
56. Galíndez Suarez, *Era of Trujillo*, 208 n. 9; F. B. Attwood's memorandum, 15 Feb. 1938, 838.00/3406, De la Rue to Duggan, 27 July 1938, 838.61A/13, DF; Trujillo to Lescot, 1 Nov. 1943, Kurt Fisher Collection, Schomburg Research Center, New York Public Library.
57. Ferdinand L. Mayer to the Secretary of State, 3 June 1939, 738.39/347; idem to idem, 1 Nov. 1938, 838.00/3430; idem to idem, 26 Nov. 1937, 738.39/146; idem to idem, 1 Dec. 1937, 738.39/149; De la Rue to Mayer, 21 Dec. 1937, 838.51/3520; Franklin B. Atwood to the Secretary of State, 5 Nov. 1937, 738.39/78, DF.
58. Galíndez Suarez, *Era of Trujillo*, 206; Sumner Welles' memorandum of a conversation with Andres Pastoriza, 5 Nov. 1937, 738.39/97, DF.
59. De la Rue's memorandum, 17 Sept. 1940, 838.51/4070; Mayer to the Secretary of State, 23 Dec. 1939, and enclosure, 838.00/344; idem to idem, 13 Dec. 1938, 838.00/3440, DF.
60. Mayer to the Secretary of State, 9 Nov. 1938, 838.00/3434; idem to idem, 8 Dec. 1938, 838.00/3438, DF.
61. Walmsley's memorandum, 24 Dec. 1941, 838.51/4398, DF.
62. Philip Bonsal to Stettinius, 14 Oct. 1943, 838.001/Lescot, Elie/161, DF; Trujillo to Lescot, 1 Nov. 1943, Kurt Fisher Collection; Charles Hauch to Cabot, 24 Oct. 1944, 838.001/Lescot, Elie/10-2444; Frank P. Corrigan to the Secretary of State, 12 July 1944; Orme Wilson to the Secretary of State, 13 July 1944, 838.001/Lescot, Elie/1344, DF.
63. Hull to Roosevelt, 30 Aug. 1943, 838.001/Lescot, Elie/78, DF; Associated Negro Press Release, 15 Apr. 1942.
64. J. C. White to the Secretary of State, 16 Sept. 1943, 838.001/Lescot, Elie/98; Military Intelligence Division, *Events Tending to Aggravate the Race Question*, 20 May 1943, 838.001/Lescot, Elie/81, DF.
65. John M. Blum, *The Price of Vision: The Diary of Henry A. Wallace, 1942–1946*, (Boston, 1973); Stettinius's memorandum, 14 Oct. 1943, 838.001/Lescot, Elie/136.
66. Lescot to Roosevelt, 27 Oct. 1944; Roosevelt to Lescot, 14 Dec. 1944,

838.001/Lescot, Elie/10-2744; Elliott Briggs to the Secretary of State, 4 Dec. 1944, 838.001/Lescot, Elie/12-444; Wilson to the Secretary of State, 6 Dec. 1944, 838.001/Lescot, Elie/12-644; Norman Armour's memorandum, 27 Oct. 1944; Neal and Hauch's memorandum, 21 Dec. 1944; 838.001/Lescot, Elie/10-2744; Justice Department memorandum, 29 Dec. 1944, 738.39/12-1644, DF.

67. Captain John A. Butler, USNA, Military Intelligence Report, *Dominican Republic, Political Forces, Foreign Penetration,* 19 June 1941, 838.001/Lescot, Elie/161. On Spanish Republican and Jewish refugees, see Galíndez Suarez, *Era of Trujillo,* 214, 215, and Fiehrer, "Political Violence," 16.

68. William E. DeCourcy to the Secretary of State, 16 Dec. 1949, 838.00W/12-1649, DF.

69. Bernard Diederich and Al Burt, *Papa Doc* (New York, 1969), 57; Crassweller, *Trujillo,* 242–48, 353; State Department, Office of Intelligence Research, no. 5155, "Alleged Complicity of the Dominican Government in Haitian Assassination Plot," 10 Jan. 1950; Charles D. Ameringer, *The Democratic Left in Exile* (Coral Gables, Fla., 1974), 104–5.

70. Ameringer, *Democratic Left in Exile,* 105–7; Thomas Mann's memorandum, 13 Jan. 1950, in *Foreign Relations of the United States, 1950,* 2:644–49.

71. Barber to Woodward, et al., 19 Mar. 1947, 838.00/3-1947, DF.

72. Donnelly (Caracas) to the Secretary of State, 16 Jan. 1948, 838.2331/1-1648; DeCourcy to the Secretary of State, 21 Dec. 1948, 737.38/12-2148; idem to idem, 28 Dec. 1948, 838.00W/12-2748, DF.

73. Memorandum of a conversation with Secretary Dillon, Senator Smathers, et al., 16 May 1960; Dillon's memorandum for the President, 12 May 1960, Eisenhower Library, Declassified Documents Reference Collection (DDRC) (Washington, D.C., 1976–77); Ernest V. Siracusa's memorandum, 4 Aug. 1949, *Foreign Relations of the United States, 1949,* 456; Milton K. Wells to the Secretary of State, 12 May 1949, ibid., 444, 445.

74. Allan Dawson to the Secretary of State, 8 Nov. 1945, 838.00/11-845; see also J. C. White to the Secretary of State, 12 Apr. 1941, 838.00/3594, DF; Galíndez Suarez, *Era of Trujillo,* 38, 209; Joe Alexis Morris, "Cruel Beauty of the Caribbean," *Saturday Evening Post,* 17 Nov. 1951, 173.

9. Toward the Third World

1. State Department, "Political and Economic Relations of the United States and Haiti," 16 Apr. 1951, *Foreign Relations of the United States, 1951,* 2:1462;

273 Notes to Pages 163–166

O. Ernest Moore, *Haiti: Its Stagnant Society and Shackled Economy* (New York, 1972), 67.

2. Orme Wilson to the Secretary of State, 17 Aug. 1946, State Department Decimal File (DF), 838.00/8-1746; Harold Tittmann to the Secretary of State, 10 Mar. 1947, DF, 838.00/3-1047; William DeCourcy to the Secretary of State, 12 Jan. 1949, DF, 838.00/1-1249.

3. MOP, *Actes et principes*, 24 Mar. 1949; Alex Dupuy, *Haiti in the World Economy* (Boulder, Colo., 1989), 147; Charles Hauch's memorandum, 27 Dec. 1946, *Foreign Relations of the United States, 1946*, 947; *Haïti-Progrès*, 15–21 June 1988, 8.

4. Wilson to the Secretary of State, 18 Aug. 1946, 912–15; Dean Acheson to Wilson, 21 Aug. 1946, 915–16; Charles Hauch's memorandum of a conversation with Spruille Braden et al., 26 Aug. 1946, 919; Braden to Harold Tittmann, 3 Oct. 1946, 922, 923–24; Acheson to Tittmann, 4 Oct. 1946, 924–25; Tittmann to the Secretary of State, 20 Nov. 1946, 929; Hauch's memorandum, 12 Dec. 1946, 930; W. H. Williams and Thomas Pearson to Tittmann, enclosed with Tittmann to the Secretary of State, 9 Nov. 1946, 937. *Foreign Relations of the United States, 1946*.

5. DeCourcy to the Secretary of State, 20 Dec. 1948, 838.00/12-2048, DF.

6. Ibid.; Lester D. Langley, *America and the Americas* (Athens, Ga., 1989), 168; State Department, "Political and Economic Relations of the United States and Haiti," 1461.

7. Tittmann to the Secretary of State, 13 Dec. 1947, DF, 838.00/12-1347; Wilson to the Secretary of State, 22 Jan. 1946, 838.00/1-2246.

8. Bernard Diederich and Al Burt, *Papa Doc* (New York, 1969), 56–58; J. Michael Dash, *Haiti and the United States: National Stereotypes and the Literary Imagination* (New York, 1988), 93–94; Kern Delince, *Armée et politique en Haïti* (Paris, 1979), 114; Dean Acheson to the diplomatic representatives in the American Republics, 26 Mar. 1946, *Foreign Relations of the United States, 1946*, 910–11; *Newsweek*, 23 Oct. 1950, 44.

9. Carlo A. Désinor, *L'affaire jumelle* (Port-au-Prince: n.d.) 50, 51; Kansas City *Call*, 15 Feb. 1950.

10. Désinor, *L'affaire jumelle*, 50, 51; *Washington Evening Star*, 26 Oct. 1950.

11. Jean A. Magloire, *Pour défendre la mémoire d'Illustre Président Dumarsais Estimé*, (Port-au-Prince, 1957); DeCourcy to the Secretary of State, 15 Nov. 1949, DF, 838.00/11-1549.

12. State Department, "Political and Economic Relations of the United States and Haiti," 1460. Désinor, *L'affaire jumelle*, 50, 51; *Newsweek*, 23 Oct. 1950, 44; Diederich and Burt, *Papa Doc*, 61.

13. Moore, *Haiti*, 234, 235, 238–39; State Department, "Political and Economic Relations of the United States and Haiti," 1457.
14. Diederich and Burt, *Papa Doc*, 65–66.
15. Ibid., 74, 75.
16. *Nation* 180 (26 Mar. 1955):256, and 183 (22 Dec. 1956):530; Désinor, *L'affaire jumelle*, 46, 47; Michel Hector, *Syndicalisme et socialisme en Haïti, 1932–1970* (Port-au-Prince, c. 1987), 91; *Time*, 14 Jan. 1957, 32.
17. Patrick Bellegarde-Smith, "Class Struggle in Contemporary Haitian Politics," *Journal of Caribbean Studies* 2 (Spring 1981):120, 121; Delince, *Armée et politique*, 114–15; *Haïti-Progrès*, 9–15 Dec. 1987.
18. Bellegarde-Smith, "Class Struggle," 121–23.
19. Diederich and Burt, *Papa Doc*, 78; Bellegarde-Smith, "Class Struggle," 118; *Haïti-Progrès*, 22–28 June 1988, 8.
20. Simon Fass, *Political Economy in Haiti* (Boulder, Colo., 1988), 26; State Department, "Political and Economic Relations of the United States and Haiti," 16 Apr. 1951, *Foreign Relations of the United States, 1951*, 2:1456.
21. Fass, *Political Economy in Haiti*, 26.
22. Claude Erb, "Prelude to Point Four: The Institute of Inter-American Affairs," *Diplomatic History* 9 (Summer 1985):249–50.
23. Ibid., 253, 260, 261.
24. Joint Chiefs of Staff, "Foreign Policy of the United States," 10 Feb. 1946, quoted in Melvyn P. Leffler, "The American Conception of National Security and the Beginning of the Cold War, 1945–48," *American Historical Review* 89 (April 1984):354.
25. Leffler, "American Conception," 353, 356; Henry Wallace, diary entry, 28 Aug. 1946, in John Blum, ed., *The Price of Vision* (Boston, 1973), 611.
26. Robert A. Packenham, *Liberal America and the Third World* (Princeton, N.J., 1973), 25–49.
27. Walter LaFeber, *The American Age: United States Foreign Policy at Home and Abroad Since 1750* (New York, 1989), 465.
28. Packenham, *Liberal America*, 49–58; Stephen G. Rabe, "Controlling Revolutions: Latin America, the Alliance for Progress and Cold War Anti-Communism," in *Kennedy's Quest for Victory: American Foreign Policy, 1961–1963*, edited by Thomas G. Paterson (New York, 1989), 117.
29. O. Ernest Moore, *Haiti: Its Stagnant Society and Shackled Economy* (New York, 1972) 68, 92–93, 136–37; Michel-Rolph Trouillot, *Haiti: State Against Nation* (New York, 1990), 140–41.
30. Moore, *Haiti*, 98–99; Edmund Wilson, "UNESCO at Marbial," *Reporter* 2 (23 May 1950):29–33.

31. LaFeber, *American Age*, 538–39.
32. Rabe, "Controlling Revolutions," 109; U.S. Senate Report 94-465, "Alleged Assassination Plots Involving Foreign Leaders," Washington, D.C., 1975, 191–92.
33. Timmons to the Secretary of State, 18 Dec. 1963, 7:53 p.m., Johnson Library, Declassified Documents Reference Collection (DDRC); Moore, *Haiti*, 97.
34. Packenham, *Liberal America*, 61–68.
35. Rabe, "Controlling Revolutions," 107, 110–12.
36. Ibid., 122.
37. Packenham, *Liberal America*, 71–72; LaFeber, *American Age*, 573.
38. Packenham, *Liberal America*, 73, 74.
39. Ibid., 75.
40. *New York Times*, 13 Oct. 1962, 52:1.
41. Moore, *Haiti*, 96–97.
42. Packenham, *Liberal America*, 94, 94 n. 56; Rabe, "Controlling Revolutions," 113.
43. Packenham, *Liberal America*, 94–95.
44. Ibid., 95, 96.
45. *New York Times*, 20 Mar. 1964, quoted in Packenham, *Liberal America*, 96; Moore, *Haiti*, 103.
46. Packenham, *Liberal America*, 96.
47. Department of State, memorandum of a conversation with René Chalmers, et al., 31 Jan. 1964; Timmons to Assistant Secretary of State Mann and Kennedy Crockett, 17 Jan. 1965, Johnson Library, DDRC; Robert Debs Heinl and Nancy Gordon Heinl, *Written in Blood: The Story of the Haitian People: 1492–1971* (Boston, 1971), 644 n. 58.
48. Rusk to the President, 14 Oct. 1966, Johnson Library, DDRC; Moore, *Haiti*, 103–4, 105; Robert Maguire, "Bottom-up Development in Haiti," Inter-American Foundation, IAF Paper no. 1, Oct. 1979.
49. Alex Dupuy, *Haiti in the World Economy: Class, Race, and Underdevelopment Since 1799* (Boulder, Colo., 1989), 167; Trouillot, *Haiti*, 207; James Ferguson, *Papa Doc, Baby Doc: Haiti and the Duvaliers* (London, 1987), 55; Georges A. Fauriol, *Foreign Policy Behavior of Caribbean States: Guyana, Haiti, and Jamaica* (Lanham, Md., 1984), 160.
50. Rod Prince, *Haiti, Family Business* (London, 1985), 72, 73.

10. The Duvalier Dictatorship: The Consolidation

1. Bernard Diederich and Al Burt, *Papa Doc: The Truth About Haiti Today* (New York, 1969), 101–2, 105; for Kébreau, Carlo A. Désinor, *L'affaire jumelle* (Port-au-Prince: n.d.), 177n.

2. Robert D. Heinl and Nancy G. Heinl, *Written in Blood: The Story of the Haitian People* (Boston, 1978), 591.

3. Elizabeth Abbott, *Haiti: The Duvalier Years* (New York, 1988), 76–77.

4. Heinl and Heinl, *Written in Blood*, 591.

5. Robert D. Crassweller, *Trujillo: The Life and Times of a Caribbean Dictator* (New York, 1966), 352.

6. Ibid., 347; George Fauriol, *Foreign Policy Behavior of Caribbean States: Guyana, Haiti, Jamaica* (Lanham, Md., 1984), 154.

7. Heinl and Heinl, *Written in Blood*, 590. Heinl and Heinl claim that Prío paid $20,000 and Batista $4 million. Alternative figures of $200,000 and $1 million are offered by Warren Hinckle and William W. Turner, *The Fish is Red: The Story of the Secret War Against Castro* (New York, 1981), 235; Crassweller, *Trujillo*, 353.

8. L. D. Mallory's memorandum of conversation with Acting Secretary Dillon, et al., 16 May 1960, Department of State; Douglas Dillon's memorandum for the President, 12 May 1960, Eisenhower Library, Declassified Documents Reference Collection (DDRC).

9. Fauriol, *Foreign Policy Behavior*, 154; Stephen G. Rabe, "Controlling Revolutions: Latin America, the Alliance for Progress and Cold War Anti-Communism," in *Kennedy's Quest for Victory: American Foreign Policy, 1961–1963*, edited by Thomas G. Paterson (New York, 1989), 109.

10. Robert D. Tomasek, "The Haiti-Dominican Republic Controversy of 1963 and the OAS," *Orbis* (Pa.) 12 (Spring 1968):299–300; Jesus Galíndez Suarez, *The Era of Trujillo* (Tucson, Ariz., 1973), 65.

11. Fauriol, *Foreign Policy Behavior*, 156.

12. Ibid., 154, 155; Rod Prince, *Haiti, Family Business* (London, 1985), 75; Tomasek, "The Haiti-Dominican Republic Controversy," 303, 308, 310, 312.

13. Stephen G. Rabe, *Eisenhower and Latin America* (Chapel Hill, 1988), 87.

14. Diederich and Burt, *Papa Doc*, 107–10.

15. Rabe, *Eisenhower and Latin America*, 88.

16. Ibid., 89.

17. Ibid., 88–89, 103–6; Stephen G. Rabe, "The Johnson (Eisenhower?) Doctrine for Latin America," *Diplomatic History* 9 (Winter 1985):8.

18. John Bartlow Martin, *U.S. Policy in the Caribbean* (Boulder, Colo., 1978), 50–51; Rabe, "Controlling Revolutions," 108.
19. Dean Rusk, *As I Saw It* (New York, 1990); Senate Report 94-465, "Alleged Assassination Plots Involving Foreign Leaders," Washington, D.C., 1975, 213–15.
20. Rabe, "Controlling Revolutions," 114, 115–16.
21. Ibid., 116.
22. *New York Times*, 8 Apr. 1961, 2:5; Diederich and Burt, *Papa Doc*, 167–68; James Ferguson, *Papa Doc, Baby Doc* (Oxford and New York, 1987), 74–75.
23. *New York Times*, 27 Oct. 1962, 9:1.
24. Ferguson, *Papa Doc, Baby Doc*, 44. See also Timmons to the Secretary of State, 18 Dec. 1963, 7:53 p.m., Johnson Library, DDRC.
25. Rabe, "Controlling Revolutions," 117.
26. Ibid., 118–19.
27. *New York Times*, 28 May 1961, 1:6, 2:6; 15 May 1961, 10:8; 29 May 1961, 6:2; 31 May 1961, 10:4, 5.
28. Heinl and Heinl, *Written in Blood*, 608; Diederich and Burt, *Papa Doc*, 188, 195, 198.
29. Diederich and Burt, *Papa Doc*, 198–99; Kern Delince, *Armée et politique en Haïti* (Paris, 1979), 115; Abbott, *Haiti*, 107–8.
30. Benson E. L. Timmons III to Dean Rusk, 15 July 1964, Johnson Library, DDRC.
31. Diederich and Burt, *Papa Doc*, 194; Hinckle and Turner, *Fish is Red*, 238, 242, 244; Charles D. Ameringer, *The Democratic Left in Exile* (Coral Gables, 1974), 271; *Chicago Defender*, 9 Aug. 1958; Baltimore *Afro-American*, 16 Aug. 1958.
32. Ferguson, *Papa Doc, Baby Doc*, 46.
33. Rusk to the American Embassies in Port-au-Prince and Santo Domingo, 4 Aug. 1964; Timmons to Rusk, 22 July 1964, Johnson Library, DDRC.
34. Ralph Salerno and John S. Tompkins, *The Crime Confederation* (New York, 1969), 386–87; Henrik Krüger, *The Great Heroin Coup* (Boston, 1980), 99, 103 n. 14.
35. Timmons to the Secretary of State, 18 Aug. 1964; idem to idem, 25 July 1964, Johnson Library, DDRC; John H. Davis, *Mafia Kingfish: Carlos Marcello and the Assassination of John F. Kennedy* (New York, 1989), 312, 425; Dan E. Moldea, *The Hoffa Wars: Teamsters, Rebels, Politicians, and the Mob* (New York, 1978), 107, 321.
36. Diederich and Burt, *Papa Doc*, 238–39.

37. Timmons to the Secretary of State, 18 Dec. 1963, 8:02 p.m.; Edward G. Curtis to the Secretary of State, 12 Dec. 1963, Johnson Library, DDRC.

38. Department of State, memorandum of a conversation with Timmons, et al., 10 Feb. 1964, Johnson Library, DDRC; Washington *Star* cited in Heinl and Heinl, *Written in Blood*, 644 n. 58.

39. Timmons to the Secretary of State, 26 Aug. 1964, Johnson Library, DDRC.

40. Timmons to Rusk, 29 Apr. 1964; Fry's memorandum to the Latin American Policy Committee, Department of State, 5 May 1964, Johnson Library, DDRC.

41. Timmons to Rusk, 29 Apr. 1964.

42. Fry's memorandum to the Latin American Policy Committee.

43. Timmons to the Secretary of State, 7 Aug. 1964, 6 p.m.; idem to idem, 1 Sept. 1964, 7 p.m.; idem to idem, 1 Sept. 1964, 9:35 p.m., Johnson Library, DDRC; Heinl and Heinl, *Written in Blood*, 640–41.

44. Timmons to the Secretary of State, 7 Aug. 1964, 11 a.m., Johnson Library, DDRC.

45. U.S. embassy to the State Department, 26 Aug. 1964; Timmons to the Secretary of State, 8 Sept. 1964, Johnson Library, DDRC; Heinl and Heinl, *Written in Blood*, 640–41.

46. Timmons to the Department of State, 7 Feb. 1966.

47. Hinckle and Turner, *Fish is Red*, 249, 258.

48. Ibid., 244–45.

49. Ibid., 234–35, 238, 244; Heinl and Heinl, *Written in Blood*, 598.

50. Timmons to the Secretary of State, 12 Nov. 1966, Johnson Library, DDRC; Delince, *Armée et politique en Haïti*, 115–16.

11. The Duvalier Dictatorship: Decline and Fall

1. Stephen G. Rabe, "Controlling Revolutions: Latin America, the Alliance for Progress and Cold War Anti-Communism," in *Kennedy's Quest for Victory: American Foreign Policy, 1961–1963*, edited by Thomas G. Paterson (New York, 1989), 113.

2. John H. Davis, *Mafia Kingfish: Carlos Marcello and the Assassination of John F. Kennedy* (New York, 1989), 312, 425; Robert D. Heinl and Nancy G. Heinl, *Written in Blood: The Story of the Haitian People* (Boston, 1978), 644; Michel-Rolph Trouillot, *Haiti: State Against Nation* (New York, 1990), 241 n. 11; Edward Glion Curtis to the State Department, "Politico-Economic Assessment—1963," 21 Apr. 1964; Timmons to Rusk, 24 Jan. 1964, John-

son Library, Declassified Documents Reference Collection (DDRC); Davis, *Mafia Kingfish*, 312, 425.

3. Trouillot, *Haiti*, 200–201.

4. Alex Dupuy, "Export Manufacture and Underdevelopment in Haiti," the Columbia University–New York University Consortium for Latin American and Caribbean Studies, Conference Paper no. 20, 1990.

5. Trouillot, *Haiti*, 200–201; Josh DeWind, "Elections Without Democracy?" *Cimarron* 2 (Winter 1990):75.

6. Warren Hinckle and William W. Turner, *The Fish is Red* (New York, 1981), 265; Heinl and Heinl, *Written in Blood*, 656–57.

7. Norman C. Warner to the State Department, 8 Apr. 1964, Johnson Library, DDRC; Alex Dupuy, *Haiti in the World Economy* (Boulder, Colo., 1989), 169.

8. U.S. Department of State, Human Rights Report for Fiscal Year 1978, Haiti, 77, 78.

9. Trouillot, *Haiti*, 206–8.

10. Rod Prince, *Haiti: Family Business* (London, 1985), 32–33; *Haïti Observateur*, 31 July–7 Aug. 1987, 5.

11. Prince, *Haiti*, 34; James Ferguson, *Papa Doc, Baby Doc* (New York, 1989), 61–62.

12. Ferguson, *Papa Doc, Baby Doc*, 63.

13. Dupuy, *Haiti in the World Economy*, 40, 142, 181–82; David Nicholls, "Haiti: The Rise and Fall of Duvalierism," *Third World Quarterly* 8, no. 4 (1986): 1243–44.

14. UNESCO Commission on Human Rights, Subcommittee on Prevention of Discrimination and Protection of Minorities, *Report of the Working Group on Slavery*, 24 Aug. 1979, 6–7.

15. Brenda Gayle Plummer, "Haitian Migrants and Backyard Imperialism," *Race and Class* 26, no. 4 (1985):41.

16. Anthony P. Maingot, "Caribbean International Relations," in *The Modern Caribbean*, edited by Franklin W. Knight and Colin A. Palmer (Chapel Hill, N.C., 1989); Philip Wheaton, "Trilateralism and the Caribbean: Tying Up 'Loose Strings' in the Western Hemisphere," in *Trilateralism*, edited by Holly Sklar (Boston, 1980), 407–8, 411–14.

17. Carolyn Fowler, "The Emergence of the Independent Press in Haiti, 1971–1980," *The Black Collegian*, April–May, 1981, 149–51; Ferguson, *Papa Doc, Baby Doc*, 67–68.

18. George Fauriol, *Foreign Policy Behavior of Caribbean States: Guyana, Haiti, Jamaica* (Lanham, Md., 1984), 137, 162.

19. Maingot, "Caribbean International Relations," 277–87.

20. Richard E. Feinberg and Richard Newfarmer, "The Caribbean Basin Initiative: Bold Plan or Empty Promise?" in *From Gunboats to Diplomacy: New U.S. Policies for Latin America*, edited by Richard Newfarmer (Baltimore, 1984), 210–12, 222–26; Lester Langley, *America and the Americas* (Athens, Ga., 1989), 247; Dupuy, *Haiti in the World Economy*, 174.

21. Rep. Walter E. Fauntroy, "The United States Impact on Haiti and the Haitian Refugees," in U.S. House of Representatives, Committee on the Judiciary, Oversight Hearings Before the Subcommittee on Immigration, Refugees, and International Law, "Caribbean Migration," 96th Cong., 2d sess., 1980.

22. Jenny Pearce, *Under the Eagle* (London, 1982), 201.

23. Fowler, "Emergence," 149–51; Georges Fauriol, "The Duvaliers and Haiti," *Orbis* (Pa.) 32 (Fall 1988), 601.

24. Plummer, "Haitian Migrants," 35.

25. Ibid.; Ferguson, *Papa Doc, Baby Doc*, 64–65; *Washington Post*, 2 Sept. 1981.

26. Patrick Bellegarde-Smith, *Haiti: The Breached Citadel* (Boulder, Colo., 1990), 129–30; Cynthia Enloe, *Bananas, Beaches, and Bases: Making Feminist Sense of International Politics* (Berkeley, Colo., 1990), 31–32.

27. Fauriol, "The Duvaliers and Haiti," 600.

28. Plummer, "Haitian Migrants," 41; Fauriol, "Duvaliers and Haiti," 603–5.

29. Josh DeWind and David H. Kinley III, *Aiding Migration: The Impact of International Assistance on Haiti* (Boulder, Colo., 1988), 32–34; Ferguson, *Papa Doc, Baby Doc*, 63–65.

30. Fauntroy, "United States Impact," 158, 159.

31. Ferguson, *Papa Doc, Baby Doc*, 82.

32. Department of State, Fry's memorandum to the Latin American Policy Committee, 5 May 1964; Timmons to Rusk, 23 Jan. 1964, Johnson Library, DDRC.

33. Glenn R. Smucker, "Peasant Councils and the Politics of Community," in *Politics, Projects and People: Institutional Development in Haiti*, edited by Derick W. Brinkerhoff and Jean-Claude Zamor (New York, 1986), 95–97; DeWind and Kinley, *Aiding Migration*, 40.

34. Smucker, "Peasant Councils," 96–97; Derick W. Brinkerhoff, "Resource Transfers and Institutional Sustainability: HACHO and Haiti's Northwest," in *Politics, Projects and People*, edited by Brinkerhoff and Zamor, 157, 181.

35. DeWind and Kinley, *Aiding Migration*, 158–61; Smucker, "Peasant Councils," 104.

36. Smucker, "Peasant Councils," 104.

37. Ibid., 103, 110; Dupuy, *Haiti in the World Economy*, 169.

38. DeWind and Kinley, *Aiding Migration*, 35; Smucker, "Peasant Councils," 105, 101, 102; Jon E. Rohde, "The Rural Health Delivery System Project: Initiative and Inertia in the Ministry of Health," in *Politics, Projects and People*, edited by Brinkerhoff and Zamor, 136.

39. Simon Fass, *Political Economy in Haiti: The Drama of Survival* (New Brunswick, N.J., 1988), 22; Smucker, "Peasant Councils," 100–101; *New York Times*, 20 Dec. 1982, 5:1.

40. Smucker, "Peasant Councils," 101, 102, 104; DeWind and Kinley, *Aiding Migration*, 35; Amy Wilentz, *The Rainy Season: Haiti Since Duvalier* (New York, 1989), 257–61.

41. Bellegarde-Smith, *Haiti*, 103–4; Wilentz, *Rainy Season*, 105–6.

42. Trouillot, *Haiti*, 219; Ferguson, *Papa Doc, Baby Doc*, 76–77; Bellegarde-Smith, *Haiti*, 103.

43. Ferguson, *Papa Doc, Baby Doc*, 76–77; Bellegarde-Smith, *Haiti*, 147; Wilentz, *Rainy Season*, 126–27.

44. Elizabeth Abbott, *Haiti: The Duvalier Years* (New York, 1988), 262–64.

45. Ferguson, *Papa Doc, Baby Doc*, 94; Trouillot, *Haiti*, 218.

46. Trouillot, *Haiti*, 217; Fauriol, "Duvaliers and Haiti," 601; Ferguson, *Papa Doc, Baby Doc*, 88.

47. Danny Lyon, *Merci Gonaïves* (Clintondale, N.Y., 1988), 22–32; Fass, *Political Economy in Haiti*, 254, 255; Ferguson, *Papa Doc, Baby Doc*, 92–97.

48. Ferguson, *Papa Doc, Baby Doc*, 117; Abbott, *Haiti*, 320–21; George Shultz to M. Carl Holman, 21 July 1986, Joint Center for Political Studies, Washington, D.C., Vertical File.

12. The Balance Sheet

1. George Kennan's memorandum, "Latin America as a Problem in U.S. Foreign Policy," 20 Mar. 1950, *Foreign Relations of the United States, 1950*, 2:600, 601.

2. William Bayard Hale, "With the Knox Mission to Central America," *World's Work*, clipping in Philander C. Knox Papers, Library of Congress; Kennan, "Latin America," 602.

3. Michel-Rolph Trouillot, *Haiti: State Against Nation* (New York, 1990), 200–201.

4. Dean Rusk to Robert D. Heinl, Jr., 23 Sept. 1975, in Robert Debs Heinl and Nancy Gordon Heinl, *Written in Blood: The Story of the Haitian People: 1492–1971* (Boston, 1971), 622.
5. Barry Bluestone and Bennett Harrison, *The Deindustrialization of America* (New York, 1982).
6. Alex Dupuy, "Export Manufacture and Underdevelopment in Haiti," the Columbia University–New York University Consortium for Latin American and Caribbean Studies, Conference Paper no. 20, 1990.
7. Annette Fuentes and Barbara Ehrenreich, *Women in the Global Factory* (Boston, 1987), Cynthia Enloe, *Bananas, Beaches, and Bases: Making Feminist Sense of International Politics* (Berkeley, 1989), 160–69; John Horton and Eun-Jin Lee, "Degraded Work and Devalued Labor: The Proletarianization of Women in the Semiconductor Industry," in Joan Smith, et al., *Racism, Sexism, and the World-System* (New York, 1988), 137–51; Josh DeWind, "Elections Without Democracy? The Impact of United States Economic Assistance on Politics in Haiti," *Cimarron* 2 (Winter 1990):73.
8. Marta E. Gimenez, "Minorities and the World-System: Theoretical and Political Implications of the Internationalization of Minorities," in Smith, et al., *Racism, Sexism, and the World-System*, 41–43; Peter F. Bell, "Capital and Gender in the Third World: Theoretical Analysis of the Current Crisis," in ibid., 81.
9. Bell, "Capital and Gender," 79–80, 81; *Livre bleu d'Haïti/Blue Book of Haiti* (New York, 1920), 213.
10. Martha Cooley, "Haiti: The AIDS Stigma," *NACLA* 17, no. 5 (1983), 47–48; Fritz N. Cinéas, "Haitian Ambassador Deplores AIDS Connection," *New England Journal of Medicine* 309 (1983):668–99; Alexander Moore and Ronald D. Le Baron, "The Case for a Haitian Origin of the AIDS Epidemic," in *The Social Dimensions of AIDS: Method and Theory*, edited by Douglas A. Feldman and Thomas M. Johnson (New York, 1986).
11. *Haiti Insight*, April 1990, 3.
12. Trouillot, *Haiti*, 200–201; Anthony P. Maingot, "Caribbean International Relations," in *The Modern Caribbean*, edited by Franklin W. Knight and Colin A. Palmer (Chapel Hill, N.C., 1989).
13. U.S. Department of State, report, "Libyan Activities in the Western Hemisphere," July 1986, Joint Center for Political Studies, Washington, D.C., Vertical File.
14. Georges Fauriol, "The Duvaliers and Haiti," *Orbis* (Pa.) 32 (Fall 1988), 604.

15. Josh DeWind, "Elections Without Democracy?" *Cimarron* 2 (Winter 1990), 66, 67; Alex Dupuy, *Haiti in the World Economy* (Boulder, 1989), 186, 188.
16. James Ferguson, *Haiti and the Duvaliers* (London, 1987), 121–22.
17. Organization of American States, "Report on the Situation of Human Rights in Haiti," May 1990 (Washington, D.C.), 12, 16.
18. Elizabeth Abbott, *Haiti: The Duvalier Years* (New York, 1988), 333; David Nicholls, "Haiti: The Rise and Fall of Duvalierism," *Third World Quarterly* 8, no. 4 (1986):1252; Ferguson, *Haiti and the Duvaliers*, 126.
19. Abbott, *Haiti*, 388; Nicholls, "Haiti: The Rise and Fall of Duvalierism," 1251; DeWind, "Elections Without Democracy?" 73.
20. Robert E. Maguire, "Haiti's Emerging Peasant Movement," *Cimarron* 2 (Winter 1990):28–44; Nicholls, "Haiti," 1252; *Haïti-Observateur*, 31 July–7 Aug. 1987, 1, 6, 12, 25, 27, 31.
21. Dupuy, *Haiti in the World Economy*, 192–93; Organization of American States (OAS), "Human Rights in Haiti," 12.
22. Ferguson, *Haiti and the Duvaliers*, 140–41, 147, 154–55.
23. Fauriol, "Duvaliers and Haiti," 604; OAS, "Human Rights in Haiti," 13.
24. Amy Wilentz, *The Rainy Season* (New York, 1989), 296, 298; *Haïti-Observateur*, 10–17 July 1987, 31.
25. *Haïti-Observateur*, 10–17 July 1987, 14; 31 July–7 Aug. 1987, 9.
26. *Haïti Progrès*, 18–24 Nov. 1987, 2; Wilentz, *Rainy Season*, 301, 304.
27. Wilentz, *Rainy Season*, 294–96.
28. Ferguson, *Haiti and the Duvaliers*, 175–77; *Haïti-Observateur*, 4–11 Dec. 1987, 4; OAS, "Human Rights in Haiti," 13.
29. Fauriol, "Duvaliers and Haiti," 605; Ferguson, *Haiti and the Duvaliers*, 178; *Haïti-Observateur*, 4–11 Dec. 1987, 2, 24.
30. Ferguson, *Haiti and the Duvaliers*, 132–33.
31. Ibid., 137–38; Wilentz, *Rainy Season*, 132.
32. Ferguson, *Haiti and the Duvaliers*, 188–90, 299–300, 308; DeWind, "Elections Without Democracy?" 74–75.
33. DeWind, "Elections Without Democracy?" 70.
34. Larman C. Wilson, "Military Rule and the Hopes for Democracy in Haiti: The Limits of U.S. Foreign Policy," the Columbia University–New York University Consortium for Latin American and Caribbean Studies, Conference Paper no. 22, 1990, p. 10; Ferguson, *Haiti and the Duvaliers*, 182, 183.
35. Ferguson, *Haiti and the Duvaliers*, 183.

36. Dupuy, *Haiti in the World Economy*, 197; Abbott, *Haiti*, 365.
37. Trouillot, *Haiti*, 223; OAS, "Human Rights in Haiti," 14; Wilson, "Military Rule," 12–14.
38. *Haïti-Observateur*, 24 June–1 July 1988, 1–4, 7, 9–16, 20–22, 26; *Haïti Progrès*, 22–28 June 1988, 1, 2, 5, 26.
39. Abbott, *Haiti*, 341; OAS, "Human Rights in Haiti," 14, 15.
40. Patrick Bellegarde-Smith, *Haiti: The Breached Citadel* (Boulder, Colo., 1990), 176; Wilentz, *Rainy Season*, 339.
41. Wilentz, *Rainy Season*, 22.
42. DeWind, "Elections Without Democracy?" 71–72; "Anatomy of a Failed Coup," *Haiti Insight*, May 1989, 2.
43. Wilson, "Military Rule and the Hopes for Democracy in Haiti," 18; Americas Watch/National Coalition for Haitian Refugees, Report, "Human Rights in Haiti," 11 Sept. 1989, 12.
44. DeWind, "Elections Without Democracy?" 66–67, 80.
45. OAS, "Human Rights in Haiti," 12–13.
46. *Haiti Insight*, December 1989, 4; *Haïti-Observateur*, 10–17 Jan. 1990, 6.
47. OAS, "Human Rights in Haiti," 18.
48. Ibid., 18–19, 39.
49. DeWind, "Elections Without Democracy?" 76; OAS, "Human Rights in Haiti," 20, 21; *Haiti Insight*, February–March 1990, 1, 6, 8.
50. OAS, "Human Rights in Haiti," 21.
51. *Haiti Insight*, February–March 1990, 1; April 1990, 1–2.
52. Ibid., Summer 1990, 1. DeWind, "Elections Without Democracy?" 78.
53. DeWind, "Elections Without Democracy?" 78; *Haiti Insight*, Summer 1990, 2.
54. DeWind, "Elections Without Democracy?" 79.
55. Wilentz, *Rainy Season*, 137.
56. DeWind, "Elections Without Democracy?" 79.
57. Heinl and Heinl, *Written in Blood*, 620.
58. Ibid., 619.
59. Associated Negro Press, release; 23 June 1937, Claude Barnett Papers, Chicago Historical Society.
60. Heinl and Heinl, *Written in Blood*, 619.
61. *Haïti Observateur*, 6–13 Nov. 1991, pp. 1, 7; *Washington Post*, 8 Oct. 1991, A1:1–2, A14:1–2; *Haïti-Progrès*, 13–19 Nov. 1991, pp. 2, 3, 8, 9.
62. *Haïti Observateur*, 6–13 Nov. 1991, pp. 3, 4, 10, 19; Jean-Bertrand Aristide,

"Restore the Road to Democracy," *New York Times*, 27 Oct. 1991, reprinted in *Haïti Observateur*, 6–13 Nov. 1991, p. 12; *Washington Post*, 9 Oct. 1991, A1:6, A20:1, 6.

63. *Haïti-Progrès*, 13–19 Nov. 1991, p. 11; *Haïti Observateur*, 6–12 Nov. 1991, p. 7.

64. *Washington Post*, 8 Oct. 1991, A1:3, 4, A14:1–2; 9 Oct. 1991, A20:4.

65. *Washington Post*, 25 Oct. 1991, A19:1, A22:1, A22:2.

66. *Haïti-Progrès*, 13–19 Nov. 1991, p. 15.

67. *Ibid*; *Haïti Observateur*, 20–27 Nov. 1991, pp. 1–2.

Bibliographical Essay

Several recent, thorough bibliographies are available to students of Haiti. These include Michel S. Laguerre, *The Complete Haitiana: A Bibliographic Guide to the Scholarly Literature, 1900–1980*, 2 vols. (New York, 1982), which makes a prodigious effort to compile materials in many languages and on a wide variety of subjects. Robert Lawless, *Haiti: A Research Handbook* (New York, 1990) lists the growing number of English language and Haitian Creole sources on Haiti. Another useful reference book is Roland I. Perusse, *Historical Dictionary of Haiti* (Metuchen, N.J., 1977).

Haiti is the second oldest American republic but perhaps the least understood. The conventional emphases on exotica and on lurid, picturesque descriptions of Haitian history and culture have often deprived serious readers of the insights that careful study affords. This bibliographical essay highlights works that present Haiti's role in world affairs, that view its history and society as comprehensible, and that examine it in a hemispheric context. Fortunately, several newer works situate Haiti among other Latin American republics. These include Patrick Bellegarde-Smith, *Haiti: The Breached Citadel* (Boulder, Colo., 1990) and Michel-Rolph Trouillot, *Haiti: State Against Nation* (New York, 1990). Gordon K. Lewis, *Main Currents in Caribbean Thought* (New York, 1983) is an intellectual history that includes consideration of the voluminous Haitian canon. Other general works, including Franklin W. Knight, *The Caribbean*, 2d ed. (New York, 1990) and Lester D. Langley, *America and the Americas* (Athens, Ga., 1989) view Haiti as an intrinsic part of the Western experience. An older work, James Leyburn, *The Haitian People* (New Haven, Conn., 1941), still provides one of the best treatments of class and color dynamics in Haitian society. Another, David Nicholls's still controversial *From Dessalines to Duvalier: Race, Colour, and National Independence in Haiti* (Cambridge, Eng., 1979), traces the motifs of race and color in Haitian culture and politics.

There is a large body of literature on colonial Saint-Domingue and on the Haitian Revolution. A substantial part of this consists of eyewitness accounts and travel narratives by European residents and observers. These works, published in the late eighteenth or early nineteenth centuries, are for the most part found in the rare book rooms of academic or metropolitan central libraries. They can be accessed through Francis Anthony Gaimari, Jr.'s master's thesis, "Historiographical and Bibliographical Survey of Primary and Secondary Source Materials Relevant to the Study of the Haitian Revolution," University of Florida, 1977, and Magdaline W. Shannon, *Bibliography of Saint Domingue: Especially for the Period of 1700–1804* (Iowa City, Iowa, 1973). A very detailed and comprehensive study of the Haitian Revolution is contained in a multivolume, early twentieth-century study by Beaubrun Ardouin, *Etudes sur l'histoire d'Haïti* (Port-au-Prince, 1924–30). Materials that relate revolutionary politics to the worldwide liberal republican enterprise of the eighteenth century are comparatively scarce. David Brion Davis, *The Problem of Slavery in the Age of Revolution, 1770–1823* (Ithaca, N.Y., 1969), makes some information about the impact of the Haitian, North American, and European revolutionary experiences upon one another available, but Haiti remains clearly peripheral in Davis's treatment. Better for this purpose is Franklin W. Knight, "The American Revolution and the Caribbean," in *Slavery and Freedom in the Age of the American Revolution*, edited by Ira Berlin and Ronald Hoffman (Baltimore, 1983); and an enduring classic that has withstood revisionist assault, C. L. R. James, *The Black Jacobins* (New York, 1938). Thomas O. Ott, *The Haitian Revolution, 1789–1804* (Knoxville, Tenn., 1973), also evaluates the revolutionary era in Haiti.

The recent French bicentennial focused scholarly attention on the relative weight of European or indigenous influences on the Haitian Revolution. This debate entails investigation of the political character of ethnicity, slave resistance, and race relations in colonial Saint-Domingue. Jean Fouchard, *The Haitian Maroons* (New York, 1981), and David Geggus, "Slave Resistance Studies and the Saint Domingue Slave Revolt: Some Preliminary Considerations," Florida International University, Latin American and Caribbean Center, Occasional Paper no. 4 (Winter 1983), address the question. The theme is taken up by Eugene D. Genovese, *From Rebellion to Revolution: Afro-American Slave Revolts in the Making of the New World* (Baton Rouge, La., 1979). None of these authors are in agreement, and the points of debate furnish ample food for thought. Henock Trouillot, "La guerre de l'independance en Haïti," 3 parts, *Revista Historica de las Americas* 72–74 (1971), is an original treatment of ethnicity in the revolutionary context. *Maroon Societies: Slave Rebel Communities in the Americas*, compiled by Richard Price (Garden City, N.Y., 1973), provides a useful overview of maroons, or slave fugitives, in hemispheric perspective.

The struggle against the French culminated in national independence, and

Haitians then confronted the task of constructing a polity and economy from the ruins of plantation agriculture and involuntary servitude. This process is perceptively probed in Michel-Rolph Trouillot, *Haiti, State Against Nation* (New York, 1990). Studies of Haitian leadership and state policies include an early collection of documents compiled by an Afro-American expatriate civil servant in Haiti, Prince Saunders. Prince Saunders, *Haytian Papers: A Collection of Very Interesting Proclamations and Other Official Documents . . .* (Boston, 1818). Letters exchanged between King Henri Christophe and the British abolitionist Thomas Clarkson further reveal public policy delineation. These appear in *Henry Christophe and Thomas Clarkson: A Correspondence*, edited by Earl Leslie Griggs and Clifford H. Prator (Berkeley, Calif., 1952). See also Hubert Cole, *Christophe, King of Haiti* (New York, 1967), and Guerin Montilus, "Africa in Diaspora: The Myth of Dahomey in Haiti," *Journal of Caribbean Studies* 2 (Spring 1981):73–84, on ethnicity's continuing role during the early independence years.

In a world still characterized by slavery and racism, Haitian statesmen made efforts to turn these chauvinisms to their account. They took advantage of increasing racial friction and growing black nationalist sentiment in North America by endorsing colonization schemes that might strengthen Haiti and improve relations with the United States. Floyd J. Miller, *The Search for a Black Nationality* (Urbana, Ill., 1975), explores these. David M. Streifford, "The American Colonization Society: An Application of Republican Ideology to Early Antebellum Reform," *Journal of Southern History* 45 (May 1979):201–20, sets colonization against the backdrop of U.S. domestic politics in the nineteenth century.

Haiti and the United States did not enjoy full diplomatic relations until Confederate secession permitted Washington to recognize a black republic founded by slave insurrectionists. The most readily available primary sources for the limited commercial relations between the two nations consist of U.S. consular dispatches from Aux Cayes and Cap-Haïtien, which are extant from 1797 to 1906, and from Port-au-Prince from 1835 to 1906. The National Archives, Washington, D.C., has microfilmed these records. Consular dispatches from St. Marc are available from 1861 to 1891. The troubled but intriguing history of Haitian-American relations in the antebellum period is covered in Alfred N. Hunt, *Haiti's Influence on Antebellum America* (Baton Rouge, La., 1988), and in the standard diplomatic history of the nineteenth century, Rayford Logan, *The Diplomatic Relations of the United States with Haiti, 1776–1891* (Chapel Hill, N.C., 1941). Robert May, *The Southern Dream of a Caribbean Empire*

(Baton Rouge, La., 1973), is also useful for a broader view of the conditions that made Haitians distrust the United States during that epoch.

Beginning with the pioneer Haitian social scientist Edmond Paul, scholars have grappled with the Haitian economy's thorny problems since the nineteenth century. More recent work includes an assessment of the relationship between foreign aid and migration patterns, Josh DeWind and David H. Kinley III, *Aiding Migration: The Impact of International Assistance on Haiti* (Boulder, Colo., 1988), and four analyses of political economy. These are Alex Dupuy, *Haiti in the World Economy: Class, Race, and Underdevelopment Since 1870* (Boulder, Colo., 1989), Benoit Joachim, *Les racines du sous-developpement en Haïti* (Port-au-Prince, 1979), O. Ernest Moore, *Haiti: Its Stagnant Society and Shackled Economy* (New York, 1972), and David Nicholls, *Economic Dependence and Political Autonomy, the Haitian Experience* (Montreal, 1974). Simon Fass, *Political Economy in Haiti: The Drama of Survival* (New Brunswick, N.J., 1988), a heartbreaking study of household economy in the Port-au-Prince slum Brooklyn, balances the mostly macroeconomic analyses that dominate this literature. Paul Moral's brilliant *Le paysan haïtien* (Paris, 1961) still has no peer in its profound and nuanced treatment of the rural economy. Other important work in agricultural economics includes Mats Lundahl's *Peasants and Poverty: A Study of Haiti* (New York, 1979), and his *The Haitian Economy: Man, Land and Markets* (New York, 1983).

Anthropological studies that focus on the rural majority have dominated views of Haitian culture and society. Haitians have become increasingly an urban people, however, and interact with the international market economy and a government whose presence and activities in the city are much more pervasive than in the countryside. The anthropologist Michel S. Laguerre in *Urban Life in the Caribbean* (Cambridge, Mass., 1982) traces this transformation and its consequences. Culture and society are approached through literature in J. Michael Dash, *Literature and Ideology in Haiti, 1915–1961* (Totowa, N.J. 1981). The essays in David Nicholls, *Haiti in Caribbean Context: Ethnicity, Economy, and Revolt* (Oxford, 1985), discuss a variety of societal issues, including ethnic minorities and the status of women. Laguerre, above, details the influence of the Afro-Haitian cults on political life, and follows suit in his *Voodoo and Politics in Haiti* (New York, 1989). *Religion and Politics in Haiti*, edited by Rémy Bastien and Harold Courlander (Washington, D.C., 1966), also addresses this subject.

Haitian diplomacy is examined in Patrick Bellegarde-Smith, "Overview of

Haitian Foreign Policy and Relations," in *Haiti—Today and Tomorrow: An Interdisciplinary Study*, edited by Charles R. Foster and Albert Valdman (Lanham, Md., 1984). Michael Dash, *Haiti and the United States: National Stereotypes and the Literary Imagination* (New York, 1988), looks at Haitian foreign relations in the twentieth century from a cultural perspective. For the early twentieth century, see Brenda Gayle Plummer, *Haiti and the Great Powers, 1902–1915* (Baton Rouge, La., 1988). Georges Fauriol's comparative study, *Foreign Policy Behavior of Caribbean States: Guyana, Haiti, and Jamaica* (Lanham, Md., 1984), places Haiti in regional context. David Healy, *Gunboat Diplomacy in the Wilson Era, The U.S. Navy in Haiti, 1915–1916* (Madison, Wis., 1976), is a monograph on the early U.S. military occupation of Haiti. Haitian accounts of the occupation include Suzy Castor, *La ocupación norteamericana de Haití y sus consecuencias (1915–1934)* (Mexico City, 1971), and Kethly Millet, *Les paysans haïtiens et l'occupation américaine* (La Salle, Canada, 1978). An earlier general history of U.S.-Haitian relations is Ludwell Lee Montague, *Haiti and the United States, 1714–1938* (Durham, N.C., 1940). The standard work in English on the occupation as a whole is Hans Schmidt, *The United States Occupation of Haiti, 1915–1934* (New Brunswick, N.J., 1971). Dana G. Munro, a former minister to Haiti, wrote *The United States and the Caribbean Republics, 1921–1933* (Princeton, N.J., 1974). He provides an overview of Haitian-U.S. relations during the occupation years. Munro also wrote *Intervention and Dollar Diplomacy in the Caribbean, 1900–1921* (Princeton, N.J., 1964), which contains another account from the State Department view. Former envoy John Bartlow Martin focuses on the mid-twentieth century in *U.S. Policy in the Caribbean* (Boulder, Colo., 1978). Primary source materials in print include the National Archives' ongoing microfilm publication of the State Department Numerical and Decimal Files. These comprise records of relations between Haiti and the United States and Haiti and other countries. Instructions to the U.S. legation in Port-au-Prince from the State Department and notes from the Haitian legation to the State Department have also been filmed.

Haiti maintained relations with other nations that influenced the character of its interactions with the United States. The Dominican Republic, France, and Germany were the most important of these. For the Dominican Republic, see Rayford W. Logan, *Haiti and the Dominican Republic* (New York, 1968), G. Pope Atkins and Larman C. Wilson, *The United States and the Trujillo Regime* (New Brunswick, N.J., 1972), Thomas Fiehrer, "Political Violence in the Periphery: The Haitian Massacre of 1937," *Race and Class* 32 (October–

December 1990):1–20, and Robert D. Crassweller, *Trujillo: The Life and Times of a Caribbean Dictator* (New York, 1966). Relations with France and Germany during the nineteenth century are reviewed in Jacques-Nicolas Léger, *La politique extérieure d'Haïti* (Paris, 1886), and Anténor Firmin, *Diplomates et diplomatie* (Cap-Haïtien, 1899). Useful recent studies are C. M. Andrew, *Théophile Declassé and the Making of the Entente Cordiale: A Reappraisal of French Foreign Policy 1898–1905* (New York, 1968), and Holger H. Herwig, *The Politics of Frustration: The United States in German Naval Planning, 1889–1941* (Boston, 1976). Warren Kneer's *Great Britain and the Caribbean, 1901–1913, A Study in Anglo-American Relations* (Lansing, Mich., 1975), has an instructive chapter on Haiti in British and U.S. calculations.

The period between the end of the U.S. occupation and the rise of François Duvalier has yet to find its chroniclers. Patrick Bellegarde-Smith pioneers here with *In the Shadow of Powers: Dantès Bellegarde in Haitian Social Thought* (Atlantic Highlands, N.J., 1985). The 1934–57 era marks the "discovery" of Haiti by the tourist industry and the international art world. Some impressionistic writing by Herbert Gold, a U.S. citizen living in Haiti, gives a sense of the climate of the times. See Herbert Gold, *My Last Two Thousand Years* (New York, 1972), and also his "Americans in the Port of Princes," *Yale Review* (Autumn 1954): 85–98. This trend is continued in Selden Rodman, "U.S. Tourists in Haiti," *Americas* 6 (October 1954): 32–33.

The Duvalier period generated a considerable literature. Some of the works described above, notably those of Bellegarde-Smith, Dupuy, Laguerre, and Trouillot, explain the dictatorship even though they embrace much broader terrain. Gérard Pierre-Charles, *Radiografía de una dictadura* (Mexico City, 1969), is an earlier effort to dissect the Duvalier phenomenon. General—and less analytical—studies include such older works as Bernard Diederich and Al Burt, *Papa Doc: The Truth About Haiti Today* (New York, 1969). More recent are James Ferguson, *Papa Doc, Baby Doc: Haiti and the Duvaliers* (London, 1987), and Rod Prince, *Haiti, Family Business* (London, 1985). Graham Greene tried to depict the atmosphere of the early 1960s in his novel *The Comedians* (New York, 1966), a book that many Haitians continue to criticize sharply.

Charles D. Ameringer, *The Democratic Left in Exile* (Coral Gables, Fla., 1974), is about the noncommunist Caribbean Legion. It relates anti-Duvalier exiles' efforts to overthrow the regime in the 1960s and shows them acting out of motives common to all regional insurgents. The U.S. naval attaché to Haiti from 1958 to 1963 and his wife wrote a general history of Haiti whose most authoritative sections concern their experiences and reactions to events of the period. Robert Debs Heinl and Nancy Gordon Heinl, *Written in Blood: The History of the Haitian People* (Boston, 1978), in other respects marks no improvement over the sensationalistic literature of the nineteenth century. Kern Delince, *Armée et Politique en Haïti* (Paris, 1979), is one of the few texts that analyzes the army as an institution and explores its relationship to the polity.

Many Haitians responded to the austerities and brutalities of the Duvalier years by migrating. Circular migration to the Dominican republic had long existed and expanded during this period. The enslavement of Haitian agricultural workers by corporate growers with Haitian and Dominican official collusion is chronicled in Maurice Lemoine, *Bitter Sugar: Slaves Today in the Caribbean* (Chicago, 1985). For Haitian migration to American countries other than the United States, see Paul Dejean, *The Haitians in Quebec* (Ottawa, 1980), and Dawn I. Marshall, "Haitian Migration to the Bahamas," in *The Contemporary Caribbean: A Sociological Reader*, edited by Susan Craig (Maracas, Trinidad, 1981), 110–27.

Events moved rapidly in Haiti following Jean-Claude Duvalier's departure. Much writing after the *dechoukaj*, or "uprooting," has consequently been journalistic in tone. Some analytical studies are emerging, however, including *Politics, Projects and People: Institutional Development in Haiti*, edited by Derick W. Brinkerhoff and Jean-Claude Zamor (New York, 1986), Anthony Maingot, "Haiti: Problems of a Transition to Democracy in an Authoritarian Soft State," *Journal of Interamerican Studies and World Affairs* 28, no. 4 (1987):75–102, and David Nicholls, "Haiti: The Rise and Fall of Duvalierism," *Third World Quarterly* 8 (1986):1239–52. Elizabeth Abbott's seemingly timely *Haiti: The Duvaliers and Their Legacy* (New York, 1988) strives for and often achieves objectivity. As the sister-in-law of General Henri Namphy, however, she illustrates some biases. Amy Wilentz, *The Rainy Season: Haiti Since Duvalier* (New York, 1989), evokes the miseries and aspirations of ordinary Haitians.

The growing Haitian community in the United States and other nations, and its relationship to its country of origin as well as its hosts, has generated new literature. Gilburt Loescher and John Scanlan, "Human Rights, U.S. Foreign Policy, and Haitian Refugees," *Journal of Interamerican Studies and World Affairs* 26 (1984):313–56 assess the implications of Haitian immigration for foreign relations. Naomi Flink Zucker, "The Haitians versus the United States: The Courts as Last Resort," *Annals of the American Academy of Political and Social Science*, no. 467 (1983):151–62 reviews legal aspects. Haitians in Miami,

Florida, are observed in Alex Stepick, "The Roots of Haitian Migration," in *Haiti—Today and Tomorrow: An Interdisciplinary Study*, edited by Charles R. Foster and Albert Valdman (Lanham, Md., 1984), 337–49, and Stepick's "Flight into Despair: A Profile of Recent Haitian Refugees in South Florida," *International Migration Review* 21 (1986):329–50. For Haitians in New York: Michel S. Laguerre, *American Odyssey: Haitians in New York City* (New York, 1984).

Index